White Women Writing White

White Women Writing White

Identity and Representation
in (Post-)Apartheid
Literatures of South Africa

Mary West

dp *davidphilip*

First published in 2009 by David Philip Publishers
An imprint of New Africa Books (Pty) Ltd
99 Garfield Road, Claremont, 7700, South Africa

© in text: Mary West
© in published edition: New Africa Books (Pty) Ltd

All rights reserved. No part of this publication may be reproduced, stored in a retrieval system, or transmitted in any form or by any means, electronic, mechanical, photocopying, recording or otherwise, without prior written permission of the publishers.

ISBN: 978-0-86486-715-5

Editor: Helen Hacksley
Text design and layout: Claudine Willatt-Bate
Proofreader: Sean Fraser
Index: Jennifer Stern
Cover design: Nic Jooste, Comet Design
Printed and bound by Digital Print Solutions

Contents

Acknowledgements vii

1. **Whiteness and Women's Writing** 1
   Introduction 1
   White Women's Writing: Gender and Genre 5
   Positioning this Study in Relation to Whiteness Studies 10
   White Western Womanhood 27
   Conclusion: Plotting a Continuum 35

2. **Complicity and Cliché in *People Like Ourselves* by Pamela Jooste
   and *One Tongue Singing* by Susan Mann** 38
   Introduction 38
   People like Ourselves and People like Them 39
   One Rainbow, One Nation, One Tongue Singing 52
   Conclusion 63

3. **The Metamorphosis of the Sole/Soul: Shades of Whiteness
   in Antjie Krog's *A Change of Tongue*** 65
   Introduction 65
   Unsettling Generic (and Other) Boundaries 66
   Metamorphosis of the Sole/Soul: De-/Reconstructing White Identity 70
   Defining Whiteness: Negotiating and Mediating Black Responses 81
   Redefining Whiteness: Working with Words 94
   Scatological and Eschatological Preoccupations: Latrines and Doctrines ... 96
   A Conclusion 99
   Conclusion 101

4. **The Wise Fool in the Queen's Court: 'Unfair' Commentary on White Western Womanhood in Marianne Thamm's *Fairlady* Columns** 103
   Introduction 103
   Conversations with Women... 104
   The Court Jester: In Praise of Folly................................... 107
   Goblin Boots and Ruffled Collars: On the Possibilities of Duplicity.... 110
   One Purple Leg, One Green Leg: On 'Colour' in Thamm's Columns......... 114
   A Brown Monk's Cowl and a Fool's Staff: On the Impossibilities
      of Duplicity... 121
   Conclusion.. 126

5. **The Co-ordinates of (Post-)Colonial Whiteness: A Reading of Karen Press's *Echo Location: A Guide to Sea Point for Residents and Visitors*** 130
   Introduction 130
   Charting Whiteness: The Convergence of Opposite Forces 133
   Presumptions and Anxieties: White South Africa Disintegrating 137
   Identity and the Other: 'Alida is not my name' 143
   Found Poems: Raiding the Archives 146
   Baseline Text: Advertising Excess 152
   End Poems... 155
   Conclusion.. 157

6. **Narratives of Madamhood in Suburban South Africa in Short Stories by Nadine Gordimer and Marlene van Niekerk**......... 159
   Introduction 159
   Nadine Gordimer's Short Fiction....................................... 161
   'Labour' or 'Small Finger Exercise on the Notion of Hybridity'........ 172
   Conclusion.. 187

7. **Conclusion** 189
8. **Addendum: Poems from Antjie Krog's *Kleur Kom Nooit Alleen Nie***..... 196
9. **Bibliography**.. 200

Endnotes 211
Index 225

Acknowledgements

This project would not have been possible without support. I would like to thank the Nelson Mandela Metropolitan University (NMMU) for the sabbatical period that encouraged its beginnings as a doctoral study. During that phase, my promoters, Helize van Vuuren and Kevin Goddard, read it critically and supportively, and I thank them both for their guidance. Special thanks also goes to the staff of English Studies at NMMU, especially Nancy Morkel and Janine van Rooyen for picking up much of my normal teaching load while I wrote. I am grateful for the external examiners' very positive responses to the material and their recommendations for fine-tuning it. They are Dorothy Driver, Denise deCaires Narain and Judith Coullie. Thanks also to Helen Hacksley for the technical and editorial support and Alfred LeMaitre for his initiative in getting this publication into press. I am very grateful for my family's love and encouragement, especially Luc Hosten, Jenny Miller and Joan West.

1

Whiteness and Women's Writing

*Whiteness is not, yet we continue for
many reasons to act as though it is.*
Alfred J. López (2005: 1)

*Whiteness, the condition once assumed by diverse
European settler communities, is no longer one to
be cherished. Indeed, it is no longer a nice word.*
Zoë Wicomb (2001: 159)

*I search instead for the others
the ones left over,
the ones who have escaped from these
mythologies with barely their lives*
Margaret Atwood (1998: 157)

Introduction
It was W.E.B. du Bois who, as far away and long ago as the United States in the 1930s, tried to envisage a 'political realm beyond racism' called 'Transcaucasia' (Ware & Back 2002: 23). Since then there have been many casualties, both in the United States and in other worlds colonised by the West, of global 'Caucasian' hegemony. Here in South Africa, the story of Happy Sindane that made news headlines in most local newspapers and on national TV in 2003 epitomises the extent of a white South African obsession with 'race'. Happy, a young boy of mixed racial heritage, arrived at the police station in Bronkhorstspruit, claiming to be a white boy kidnapped in infancy and reared by an African woman in a black township. His photograph, strategically obscuring the 'reliable' visual racial markers, was everywhere (in the largely white-managed media), and generated intense and very sceptical speculation (from a largely white audience) about whether indeed he was really white. We all

suspected that he was not – South Africans of all hues (though I speak here on behalf only of white South Africans) have been well trained in spotting the racial markers, no matter how concealed, that divided and continue to haunt us. Interest in the story thus quickly waned once his racial identity had been officially determined as mixed. A year later, he made the local papers in small back-page inserts, which tell of his frequent foray into petty crime and his penchant for substance abuse (*Eastern Cape Herald*, 30 November 2004). Happy is just one of the more apparent casualties, in this country, of white South Africa's vigilant defensiveness about 'race'.

The full-colour front-page photograph in the *Eastern Cape Herald* on 19 January 2005 bears witness to a more subtle and insidious form of this 'dis-ease' afflicting white identities. It depicts a set of six-year-old female triplets all dressed up neatly in uniform on their way to school for the first time. They are lily white, freshly scrubbed and rosy-cheeked with red hair and blue eyes. The picture on its own is innocent (and appealing) enough, and a welcomed shift in that girls, rather than boys, are selected to represent the symbolic moment of initiation into society. However, the scene is undercut by the scripted report directly beneath it, the headline of which will suffice to demonstrate the point: 'Bleak start to the year for township pupils, who face lack of stationery, vandalised schools.' The privileged and perfectly appointed white triplets appear here as iconographic indicators of the racial divide that dictates social (and political) realities in South Africa a decade after the country's first democratic election. One wonders why the editor selected this picture, which is diametrically opposed to the story it accompanies. Zoë Wicomb's reading of an article published in the British media provides a useful approach to the racial implications of such juxtapositions. Wicomb analyses the strategic use of photographs in support of an article in *The Guardian* (18 January 1997) on the Truth and Reconciliation Commission. What she discovers is a 'larger-than-life' picture of 'a black woman crying', although the article itself contains 'no story of black tears'. 'The report', says Wicomb, 'is at odds with the images' and the 'scripto-visual text finds its cohesion' (2001: 160) in Antjie Krog's grief and *her* tears in her capacity as journalist covering the hearings and having to listen to the horror stories emerging from the TRC. In the *Eastern Cape Herald*'s 'Back to School' story, the report is also at odds with the image, though in this case the racial dynamic of the scripto-visual text is in reverse. White normativity, which in this photograph is suggested in the regimented replication of physiognomic traits of the three pretty and more-or-less identical girls, their good (slightly overweight) healthy form, their sprightly step and their exactly matching uniforms, are all in the service metonymically of suggesting what it is that poor vandalised township schools need to aspire towards. It is not the aspiration but the representation of the aspiration that suggests the shoring up of white hegemony.

The story of Happy Sindane and the 'Back to School' media report both illustrate something of the continued effect of white normativity as a phenomenon that hinders progress in healing the racial divide that is South Africa's heritage. In this book I explore the representation of whiteness as a cultural construct in contemporary white women's writing, and I employ contemporary theories and definitions emerging largely out of a new body of work that has become known as 'whiteness studies', which focuses on 'race'[1] and representation. In the broadest possible terms, my aim has been to examine the condition of whiteness as it continues to inform identity politics in post-apartheid[2] South Africa. More specifically, my aim is to demonstrate that women's writing in post-apartheid South Africa is marked by an uneasy duality. It is a literature that, precisely because it is ambivalent (even at times duplicitous), *undoes*, at worst, inadvertently and crassly – at times, consciously and carefully, at best, self-consciously and courageously – the very project of 'reconciling' races and celebrating multiculturalism, which post-apartheid literature often champions. As a result, it is a literature that exposes the extent to which the power of whiteness, as an 'unmarked marker'[3] in a western[4] liberal humanist tradition, continues residually to 'mark' race representations and race relations in post-apartheid South Africa. The analysis attempts to plot a continuum from writers who are least to those who are most aware of whiteness as a cultural construct and of their own positionality in relation to the discursive dynamics that inform South African racial politics.

In an analysis of selected texts produced by white women, I examine the largely invisible ways in which white identity continues to suggest normativity even as it is undermined, either from contesting literatures and criticism or from within its own self-regulating discourse. In reading a representative selection of literatures[5] produced in contemporary South Africa by white women writers, I explore the ways in which white writing by women is uncomfortably both consciously in support of, and unconsciously at odds with, multicultural celebrations of rainbow nationhood. An examination such as this enables an assessment of the extent to which white identities continue to be characterised by a largely unconscious and thus unexamined set of assumptions, and a concomitant sense of entitlement that manages to hold uncertain currency, despite ten years of democracy. These assumptions are not easy to identify, and in fact often do not seem to be assumptions at all. Indeed, the very notion of normativity, as explored later in this introductory chapter, resists being read as a sense of entitlement precisely because such responses do not emerge, without paying particular attention to them, except as normative. Despite these resistances, contemporary writing emerging in South Africa is marked by a deep and abiding preoccupation with 'race'. White writing[6] in particular is characterised by an uneasy ambivalence that becomes apparent when one examines the interstitial manifestations of residual assumptions of entitlement that are at odds with emergent reconciliatory gestures. This renders a revealing duplicity that the writers under scrutiny either acknowledge and investigate or ignore and perpetuate, even at times manifesting both responses simultaneously.

The work of white women writers offers the scope for such an examination, since white women have necessarily occupied an uneasy space, falling somewhere between the phallogocentricity[7] of Cartesian subjectivity and the iconographic other of western imperialism.[8] In other words, they have often been defined by and in relation to men, who have conventionally objectified women and silenced them. The hierarchical relationship that patriarchy established may not be as powerful and as destructive in the twenty-first century as it has been in the past, in advanced western societies (which influence the mores of white South Africans), but it is nonetheless still hierarchical and women have not entirely escaped the objectification that such a relationship has inculcated.

My project demonstrates the continued and residual effect of particular discursive formations, integrally related to gender and class, that favour whiteness as a racial category, despite official policies that have begun to shift the racial marker into a less than comfortable position, and it examines the phenomena that sustain the aspiration. Perhaps the most significant element of such discursive formations is western liberal humanism, a discourse that has often been instrumental in maintaining the insularity and the assumptions that have emerged as normative.[9] The liberal humanist in the history of South Africa's political turmoil has often been the white English-speaking product of a privileged and educated background, an individual who has been allowed the comfort of disapproving of, even resisting, the apartheid regime, but from a position of relative safety, as a result of material privilege and empowerment through education (knowledge). To assess the continued effect of such discourses and to examine the extent to which whiteness as a cultural construct continues to exert its influence on race relations in post-apartheid South Africa, I analyse a selection of disparate texts to explore the positionalities of the writers in relation to their negotiations of race and belonging. By (re-)reading white women writers in the light of contemporary theories that have collectively been labelled whiteness studies, I demonstrate that racial hierarchies in post-apartheid South Africa have not been successfully renegotiated and that white normativity still holds uncertain currency.

White Women's Writing: Gender and Genre
Though white women's writing in post-apartheid South Africa is the general terrain I explore, this in itself is rather a broad category and demands a more clearly defined focus. Four major concerns have informed the selection of texts. The first consideration is the inclusion of women writers who have stayed in South Africa, and who continue to live in and write about living in this country. Though writers who live elsewhere are no less interested in examining their South African identity, theirs may necessarily be a different kind of exploration to those who have stayed in the country to experience and witness (to) the changes that the last decade has brought. Though there is potential for a comparative study in this regard, the primary focus of my project is the residue of whiteness that white woman writers in South Africa are negotiating. This is a residue of privilege and normativity that being white has historically bestowed, but which is now, in South Africa, under enormous threat in ways that it simply is not in western countries abroad.

Secondly, I examine the postulation that there is not a homogeneous, monolithic whiteness in South Africa, marked as it is by class divisions as well as by a cultural and linguistic division between English- and Afrikaans-speaking white inhabitants. In this regard, the differences have proved to be complex in examining whiteness as a (neo-)colonising force in this country. In order to explore the ramifications of this divide, the Afrikaans writers, namely Antjie Krog and Marlene van Niekerk, have been included. Both have published in English, having had their major works translated. The act of 'translation' and its association with 'transformation'[10] and other traversings is therefore also under scrutiny. Both are major voices in contemporary South Africa, with Krog's *Country of My Skull* (1998) and Van Niekerk's *Triomf* (1996) winning multiple literary awards, while both works are also seminal responses to South Africa's painful transformation from a white perspective.

Thirdly, I have deliberately endeavoured to incorporate writers who have not necessarily featured dominantly in literary scholarship because, as a feminist scholar, I am interested in listening as carefully to neglected or marginal voices as I am in acknowledging the major contributions of relatively mainstream writers such as Antjie Krog. Though Nadine Gordimer is one of the most important white woman writers in South Africa, her work has been amply researched, and is thus deliberately under-represented in this study. On the other hand, Marlene van Niekerk has not been afforded much critical attention by English South African literary scholars, whereas her representation of whiteness may be as important as Gordimer's.

Finally, rather than confining the study to literary output, the boundaries of which are in any case contested, my research includes four conventional genres, namely the novel, the 'novelistic' autobiography, poetry and short fiction, and instead of a dramatic text, the focus has been broadened to include the 'literary' journalism of Marianne Thamm. This controversial columnist writes a monthly column entitled 'Unfair Comment' for the popular South African women's magazine *Fairlady*. Her columns have also been collected in a publication entitled *Mental Floss* (2002), which shifts her work into the ambit of a literary investigation, though her more recent columns are also examined in this study. The decision to omit drama and include literary journalism,[11] to some extent, hinges on the very limited output in South Africa of dramatic material written by white women, but it is informed more significantly by Raymond Williams's examination of the ideological implications of the origins of literary studies. Williams has asked the uncomfortable question whether drama may be categorised as literature.[12] Mindful of the fact that the entire Leavisite tradition would have appeared sorely depleted without the inclusion, indeed the centrality, of Shakespeare, Williams's answer points to a shift in the definition of literature from its earliest sense of 'reading ability and reading experience' to '"taste" or "sensibility"'.[13] The multigeneric exploration in the following chapters (which purposefully includes the anomaly of popular media writing) reflects the shifts and trends in contemporary literary critical praxis ushered in by Raymond Williams, Stuart Hall and others. Their groundbreaking work has led at least partially to the displacement of literary studies (along with its bourgeois sensibilities) and to the rise of cultural studies.[14]

With this literary critical turn as a guiding principle, Chapter Two tackles a genre which the late Robert Kirby, columnist at the *Mail & Guardian,* identified as a growing trend in South African fiction: 'post-apartheid weepies written by guilt-ridden white women as they emerge from years of suppressed conscience' (2005a: 23). Two such 'weepies' characteristic of pulp fiction are the focus of Chapter Two, namely Pamela Jooste's *People Like Ourselves* (2004) and Susan Mann's *One Tongue Singing* (2005), in order to sample and gauge the extent to which empowered middle-class white women have become spokespersons for multicultural celebrations and Truth and Reconciliation confessions. The chapter offers a deconstruction of the discourse of privilege (reliant on cliché and emerging as normative), which is often an unconscious element of such projects.

Chapter Three offers a reading of Antjie Krog's *A Change of Tongue* (2003), a book that may also be defined within and against the 'testimony', offering the writer's personal response to the difficulties of transformation within the first decade of South African democracy. The autobiographical aspect of Krog's project is clearly difficult to dispute, but the writer resists easy categorisation in her postmodernist propensity to unsettle the boundaries between truth and fiction.[15] Indeed, she may be read as setting herself up as a character in the text, fictionalising aspects of her experience and personalising very public debates. In doing so, she becomes a spokesperson or representative voice, reflecting a general white South African response to transformation. Krog's positionality in relation to the politics of post-apartheid South Africa is the key exploration in the text. In her dual capacity as writer and subject, she constantly confronts her own defensiveness, her own sense of normalcy and her own sense of alienation, in relation to multiple encounters with people whose politics do not necessarily concur with her own. This work exemplifies the ambivalence of resisting and enacting white normativity that is central to my study, and it is an ambivalence suggesting that the ideological hopes she expressed in her earlier work, *Country of My Skull* (1998), have not been sustainable, and that her sense of belonging as a white person in Africa is in jeopardy.

In Chapter Four, I examine the journalism of Marianne Thamm because it is in magazines and newspapers rather than in 'high' literature that one encounters a more widely read selection of written responses to the politics of identity facing white South African women. In the case of Thamm, I explore the inclusion of an obviously contending voice writing *against* the general tenets of *Fairlady*, the magazine that ironically publishes her work. The ambivalence that emerges in this chapter relates to the uncomfortable role she is forced to play. In this regard, Thamm's critique of the mores governing bourgeois white womanhood is read in relation to her role, that of the traditional court jester, whose licence to criticise is earned at some expense. The chapter examines the duplicity of the 'Wise Fool' as reflecting the duplicity of *Fairlady*, a magazine devoted almost entirely to reinforcing white western feminine normativity, whilst consciously representing itself as a magazine with a 'social conscience'. However, an alternative reading is posited in examining the transgressive potential of Thamm's journalistic practice.

A collection of poems written by Karen Press is the focus of Chapter Five. Her work offers a powerful engagement with a white South African crisis of belonging. In *Echo Location: A Guide to Sea Point for Residents and Visitors* (1998), Press facetiously camouflages what is a collection of poems by invoking a more marketable kind of publication in the title, the ubiquitous tourist brochure. She nonetheless engages quite overtly with the implications of cartography, mapping the co-ordinates of a New South Africa in which the imperial maps of discovery have been exposed as a violent 'renaming [of] spaces in a symbolic and literal act of mastery and control' (Ashcroft, Griffiths, Tiffin 1998: 32). Press's inclusion of poems reflecting multiple perspectives (which offer first-person accounts, 'found poems', snippets of overheard conversation, and a few characters whose stories are narrated) renders the work a complex set of interactions. The whole is expertly negotiated by the poet-observer whose view of Sea Point takes in the sweep of history and attempts to plot an alternative set of co-ordinates, while remaining aware of the paradoxes and impasses in contemporary race relations that hinder progress.

Chapter Six offers a detailed reading of four short stories, written by Nadine Gordimer and Marlene van Niekerk, respectively. I have chosen these stories[16] as they represent two established South African women writers who both focus on aspects of white 'madamhood'. The stories are thus deliberately juxtaposed to trace an anxious and tragic impasse in white responses to suburbia (the place of enactment of white bourgeois mores) which both writers ruthlessly interrogate. The inclusion in this chapter of three Gordimer short stories (which were written during apartheid) hinges on the comparative value they offer in tracing the anxieties of white madamhood, raging on unabated, as Van Niekerk's story suggests.

This brief summary of the trajectory my study follows needs to be viewed in relation to a number of contextualising factors, which the remainder of this chapter plots. However, there are two more introductory aspects that act as a further justification for a book focussing exclusively on white women writers in contemporary South Africa. The first of these emerges in an article on the subject, by Fred de Vries, writing for *This Day* sometime before the newspaper's untimely demise in 2004. Entitled 'Singular White Females', and obviously ironically echoing the movie title *Single White Female*, which in turn recalls advertisements in the 'Social' or 'Matchmaking' sections of newspaper classifieds, the article explores the trend in post-apartheid popular fiction towards the increasing emergence of white women's fiction in English. Though some of the fiction De Vries explores may be perceived as not worthy of scholarly consideration, one of the primary objectives of this study is to bring together a constellation of texts that have the most currency in white suburban spaces and demonstrate some of the major influences and trends in social thinking that characterise contemporary white South Africa. Even Karen Press's *Echo Location* is presented in such a way as to attract a wider readership than poetry usually receives, with its inclusion of photographs, a map and a baseline text aimed at satisfying the appetites of the consumer-traveller. The texts selected, albeit with varying degrees of probability, might readily be described as 'easily digestible' or 'highly readable' in the parlance of typical book reviews in local newspapers, and may consequently be considered unworthy of serious scholarly attention. This is at least one of the preconceptions a study such as this aims to foreground in its adoption of cultural criticism as a frame of reference. Thus, for example, the short story anthology, the autobiographical novel, the popular women's magazine, popular fiction in the form of the 'post-apartheid weepy', and a collection of poems with pictures and a scrolling menu are juxtaposed to provide a sampling of multi-generic written responses to the politics of post-apartheid identity by white women in contemporary South Africa.

The list of established and emerging white women writers presented by Fred de Vries in 'Singular White Females' is extensive, from Nadine Gordimer and Marlene van Niekerk through to Diane Awerbuck and Jo-Anne Richards. De Vries's proposition regarding the proliferation of popular fiction by new writers is worth considering: he suggests that it has something to do with 'an urge to describe the complexities of post-apartheid life and the manic-depressive character of South Africa' (2004a: 10). Though there may be strong evidence to support the kind of psychological illness he has in mind, it may not be a 'South African' phenomenon *per se*. Rather, it may be very specifically a *white* South African mental dis-ease, and though De Vries's exploration of the trend is both well researched and convincingly argued, it is in moments such as this that he makes a characteristic white error in that his 'South Africans' clearly refers primarily to white South Africans. This is the kind of signifying slippage I examine – those hidden assumptions of universality that emerge out of a profound but largely unconscious, or at least unacknowledged, sense of white normalcy. In the less guarded, more popular kinds of writing emerging in post-apartheid South Africa by white women, it is precisely this aspect of white subjectivity that is under scrutiny.

The second introductory observation that is intended to contextualise this study emerges in response to an article entitled 'Burden of Whiteness', published in the *Mail & Guardian*, which draws attention to a post-apartheid sense of white displacement and white anxiety. It features, among other things, the responses in the visitors' book to the exhibition of Michelle Booth's photographic interrogation of whiteness at the Rosebank Gallery, which in broken English express a frustrated defensiveness that has become one of the hallmarks of white responses to post-apartheid South Africa:

> I take umbridge [sic] at Booth and her elk [sic] who continually perport [sic] to 'speak' for all white South Africans [...] I'm not for one moment, at all ashamed of my whiteness and have nothing whatsoever to be embarassed [sic] about for having a white skin.

And:

> The most powerful thing about your 'art work' is the blatant racism you display toward people of your own colour.

As the journalist rightly points out, these gut responses, despite the shocking level of inarticulacy, are very revealing because they reflect 'an ongoing belief among white South Africans that whiteness is beyond scrutiny' (2004: *Mail & Guardian* Archives: http://archive.mg.co.za). However, it is perhaps Liese van der Watt's reading that is the most valuable in accounting for the extreme defensiveness evident in such responses. She notes that, increasingly, television advertisements are demonstrating an anxiety around whiteness, which has had the effect of foregrounding whiteness:

> In some cases this awareness has made [white people] retreat more and more into their cluster homes and suburbs [...] Many [of them] have experienced a form of psychological emigration from this country.

The extent of this psychological migration, together with the inevitable defensiveness and anxiety that emerge in its wake, is an aspect of white identity examined in the texts selected here. Gail Smith, writing in *This Day*, notes a general reluctance among white people to 'face up to the politics of privilege' (2004: 9), and quotes Michelle Booth's parting words in an interview she conducted: 'In my observation black people are fed up, they don't want to conscientise white people anymore. And I can understand that, which is why I began to speak about it' (2004: 9). A significant part of my project in this book is to acknowledge and examine the 'politics of privilege' that governs white responses to post-apartheid South Africa, in recognition of the understandable reticence among black South Africans in having to bear the burden of white defensiveness.

Positioning this Study in Relation to Whiteness Studies
This section consists of three subsections, namely, whiteness studies in the United States, whiteness as a post-colonial concern and whiteness studies in South Africa. Though there are obvious interrelations between these academic inquiries, the divisions are used as an ordering principle but at the expense, on occasion, of

chronology. Before giving a necessarily brief overview of this proliferating field of study as it has emerged in the United States and beyond, it is important to explore in a general sense what is understood by 'whiteness', although the preceding discussion has, to some extent, introduced the salient aspects of its appearance in contemporary theorisation.

The first observation in this regard hinges on the distinction between 'whiteness' and complementary concepts that portray black identity, for example. In the United States, 'Black Power' was the African-American response to white supremacy, and later, in South Africa, Steve Biko introduced the notion of 'Black Consciousness' to counter white racism.[17] Both versions are thus essentialising responses to the continued effects of an essentialising racial hierarchy that favours the white community. 'Whiteness' as a concept carries with it the implication of an invisible but powerful abstraction that other groups have *experienced* as monolithic. This is not to say that whiteness as a cultural category *is* monolithic, but to understand how the politics of privilege is experienced by those who are white-identified[18] and those who are not.

The second observation in contextualising the concept of whiteness is to distinguish between skin colour or pigmentation and ideological identification. Whiteness has in fact very little to do with pigmentation, but it emerges as an identification that is premised on the historical fact that white settlers of mainly European extraction colonised large tracts of the rest of the world. This initiated an unequal relationship between the lighter-skinned settler and the darker-skinned native, and consequently between the descendants of the settler and the native. The history of that relationship in South Africa is clearly more charged because it is more recent than in other colonised worlds – it has only been just over a decade since the official dismantling of apartheid structures.

The third observation is that whiteness emerges, because of the lingering effects of such a hierarchy, as an aspiration and an identification that is ideologically (re-)produced. In that sense, it is a sociocultural construct that has been brought into being, rather than a 'natural' identity, which is why many contemporary theorists favour the use of 'identification' as opposed to 'identity', in examining racial/cultural/gender politics. The fourth and final observation, and possibly the most contentious one, is that despite ten years of democracy, and despite official efforts to realign racial politics, whiteness in South Africa continues to exude a powerful sense of normativity. This normativity has recently been overlaid with defensiveness, an ambivalent combination that resists rather than assists the process of reconciliation, and in many ways deepens the racial divisions. Though there are studies emerging in cultural theory and criticism that examine the *fluidity* of racial identification, my work specifically examines the *fixity* of such identification, and though it recognises a growing sense of white displacement, it focuses on whiteness as a central and abiding affiliation, even for those who are not necessarily white-skinned. As a result, whiteness operates as a cultural force, which to some extent relieves white people of having to negotiate their whiteness, except as defensiveness. The fixity of racial identification is often understood in terms of reification and valorisation, both concepts emerging out of Marxist critiques of power relations, and denoting the invisible ways in which ideology operates to essentialise and naturalise constructed differences.

This reifying tendency may best be understood in relation to a hegemonic privileging of the white western self. Raka Shome defines 'whiteness' as a 'power-laden discursive formation that privileges, secures, and normalises the cultural space of the white Western subject' and notes in particular the reproductivity inherent in the neocolonial and figurative 'travelling' of white cultural products, including academic texts (1999: 108).[19] Shome's inclusion of 'academic texts' in her catalogue of transferable cultural products makes it necessary to take cognisance of the reproductivity of white normalcy in textual production and reception, or how certain ideas flourish as a result of the publishing industry and the readers who support it, though the latter formulation might well also work in reverse. Shome is not the first to have observed the imperialist nature of academic knowledge. Edward Said's groundbreaking work, *Orientalism* (1978), in which he examines the complicity of academic and scientific knowledge in justifying and maintaining colonial power in the East, though subsequently contested, changed the landscape of literary-critical methodology irreversibly (Young 2004: 165–168) in compelling scholars to uncover the complicities hidden in their own critical practice. This point will be taken up later in response to positioning myself in relation to the material and approaches included in this study. For the purposes of this introduction, however, it is important to note the centrality of post-colonialism as the theory and the practice most influential in bringing whiteness studies into being.

The white western self that Shome suggests as occupying a privileged space in global discourses has been subjected to a critical gaze from white western women long before the advent of whiteness studies, and at this juncture it is necessary to mention just two representative writers whose work not only anticipates the study of whiteness but who also feature in this study, namely, Virginia Woolf and Margaret

Atwood. In the first few decades of the twentieth century, Virginia Woolf, in *A Room of One's Own*, succinctly identified a white woman's dis-ease in a male-favouring world. She noted that a woman may not feel that she is the 'natural inheritor of [...] civilisation [and] becomes, on the contrary, outside of it, alien and critical' (1945: 96), an insight that still holds currency at the beginning of the twenty-first century, despite the three waves of western feminism that the last century or so has produced. There is certainly some evidence in white women's writing of such an 'alien' and 'critical' positionality, but there is also evidence to suggest that white women, having been co-opted historically as the mothers of the empire's civilising mission, are bearers of the residual attitudes, or 'discursive repertoires'[20] informing that role. These discursive repertoires are still apparent in white suburban madamhood in South Africa.

Whereas Woolf may not have always been aware of the implications of race (and class) in her feminist practice, Margaret Atwood, as a post-colonial female settler writer of the mid-twentieth century, brings to bear both feminist and post-colonial preoccupations in her literary and critical practice. I wish to add a peculiarly white South African category to her widely acclaimed, though admittedly dated, plotting, in *Survival: A Thematic Guide to Canadian Literature* (1972), of the primary national symbolic motifs in British, American and Canadian literature respectively. Atwood has identified 'The Frontier' as exemplifying American literary preoccupations, 'The Island' as characteristic of British literary production, and 'Survival' as the corresponding symbol for Canadian literature (1996: 31–32). It may be argued, taking note of Atwood's own admission of the danger in making sweeping generalisations, that 'Be-longing' (the very word containing a sense of Lacanian lack and the deferral of any possible fulfilment of desire) is the national obsession in literature produced in South Africa by white writers, and more particularly, by white women writers. 'Be-longing' manifests itself in a heightened sense of insecurity, even physical threat. As J.M. Coetzee's 1980s book title so aptly demonstrates, in the present continuous, white South Africans are 'Waiting for the Barbarians' and the 'barbarians', in the white South African psyche, are *still* just over the hill, just beyond the horizon, just on the other side of the high-security six-foot suburban vibracrete wall.

In addition to Atwood's plotting of national symbolic motifs, her 'four basic victim positions' (1996: 37–39) may be productively deployed in assessing the level of awareness evident in each of the texts under scrutiny in this study, of the writers' own positionality on the continuum plotted in this study. 'Position One: To deny the fact that you are a victim' right through to 'Position Four: To be a creative non-victim'[21] may be variously and fruitfully used to gauge white South Africa's response to 'home'. Like Canada, South Africa is an ex-British colony, but unlike Canada, the white 'victims' in South Africa are much more likely to have been defined historically (perhaps even presently), as oppressors, rather than oppressed, victimisers, rather than victims, and the 'Victim Position' grid can thus not be overlaid onto white South Africa without some fairly major realignments. How have white women writers negotiated their precarious in-between position and moved towards Position Four: being a 'creative non-victim', and a creative non-perpetrator, of gender and racial biases, respectively? These and other related questions will form the basis of the investigation of white women writing white.

Whiteness Studies in the United States

The now flourishing study of whiteness as a discreet field of investigation has developed only in the last two decades. In the United States, the critique of whiteness emerges in a number of interrelated, cross-disciplinary investigations. David Roediger's 1991 study of left-wing US labour history, entitled *The Wages of Whiteness*, for example, is regarded as a seminal study in foregrounding whiteness, its association with class consciousness, and the civil notions of normalcy with which it inevitably became associated. In addition, Toni Morrison's *Playing in the Dark: Whiteness and the Literary Imagination* (1992) has been regarded as groundbreaking in its turning of the critical gaze away from those who have been defined and represented in American literature, towards those who define and represent. Furthermore, Ruth Frankenberg's pioneering work, *The Social Construction of Whiteness: White Women, Race Matters* (1993), is a sociological study of the conditioning or socialising that marks whiteness as normative and invisible in American society. Subsequent to her publication, there have been a plethora of cross-disciplinary studies that have contributed to making whiteness visible and understanding its impact on identity politics. Three important titles are Valerie Babb's *Whiteness Visible: The Meaning of Whiteness in American Literature and Culture* (1998), *Out of Whiteness: Color, Politics, and Culture* (2002) by Vron Ware and Les Back, and most recently, a collection of essays edited by Alfred J. López and entitled *Postcolonial Whiteness: A Critical Reader on Race and Empire* (2005), the latter suggesting that whiteness studies is becoming a global phenomenon, as opposed to an exclusively American preoccupation.

These and other studies of whiteness have made it possible to think about white identities as constructed in relation to the other, and to consider whiteness as an 'imagined identity' that is still powerfully 'real', and it is this ambivalence or doubleness that makes whiteness studies a complex and contested terrain. Eric Lott's definition of 'whiteness' is one of the most succinct, especially with regard to his valuable suggestion that 'whiteness is a constructed imagined identity which, especially in the US, requires continual effort to sustain' (1999: 241). This is a concept he adapts from Benedict Anderson's reading of the nation state as an 'imagined community', and which foregrounds the constructedness of identity and identification in the service of promoting modern liberal democracies. It is thus necessary to elaborate on a theory of whiteness as an imagined identity by foregrounding the most relevant aspects of what has emerged as a burgeoning topic in contemporary American debates on identity and representation, and to suggest the relevance of these studies in relation to the texts examined in my study.

Toni Morrison's *Playing in the Dark* (1992) remains one of the most powerful critiques of literary production in the service of whiteness. Her work adopts and extends Virginia Woolf's 'alien' and 'critical' position and reinforces Margaret Atwood's reading of the literary preoccupations of the white settler. She suggests that 'until recently, and regardless of the race of the author, the readers of virtually all American fiction have been positioned as white' (1992: xii). According to Morrison, while 'cultural identities are formed and informed by a nation's literature [...] what seemed to be on the "mind" of the literature of the United States was the self-conscious but highly problematic construction of the American as a new white man' (1992: 39). Some of the texts I examine in the following chapters might well emerge out of such a preoccupation, though with a necessarily more accommodating post-apartheid multicultural backdrop. This backdrop manages to camouflage some of the more obvious ways in which whiteness continues to thrive as a cultural affiliation, and with the proviso that in women's writing it is arguably the self-conscious construction of the newly liberated white woman that is at stake. Morrison's reading of the representation of African-Americans in literature written by white writers is reflected in this project. She notes that the 'normal, unracialised, illusory white world [...] [provides] a fictional backdrop' (1992: 16), which throws into relief the 'fabrication of an Africanist persona' (1992: 17), a fabrication that says more about the self than the other. Her concluding remarks are pertinent for this study. She emphasises the point that her work is 'not about a particular author's attitudes towards race' (difficult to gauge with any measure of empirical certainty), nor whether they have produced 'racist or non-racist literature'. Her project might more usefully be read as 'an effort to avert the critical gaze from the racial object to the racial subject, from the described and imagined to the describers and imaginers, from the serving to the served' (1992: 90). My aim in this project is also not to level charges of racism but to pay attention to the moments in which the implied ideological preoccupations of the writer are revealed.

Another pioneer in the field of whiteness studies, Ruth Frankenberg, in *The Social Construction of Whiteness: White Women, Race Matters*, suggests that 'white people are "raced", just as men are "gendered"' (1993: 1), but 'the white Western self as a racial being has for the most part remained unexamined and unnamed' (1993: 17). Frankenberg's sociological study examines the possibility of reading whiteness not as skin colour but as a complex dynamic of identification, one which continues to exhibit the prejudices that were informed by pigment gradations (in outdated scientific discourses) and that continue to govern signifying associations. This introduces the possibility of whiteness being renegotiated and possibly even fluidified. However, in order to move towards these possibilities, the task of contemporary scholarship must still be to uncover the residual elements of racist discourse that hamper any effective renegotiation. Significantly, for the purposes of my study, Frankenberg sees her project as 'documenting the traces of colonial discourses in white women's thinking' (1993: 17). Commenting on the responses of some of the women she interviewed, she notes that a common reaction to her questions was markedly defensive, '"history was not their fault" – they merely inherited it, as its willing or unwilling beneficiaries' (1993: 238). In some ways this project advances Frankenberg's earlier one, though rather than a sociological study, this one relies on textual production across multiple genres and media.

In South Africa, white women's writing also exhibits the defensiveness that Frankenberg has identified in her investigation of American white responses, in that there are similar 'discursive repertoires' shaping their representations, repertoires which these women writers have 'lived, negotiated, appropriated, and rejected, [in some cases] more consciously and intentionally than in others' (1993: 290). Perhaps the most challenging aspect of this project is the attempt to place these writers on a continuum from least to most aware of their own positionality with regard to race in their contributions to post-apartheid literature. It is challenging because the predictable defensiveness that emanates from the necessarily privileged positions assumed by middle-class white South African women is closely linked to the acute sense of ambivalence that marks their responses to race and belonging in post-apartheid South Africa. In *Displacing Whiteness: Essays in Social and Cultural Criticism* (1997), Frankenberg, the editor, suggests that the most important aspect of approaching race studies from this angle (or studying racial dynamics in textual representations) is in asking 'how whiteness is performed by subjects whether in daily life, in film, in literature, or in the academic corpus'. 'At times', she suggests, 'what is at stake in such research is the 'revealing' of the unnamed – the exposure of whiteness masquerading as universal' (1997: 3). One of the primary interrogations in the present study is undertaken in response to Frankenberg's identification of a 'masquerade' which may be understood as the 'performativity' of whiteness, to invoke a concept that Judith Butler examines in relation to gender[22] (1993: 125). More recently, Georgina Horrell has examined femininity as a masquerade in white women's writing in South Africa,[23] a study that adds credence to the present enterprise. The notion of masquerading and performativity will be revisited later in this chapter in more detail, with reference to the scholarship of Vikki Bell and Judith Butler respectively.

The performance of white Womanhood[24] in particular is maintained through socialisation and training. Dreama Moon, following Althusser's reading of the workings of Ideological State Apparatuses, identifies the 'tyranny of bourgeois decorum' (1999: 183) in policing the boundaries of social propriety. One of the ways in which this transpires is, according to Moon, in 'euphemistic whitespeak' (188), which is marked by the use of the passive voice and the removal of agency in discourses on American history. This allows white Americans to talk about race as if they are not 'raced' and this relieves them of having to confront their own complicity in maintaining unequal race relations (189). The example she gives, 'Africans were bought to the US to work as slaves', is echoed in so many ways in South African whitespeak, one of the most ubiquitous being a white English disavowal of any responsibility for apartheid, sentiments predictably articulated in agentless passivity. 'Whitespeak' in South Africa may constitute an interesting study on its own, but for my purposes only some of its manifestations are explored. A useful example taken from everyday experience is the reliable rejoinder, for example: 'I'm not racist. Many of my friends are … (fill in appropriate colour description), but … (fill in the racist observation).' The statement, with its inevitable qualifying tag, is very often confirmation of a firmly entrenched though completely unconscious racism. Though this is clearly a generalisation, it is included as an aside to reflect at least one of the ways in which racism operates at a level that is not intentional, even resisted, but may nonetheless be experienced as damaging.

It is precisely within liberal humanist discourse that much of the currency of whiteness as a camouflaged construct resides, as is borne out by the work, for example, of Alistair Bonnet. He argues that the 'reifying myths of Whiteness' have enabled white Americans to be generously anti-racist and progressively liberal, without having '"their" "racial" identity [...] reviled or lambasted but never made slippery, torn open or, indeed, abolished' (1997: 177–178). More significantly, in a footnote to the essay, Bonnet calls for new approaches to whiteness that challenge an emerging defensiveness among many white people who are beginning to see themselves, as a result of the decentring of western grand narratives, as a 'beleaguered ethnic minority'. He goes on to quote from a study produced by Charles Gallagher in 1995 in which American university students were interviewed. Their responses are very similar to the opinions expressed by white undergraduate students at my own institution. Now that whiteness is becoming a visible racial marker many students in Gallagher's study (and in my own classes) express a desire to find 'a legitimate, positive narrative of [their] own whiteness [...] by constructing an identity that negate[s] white oppressor charges and frame[s] whiteness as a liability' (Gallagher 1995: 177). I examine, in literary representations, manifestations of this tendency to be defensive and to claim whiteness as a beleaguered alterity in fairly insulated post-apartheid white suburban South African communities. Bonnet's comments on the irony of such responses: 'as they seek to connote an interest in whiteness, they expose the ignorance about and disinterest in the actual historical development of white identity' (1997: 190). A similar irony is evident in the tendency of writers investigated in the following chapters to invest a younger generation of white South Africans with the unrestrained capacity to surpass the racial conflicts of the past, thus freeing them from taint and responsibility. Such a tendency does little to redress past inequalities, and often promotes white defensiveness, as will be demonstrated in relation to Susan Mann's resolution of the racial conflict she explores (discussed in Chapter Two), and with reference to one of Marianne Thamm's columns in Chapter Four.

Valerie Babb has explored the complex history of white identification which has resulted in the tendency towards white exclusivity. In *Whiteness Visible: The Meaning of Whiteness in American Literature and Culture* (1998), she plots the equation in the American imaginary of whiteness and middle-class values, and more specifically, whiteness and Englishness. Among other concerns, Babb examines the 'mutability of terms betokening whiteness' (1998: 21) and discovers a 'clear hierarchy in which English is the preferred form of white' (1998: 33). In the South African context, the relevance and implications of such a hierarchisation are significant in relation to class affiliations as they are depicted in the literature under discussion, and in relation to the divide between Afrikaans- and English-speaking women. Also relevant is Babb's view of 'the paradox of whiteness' – that '[t]he devices employed in creating white hegemony are for the most part devices of exclusion. These paradoxes articulate not necessarily who or what is white but rather who or what is not white' (1998: 42). The literature discussed in the following chapters reflects aspects of white middle-class normativity. It is analysed to assess the level of engagement in negotiating the exclusions, denials and paradoxes upon which white identification is premised, with due regard to the complexities that language and cultural affiliations promote. This statement will stand as a provocative generalisation[25] in this introductory chapter. It is, however, not an arbitrary choice to have concluded this study with the work of the Afrikaans-speaking, lesbian writer, Marlene van Niekerk, whose short story, 'Labour', is read as a particularly powerful indictment of white heterosexual middle-class normativity, and the exclusions on which it depends.

These are just some of the explorations of whiteness as a construct that have emerged in the United States. In each case the major concern is to make whiteness visible, and in doing so to demonstrate the biases, privileges and normativity that promote racial hierarchies.

Whiteness as a Post-colonial Concern
In the early 1990s, before whiteness studies began to emerge in the United States, international scholarship was strongly influenced by a growing body of work by post-colonial writers and theorists. In significant ways the rise of post-colonial responses to the colonising prerogative of white subjectivity led to the emergence of whiteness studies as a discreet but related field of inquiry, as is perhaps evident in the centrality of Toni Morrison's work in this field. Her scholarship is just one example of work that has a wider post-colonial currency than its specific negotiation of American whiteness. Post-colonial criticism, however, remains sceptical of the division between whiteness studies and race studies, as the following discussion will show.

Robert Young, in *White Mythologies: Writing History and the West*, first published in 1990, delineated and consolidated a new trend in cultural theory emerging in the work of Edward Said, Homi K. Bhabha and Gayatri Spivak, among others. The publication of the second edition in 2004 marks a decade and a half of its continued relevance, which suggests the primacy of the text in mapping the last two decades of theorising whiteness. In his introductory chapter to the second edition (2004), Young coins the term *Poquismo* (or transcontinental post-colonialism) to identify a contemporary post-structuralist/post-colonial theoretical approach that 'offers a broad front for a political philosophy of activism that contests the current situation of global inequality' and 'persists in deconstructing the white mythologies through which the West sustains itself' (2004: 31). He invokes what Emmanuel Lévinas has termed 'ontological imperialism' to plot western philosophy and its tendency to 'neutralise' and 'encompass' difference in 'its long history of desire for Unity and the One' (1969: 21). Lévinas reads this ontology as an egotism 'in which the relation with the other is accomplished through its assimilation into the self' (2004: 45). Young also introduces Derrida's notion of 'a fundamental Europeanisation of world culture' and examines the implications for the ways in which Derrida has come under fire for generalisations such as this in offering a critique of 'Western metaphysics'. However, Young points out that whenever the concept of 'knowledge' is mentioned, it is often an unselfconscious and self-assured western frame of reference that is employed (2004: 49). Young suggests that the narcissism of western epistemologies might best be countered by employing Derridean and Foucauldian deconstructionist strategies, noting that they allow for an 'active critique of the Eurocentric premises of Western knowledge' by challenging such certainties from *within*, rather than from outside of 'the west'. Young's examination includes a critique of European Marxism in addressing new world politics, citing its 'self-affirming Eurocentrism' and 'patronising paternalism' (2004: 5) as reasons for its failure. Looking beyond Marxism in *Colonial Desire: Hybridity in Theory, Culture and Race* (1995), Young provides a genealogy of whiteness which, following Spivak, he identifies as 'the sovereign self of Europe' (2004: 49).

The hegemonic narratives perpetrated by the 'sovereign' western self have resulted in an estrangement which Bhabha has examined. In 'The White Stuff' (1998), an essay that assesses the proliferation of whiteness studies in the United States, he emphasises the need to make white privilege visible 'both in the sphere of public accountability and in the more intimate recesses of the soul and psyche' (1998: 24). He also suggests that the growing interest in whiteness studies should be understood in relation to the necessity of attempts to displace white normativity (1998: 21). Bhabha's own earlier work, which examines the ambivalence and paranoia evident in the coloniser's response to the native, and his condemnation of an idealistic European humanism, reinforces the necessity of attending to the construction of whiteness as a privileged identification. He defines the 'post-Enlightenment man [as] tethered to [...] his dark reflection, the shadow of the colonised man, that splits his presence, distorts his outline, breaches his boundaries, repeats his actions at a distance, disturbs and divides the very time of his being'. Bhabha also conceives of this 'ambivalent identification' as a manifestation of the coloniser, whom he regards as a 'bizarre figure of desire which splits along the axis on which it turns' (in Fanon 1967: xiv–xv). This insight emerges in Bhabha's introduction to Frantz Fanon's *Black Skin, White Masks* published in 1952. Fanon's groundbreaking work attesting to the trauma and brutality of colonisation in this and the earlier *Wretched of the Earth* (1967, first published in 1963), provide baseline approaches to the study of whiteness in their unflinching interrogation of the 'violence with which the supremacy of white values is affirmed and the aggressiveness which has permeated the victory of these values over the ways of life and of thought of the native' (1967: 33). Although post-Fanonian scholarship has offered alternatives to the violence of the Manichean divide, his mid-twentieth-century contributions (1952 and 1963) are as relevant and hard-hitting now as they were then, in understanding the psychological effects of white supremacy.

The interrogation of whiteness that Bhabha examines in the 'White Stuff', however, carries its own dangers. Indeed, he expresses his reservations in relation to Noel Ignatiev's call for the abolition of whiteness by suggesting that such abolition may never be accomplished because, as an identification, whiteness is an elusive quality that might simply continue 'its "nationalist" career under the guise of "civility", "secularism", "tolerance", or even "national culture"' (1998: 24). A similar danger in pursuing whiteness studies is articulated by Samina Najmi and Rajini Srikanth, who argue that the trend carries with it the possibility of 'eclips[ing] the universal power of whiteness'[26] (2002: 3) and obscuring the seemingly trivial but multiple ways in which liberal whites continue to benefit socially and economically in direct proportion to that 'universal' power. The range of post-apartheid writing by white women in this study has been selected to reflect as full a spectrum of responses as possible and particular attention is afforded to identifying the interstices in which claims of anti-racist liberalism recede in the face of the myriad and minute details that suggest a universal power, which is inadvertently reaffirmed.

The scepticisms that rightly come into play in undertaking projects such as these cannot be ignored, and Back (2002: 37) offers a valuable warning to scholars studying 'whiteness' in pointing to the problematic division of labour that might be the end product of jettisoning whiteness studies out of race studies as a discreet entity.[27] Ware quotes at length a piece that appeared in the *New York Times* (date not provided) by the journalist Margaret Talbot, whose response to white critique is scathing: 'Wouldn't it be easier to retreat into transfixed contemplation of one's own racial identity than to try to breathe life onto the project of integration[?]' (Ware & Back 2002: 28). The analysis undertaken in the present project is self-consciously aware of such criticisms, which may best be anticipated in posing a counter-question: isn't 'integration' dangerously affiliated with 'assimilation', and rather than a retreat into narcissistic navel-gazing, doesn't examining the manifestations of whiteness afford an opportunity to confront the universal epistemological power of whiteness? But, as Mike Hill warns, the critique of whiteness may not always succeed because it threatens 'modernity's juggernauts (e.g. liberal pluralism, majority rule, laissez-faire economics)' (1997: 3). The elements comprising Hill's juggernauts emerge as the primary justifications in liberal white politics, which, as Bhabha has suggested, continue to promote the notion of a national, imagined identity, touting concepts such as 'civility', 'secularism', 'tolerance' and 'national culture'.

The effort required to sustain such an imagined identity often goes completely unnoticed, but it is an effort that needs to be negotiated in a study such as the present one, and particularly in South Africa where whiteness as an 'identity' or an identification and an aspiration, though obviously under threat, continues to thrive in insulated enclaves of middle-class respectability.[28] One of the major reasons that such an identification manages to go unnoticed is that it seems to be no identification at all. Indeed, it simply seems ordinary to many, perhaps most white people, not only in this country, or in the United States, but almost everywhere in the western world.[29] White women have obviously not always shared the sense of normalcy because of their position in relation to men, and as such white women writers make interesting case studies in examining the extent of the natural acceptance of white normalcy.

Roland Barthes, in *Camera Lucida*, says, 'I don't know how to work upon my skin from within' (1984: 25). Precisely this problem is under scrutiny in the texts analysed in the following chapters. The questions posed will be to what extent each of the writers has recognised the difficulty of working on her 'skin from within', and how successful that work has been in dismantling some of the trappings that hold up the edifices of white womanhood. These largely invisible assumptions that underpin representations of whiteness are examined because, as Richard Dyer has pointed out, 'white power secures its dominance by seeming not to be anything in particular [and] also because when whiteness *qua* whiteness does come into focus, it is often revealed as emptiness, absence, denial or even a kind of death' (1999: 457). He goes on to suggest that contemporary post-colonial and postmodern centring of minority group issues has to some extent led to the reinforcement of the norm that 'carries on as if it is the natural, inevitable, ordinary way of being human'. Perhaps the most elusive aspect of studying whiteness is the normativity that Dyer identifies as an unconscious but powerful effect of white western hegemony precisely because it lays claim to being natural and ordinary.[30]

'The point of whiteness studies', writes Victoria Burrows, 'should be to fight racial prejudice and racism across the board – in the world, in the academy, in ideological representations in all its forms' (2004: 15). Burrows goes on to suggest that 'the most effective way for white feminists […] to assist in the work of disassembling racism is to deconstruct inwards – to keep exposing whiteness in its many protean forms in order to dismantle it' (2004: 23). This book offers a reading of the ideological implications of representations in literatures written by white women in South Africa, in order to deconstruct from within the many ways in which whiteness as a cultural construct continues to operate invisibly and normatively.

The collected insights into whiteness studies in these seminal contributions advance at least one pivotal objective in writing this book. That is in challenging (and hopefully making a contribution towards changing) the many largely invisible ways in which I and other members of my community are the natural, inevitable beneficiaries of apartheid, and the ways in which we continue to be complicit with racism in our assumption that ours is the ordinary way of being human. This study makes visible the multitude of ways in which whiteness through language and representation emerges as normative. The 'linguistic turn' post De Saussure radically changed the landscape of literary studies with its insistence on the primacy of language in constructing meaning (making it untenable to think about literature as a discreet and aesthetically powerful practice that surpasses the context in which it is/was produced). Despite De Saussure's insights there is still a very real sense in which racialised thinking, at least as it manifests itself in literary representations, has not been eroded, which in turn makes it necessary to attend to the complicities that continue to promote whiteness as transparent.

What a post-colonial study of whiteness calls for is the deconstruction of the self-sustaining white male subject of western metaphysics, a subject who remains as influential in this country in 2007 as he did during apartheid.[31] The present project attempts to bring together the strengths of post-colonial and postmodernist strategies in countering more efficiently the effects of western hegemony and the mythologies and so-called certainties deployed to sustain it. It is deconstructionist in the sense that it employs some of the strategies of a movement which, as Diane Elam has noted, is a cross-disciplinary attempt to 'destabilise both the notion of the subject and the social' (1994: 105), and expose the constructedness of autonomy and coherent subjectivity in literary representations.

Whiteness (Studies) in South Africa

A significant part of a colonial settler experience is a sense of isolation, alienation and displacement, and the residue of that historical relationship of the settler to the colonised territory has not disappeared. J.M. Coetzee has defined 'white writing' in South Africa as 'white only insofar as it is generated by the concerns of people no longer European, not yet African' (1988: 11). The deployment of the qualifying 'yet' suggests that at least in the 1980s, Coetzee held out some hope that the condition of transience would come to an end, that there may still be room in Africa for the oxymoronic notion of a 'White African'. His own emigration from South Africa, however, after writing *Disgrace*, indicates the contrary. More recently, Zoë Wicomb has read Coetzee's definition of white writing as an attempt to give whiteness a 'marked meaning, the name for something incomplete, not fully adapted to its environment, something in transition' (2001: 169). She thus interprets Coetzee's earlier intervention as anticipating the phenomenon of whiteness studies as crucial in negotiating identity politics in South Africa. The women writers represented in this study are writers who have chosen not to leave, as both Wicomb and Coetzee have done. Their work exhibits an attempt to negotiate the increasingly 'marked' sense of whiteness, and the increasingly alien position occupied by white people in post-colonial South Africa.

In this regard, Linda Peckham's insights (1990) into the role of the white writer and intellectual in South Africa are as relevant now, in many ways, as they were then. She uses the example of the film version of André Brink's *A Dry White Season* as an instance in which white South Africa's desire for 'a sense of place and identity' (1990: 373) is translated into a highly charged critique of the state's policies, but which fails to grapple with the ways in which white people have benefited from such policies. Peckham suggests that narratives such as this deploy apartheid as a backdrop against which a story of forgiveness/redemption is played out, and that rather than a backdrop 'we need to foreground the way we are framed and positioned as part of the narratives which provide continuity to apartheid'. 'If', she argues, 'we approach apartheid as subjectivity, as it inhabits and is inhabited by whites, critical understanding will not relapse into guilt, the white man's burden'. This study aims to assess the extent to which the ideological tenets of apartheid continue to operate residually, the ways in which racist principles continue to inhabit whites, and how 'guilt, the white man's burden' continues to inform contemporary textual production. In relation to guilt, as the white *woman's* burden, the genre of pulp fiction is examined because it is a genre that most readily condemns apartheid without foregrounding the framing that Peckham has identified. In addition, manifestations of the 'testimony', or the 'confessional' in emerging literature are explored and countered in examples of the 'anti-testimony' or 'anti-confessional' to expose how ineffectual the guilt mantle is in reaching (autobiographical) catharsis. Antjie Krog's *A Change of Tongue* is, amongst other things, a personal testimony in the confessional mode, though it consciously challenges the categorical as well and deliberately fictionalises aspects of the autobiographical. This work is read against Marianne Thamm's personal essays, Karen Press's semi-autobiographical poetry and Marlene van Niekerk's semi-autobiographical short story, all of which are written within and against the 'testimony'.

In addition to the dynamics that emerge in confessional-type literatures, one finds the manifestation of the 'discursive repertoires' that are characteristic of white middle-class womanhood in South Africa. In *Whiteness: The Communication of Social Identity*, Steyn offers a personal and hard-hitting response to whiteness. She argues that the challenge for white South Africans is 'to find a new relationship to the continent; to its people and their cultures; a relationship not based on the colonial assumption of the right to dominate indigenous people' (1999: 275). In response to the general exodus of whites from South Africa post 1994, she suggests that many of the whites remaining 'try to recycle the old narrative of "whiteness"' and thus place themselves 'in profound dissonance with the new circumstances in which they have to live their lives' (2001: 276). Aspects of these 'narratives of whiteness' are examined in this project. Steyn's concluding remark that white South Africans 'are indeed learning' and that this 'marks the advent of a dialogic relationship based on appreciation of difference' (1999: 276) needs to be read in relation to Grant Farred's remark that the 'real hegemony, white property, remains in place' (1999: 65).

White South African women's writing is markedly preoccupied with space, and not only domestic space but geographic space too. There is strong evidence that the writers under scrutiny, those who have stayed in South Africa, and are increasingly becoming aware of their alienation, have found it necessary to rethink their sense of belonging, and have done so largely in relation to spatial co-ordinates. In respect of white South Africa's response to space, Farred's concluding statement is hugely significant and warrants being quoted in full:

South Africa, for centuries the province of white dominance, now presents itself as an 'unhomely' space, a country rapidly becoming inhospitable to, if not uninhabitable by, its white occupants. The unhomeliness derives [...] from post-apartheid South Africa's inability to provide physical and mental sanctuary for a community accustomed to such protection by virtue of its race. (1999: 73)

This sense of 'unhomeliness' at times manifests itself quite predominantly in a desperate attempt to hold on tenaciously to a sense of 'homeliness', and at times as a conscious attempt to confront and adapt to a displacement.

Melissa Steyn's full-length sociological study, entitled *Whiteness Just Isn't What It Used To Be: White Identity in a Changing South Africa* (2001), has proved to be a seminal source in examining aspects of white 'unhomeliness'. Steyn usefully summarises a post-apartheid sense of white displacement as following: 1. Loss of Home, 2. Loss of Autonomy and Control, 3. Loss of a Sense of Relevance, 4. Loss of Guaranteed Legitimacy, and 5. Loss of Honour, Loss of Face (2001: 156–162). Though the texts I examine exhibit these symptoms to a lesser or greater extent in the experiences depicted, there is also significant evidence to suggest that middle-class white South Africans are still fiercely protecting their unselfconscious entitlement to a sense of home (belonging), autonomy, relevance, legitimacy and honour. This is not to suggest that these aspects of social living are no longer available to white South Africans *per se*, but that their loss is often experienced and represented exclusively in relation to an unexamined sense of entitlement. Equally useful is Steyn's observation that whiteness is a 'modernist' construction that 'requires force, even violence, to hold [its] binaries in a fixed ideological hierarchy' (2001: 150, 151). This is fairly easily accomplished in a new South African political dispensation, under the leadership of Thabo Mbeki, in which modernity's capitalist consumerism flourishes, and allows capital to dictate social hierarchies, which has meant that white economic privilege has not been undermined.[32] White economic privilege continues to operate as the most forceful currency in driving the value systems and seemingly inherent normativity of whiteness.

In Steyn's most recent contribution to whiteness studies (2005) she argues that it is precisely and ironically through diasporic affiliations with other mainstream white worlds that white South Africans manage to maintain their cultural privilege and normativity. She finds evidence for this in 'White Talk' (2005: 127), which offers a catalogue of responses not dissimilar to Dreama Moon's, but one which includes peculiarly South African variations. One of these examples of 'white talk' is what Steyn calls the adoption of a 'strategic anti-essentialism' in which 'whiteness appropriates Africanness expediently [...] [a] borrowing [that] is careful nevertheless to leave its real power centers intact' (2005: 127). When such discourse is employed and is pointed out, white South Africans will almost invariably counteract by suggesting that the challenge comes from one 'who is playing the race card', thus resorting to essentialising in an attempt to remain 'anti-essentialist' and liberally 'universal'. Though class is most certainly a major aspect of whiteness in this country, the white community is not homogenous in this regard. Steyn once again points to the complexities in her summation of white, English-speaking South Africans' response to apartheid:

> Drawn toward a more cosmopolitan worldview, adopting a more liberal lifestyle, showing disdain for the Afrikaner lack of 'class', preferring the case of the 'natives' over those of the Afrikaner while their own 'whiteness' was safely protected by their cultural chauvinism, these people held the moral high ground. (1999: 269)

The 'cultural chauvinism of Englishness' is particularly pertinent in relation to South African identity politics, which is why it is imperative to take seriously attempts such as that of Steyn to delineate Afrikaans and English whiteness. Simultaneously, however, one needs to be aware of the pitfalls in doing so, which may involve a reaffirmation of white hegemony because in foregrounding cultural (and class) difference, and downplaying racial dynamics, one runs the risk of reifying whiteness once again.

White Western Womanhood

Having introduced some of the most salient definitions and explorations of whiteness as a cultural construct, it is also important to consider the most pervasive ideological position adopted in this study, a position that influences the analysis of each text in subsequent chapters. Though already acknowledged, it is nonetheless important to reiterate that it is a feminist persuasion that informs this project, though Chela Sandoval's 'methodology of the oppressed' (2000: 26) allows for the inclusion of perspectives otherwise categorically divided. In summary, priority is given to those perspectives that contribute to understanding the impact of the most powerful influences in shaping white western Womanhood and in producing the role of Woman that allows for the perpetuation of classist and racist assumptions through unexamined discourses in a post-colonial space.

This brings me finally to the negotiation of my own positionality in embarking on a study of whiteness, and white women's writing. As a middle-aged, middle-class, white, English-speaking South African woman, it may be argued that in foregrounding white women's writing, I am simply reinforcing the cultural capital of whiteness inadvertently. This is a double bind that is central to the texts and writers featured in this study, and in exposing this ambivalence as it is manifest in literary and journalistic textual production, I am aware that my own position is necessarily limited. However, as long as race continues to operate as a social mechanism that impacts on power relations, it is imperative to continue the process of uncovering the ways in which racism operates.

Although there may be value in contextualising the centrality and hegemony of white western feminist theory and practice in the provision of a historical overview of the three 'waves' of western feminism, this study more readily offers an engagement with the interconnection between the politics of feminism and other political strategies. This strategy allows an examination of the universalising and essentialising assumptions that often emerge in western feminist practice. The 'oppositional and differential consciousness' that Chela Sandoval identifies as a 'methodology of the oppressed' (2000: 26) recognises and challenges the divide between theory and practice, between one theoretical approach and another, and between black women's realities and white women's realities. Such a recognition requires of the practitioner that she becomes acquainted with 'the current situation of power and self-consciously [choose and adopt] the ideological stand best suited to push against its configurations' (2000: 59). Sandoval thus brings together a disparate configuration of theorists from seemingly conflicting ideological persuasions in order to 'poach' what is needed to withstand and confront contemporary convergences of concealed and manipulative power. One space in which power is most effectively concealed and most persuasively manipulative is in hegemonic whiteness, which though it may be vulnerable in post-apartheid South Africa, is reinforced in the currency of global media practices, and in the economic power bestowed on white inhabitants historically. The following discussion is divided into three subsections for the sake of ordering but the interrelations are significant. Each subsection deals with an aspect of feminist approaches to whiteness. The first subsection deals with the implications of gender in relation to class and race, and highlights the difficulty of disentangling these positionalities, the second subsection focuses on gender as a performance and the third subsection pursues the notion of performativity as it relates to race, and introduces a psychoanalytic reading of whiteness as a 'Master Signifier'.

Class and Race

Class is a major element in the reproduction of white normativity, and more specifically, in the white western middle-class woman's contribution to maintaining the status quo. Nancy Armstrong has argued that the domestic space, or household, as we have come to inherit and understand it, came into being in the nineteenth century and that it was in the rise of fiction that the 'new family passed into the realm of common sense, where it came to justify the distribution of national wealth through wages paid to men' (1997: 918). She points towards the gaps in traditional Marxist theorisation in its refusal to acknowledge the centrality of the gendered division of labour in creating the bourgeois model of domestic femininity. Armstrong sees white western middle-class women as powerful in the domestic sphere, especially in reinforcing and perpetuating class hierarchies. She warns against a too easy and too familiar feminism 'that sinks comfortably into the rhetoric of victimisation' (1997: 919) and demands that we 'must be willing to accept the idea that, as middle-class women, we are empowered, although we are not empowered in traditionally masculine ways'. Manifestations of this 'empowered' aspect of literary production are examined in post-apartheid writing by middle-class white women in order to test Armstrong's observation that the effects set in motion by rise in literacy and the emergence of fiction written by women in the nineteenth century may still be felt today in a class-based 'systematic invasion of private life by surveillance, observation, evaluation and remediation' (1997: 919).

Here, Armstrong is clearly invoking Foucault's figure of 'Panopticism' from *Discipline and Punish* to suggest the ways in which white, middle-class, western womanhood continues to police the boundaries of propriety, in suggesting that we 'keep watch over ourselves – in mirrors, on clocks, on scales, through medical exams' (1997: 919–920), and then inflict the enactment of power onto others. The ramifications of bourgeois ideology cannot be over-emphasised in a study such as this, and it is thus important to take heed of Armstrong's explicit warning against a feminism that relies on victimisation without due consideration given to the very real ways in which white middle-class women are in fact relatively empowered, and whose primary gestures might often be largely in support of the status quo.

In this regard, Vikki Bell's *Feminist Imagination* (1999) offers an interesting contribution, one that acknowledges the difficulty of disentangling class and race. Bell sees her aim as finding a way beyond Nietzschean 'ressentiment' or what Wendy Brown has termed western feminism's penchant for 'wounded attachment' (in Bell

1999: 40). This 'particular and *owned* suffering', though it may seem necessary in effecting political change, runs the risk of 'investing in a reiteration of [women's] own powerlessness' (1999: 41). Bell argues that 'a politics fuelled solely by a sense of injustice and privation' will necessarily fail because it is always reactive rather than proactive, always marked by ambivalence because it *reacts* only to that privileged figure, 'the bourgeois white man – whose positionality is evoked as simultaneously coveted and despised' (1999: 40). In summary, Bell posits a political identification between black man and white woman, both of whom share this ambivalence towards white men, and whose political agendas might complement each other's in countering white masculine control in liberal western democracies. Though this is perhaps an over-simplification of her argument, for my purposes, it throws out two distinctly useful ideas. Firstly, Bell's reiteration of De Beauvoir's argument that the 'American Negro' and the white western woman respond completely differently to their oppression by white men:

> women are made to desire femininity, and therefore to desire their subordination. Women themselves, and the men around women, comply with these gendered regimes, such that men are 'duped' into a sense of security that these regimes uphold, whilst women *act in bad faith*, embracing femininity as an adaption to a situation in which their embodiment places them.
> (Bell, summarising De Beauvoir, 1999: 49; my emphasis)

It is precisely in this masquerade, this 'acting in bad faith', that white women differ from black men, whose mimicking of the white man is done not to conform or kowtow but to mock and deride the tyranny of the oppressor. If these are indeed authentic, though obviously generalised responses to oppression, then the possibility for identification is precarious given the conflicting agendas of each group. Bell's call for connectivity beyond 'ressentiment' is particularly problematic in South Africa, where the figure of the suburban gardener (or 'garden boy', as he is still sometimes called) provides an interesting case study against which to test her ideas, as will be demonstrated in Chapter Six, where Van Niekerk's short story, 'Labour', is read as her recognition of the impossibility of acting in good faith, or of moving beyond such 'ressentiment'.

If the possibility of identification between white women and black men is problematic so is the possibility of identification between white women and black women. As early as 1978, Adrienne Rich began to address this relationship with foresight and sensitivity in her essay entitled 'Disloyal to Civilisation: Feminism,

Racism, and Gynophobia'. Rich describes white feminists (in the late seventies) as being ridden with 'white solipsism' – not the consciously held *belief* that one race is inherently superior to all others, but a tunnel vision that simply does not see nonwhite experience or existence as precious or significant, unless in spasmodic, impotent guilt-reflexes, which have little or no long-term, continuing momentum or political usefulness'. This and the '*mythic misperceptions*' that white women harbour of black women 'which flourish in the combined soil of racism and gynophobia, the subjectivity of patriarchy', make explorations of the interactions between white and black women at times complex, at times predictable (1979: 306; emphasis in original). Rich argues that guilt-feeling paralyses white women and 'paralysis can become a convenient means of remaining passive and instrumental', thus acting as a form of hegemonic social control. In the light of these responses, part of this project is to examine the moments of 'solipsism' whether they are acknowledged or unconsciously perpetrated, and the moments when 'mythic misperception' is either entertained or counteracted.[33]

K. Davy, following Rich,[34] identifies class ideology in representations of the 'good (white) girl' that function as a 'bourgeois construct that provides white women with full access to the privileges of white womanhood'. She suggests that '"whiteness" is most *fully* mobilised at the intersection of bourgeois ideology, as the symbolism of true (white) womanhood is not that of the disenfranchised white woman, but that of the respectable "good (white) girl"' (1995: 204). Sander Gilman has read nineteenth-century constructions of optimal femininity as reinforcing this class- (and race-) based logic (1986: 248). His work uncovers the ways in which the lower-class European prostitute is similarly positioned, physiologically and iconographically, to the 'Hottentot Venus' in the nineteenth-century western imaginary. The association of whiteness and middle-class respectability culminates in a number of interrelated images and concepts that critics and writers have coined in their effort to examine the 'invisibility' of such identifications. Rich's notion 'white solipsism' (1979: 306) recalls Ralph Ellison's phrase 'Optic white, the Right White' (1952: 218). Whereas bell hooks has identified 'white right' as 'bourgeois decorum' (1994: 42), Davy suggests that such an identification may be understood as 'institutionalised whiteness' (1995: 198). All these phrases suggest a middle-class sensibility that is not as much a matter of economics as it is 'a kind of hard-earned "gentility" in the form of civility (a bedrock concept of imperialism)'. This is a position she suggests 'encompasses a plethora of values, morals, and mores that determine […] the tenets of respectability in general' (Davy 1995: 198). Davy's reading of Frye's exploration of how white girls become socialised is notable for its explication of the ambivalences facing white women:

> The white girl learns that whiteliness [sic] is dignity and respectability […] Adopting and cultivating whiteliness as an individual character seems to put it in the woman's power to lever herself up out of a kind of nonbeing (the status of women in a male supremacist social order) over into a kind of being (the status of white in a white supremacist social order. (In Davy 1995: 160)

It is this kind of socialisation that might be pivotal in attending to (post-)apartheid white South African social (and domestic) realities. Writers like Antjie Krog and Marianne Thamm show an awareness of the double bind, while Pamela Jooste and Susan Mann appear to be only partially aware, as the analysis of each will demonstrate.

The Performativity of Gender and Race

The work of Rich and Davy might just as readily be associated with queer theory as it is with feminist theory, and in addition to their work, Judith Butler (who has also been mentioned) offers a theory on gender performativity that is relevant in this project. These overlappings suggest something of the political tensions that exist within gender studies. One of these tensions emerges in relation to race: Sagri Dhairyam, in 'Racing the Lesbian, Dodging White Critics', suggests that 'Queer Theory' has come 'increasingly to be reckoned with as a critical discourse, but concomitantly writes a queer whiteness over raced queerness; it domesticates race in its elaboration of sexual difference' (1994: 26).

With this criticism in mind, there is some scope in pursuing, in relation to race, the significance of Butler's performativity theory, which she borrows from Foucault's *History of Sexuality*, and elaborates on in her deconstruction of drag. Her proposition that gender norms operate by requiring the embodiment of certain ideals of femininity and masculinity (1993: 231–232) may be redirected to entertain the following equation: white normativity operates by requiring the embodiment of certain ideals of the west, and that whiteness, far from being 'original' requires 'repeated effort to imitate its own idealisations' (1993: 125).

In addition to testing Butler's proposition, aspects of this enquiry invoke Jonathan Dollimore's notion of a queer 'transgressive aesthetic' (1991: 64) and how it relates to contemporary cultural politics, especially with regard to his reading of Foucault's analysis of sexual deviance. Dollimore summarises this position as harbouring both 'rejuvenative or insightful potential, [and] the insidious, manipulative complexities of power' in terms of the 'paradoxical relationship of deviants to it' (1991: 222).[35] Dollimore explains a 'transgressive aesthetic' specifically in relation to the work of Oscar Wilde, though his insight into how such an aesthetic operates has wider currency. Briefly summarised, it harnesses the dissidence and anger of the artist and puts these to work in trans-valuing 'the survival strategies of subordination – subterfuge, lying, evasion – [by turning them] into weapons of attack, but ever working obliquely through irony, ambiguity, mimicry and impersonation' (1991: 310). Both Thamm and Van Niekerk are read in relation to a Wildean transgressive aesthetic, and through Butler, in relation to a Foucauldian account of gender (and race) performativity.

Whiteness as Master Signifier

A psychoanalytic perspective, which reinforces the performativity of gender and race, offers the possibility of understanding the ambivalences of white western womanhood, though it is a contested terrain. Mary Ann Doane, in *Femme Fatales* sees psychoanalysis as a 'quite elaborate form of ethnography – as the writing of the ethnicity of the white western psyche' (quoted in Spillers 1997: 138). This succinctly signals the danger in adopting such a theory, the origins of which are firmly rooted in Eurocentric traditions, in critical discussions of race. Hortense Spillers warns against co-opting classical psychoanalysis, suggesting that the bourgeois household of Freud's Vienna a century ago 'generated the neurosis and its science out of a [particular] social fabric that feminist investigation has been keen to rethread' (1997: 138). Spillers' use of Lacanian psychoanalysis is firstly to wrest 'race' from the realm of the 'Real' (1997: 150), and to return it to the realm of the Symbolic. She suggests that it is important to 'unhook the psychoanalytic hermeneutic from its rigorous curative framework and recover it in a free floating realm of self-didactic possibility that might decentralise and disperse the knowing one' (1997: 153). Spillers foregrounds the role of language in constructing reality. She recognises the possibility that some of the insights that emerge in psychoanalysis may be deployed in understanding, for example, not 'hysteria' *per se*, but how hysteria was constructed as a female disease. By extension, she shows how 'race' might be similarly exposed as a construction in the service of maintaining European colonial power and its residual effects.

Kalpana Seshadri-Crooks manages the kind of recovery of a psychoanalytic hermeneutic that Hortense Spillers envisages. She summarises her main thesis as follows:

> Race is a regime of visibility that secures our investment in racial identity.
> We make such an investment because the unconscious signifier Whiteness,
> which founds the logic of racial difference, promises wholeness. (This is what
> it means to desire Whiteness: not a desire to become Caucasian[!] but, to put
> it redundantly, it is an 'insatiable desire' on the part of all raced subjects to
> overcome difference.) (2000: 21)

The centrality of Lacan's Symbolic Order in the construction of race is a major part of Seshadri-Crooks's argument, and her notion of race as a 'regime' (of visibility), in addition to her reading of whiteness as a 'master signifier', is a valuable frame of reference in negotiating the persistence of racial categorisation into the twenty-first century. Her work throws out at least two distinctly useful insights in examining whiteness. Firstly, she points to the dangers inherent in modern civil society which permits racial classification in drawing a distinction between:

> supposed ontology (the study of physical and cultural difference) and an
> epistemology (discriminatory logic) in the name of preserving a semblance of
> inter-subjectivity. Race, it suggests, is a neutral description of human difference;
> racism, it suggests, is the misappropriation of such difference. (2000: 8–9)

This practice is related to the new South African phenomenon of 'Rainbow Nationhood',[36] which promotes racialised thinking. A serviceable example of the supposed ontology of racial pragmatism appears typically in scientific discourse. In an article entitled 'Fair Enough' in *The New Scientist* (12 October 2002) Adrian Barnett attempts to answer that elusive question: 'Why are some people fair-skinned and some dark?' (2002: 34). In his purely anthropological/scientific discussion, race is conceived of exclusively in relation to UV and melanin. Interesting enough, but what is not 'fair enough' is that not even a passing glance is given in the piece to the crises engendered by these UV/melanin markings.

The second illuminating point to be gleaned from Seshadri-Crooks is in her useful discussion of Herman Melville's *Moby Dick*. The following passage from Melville's 1851 novel provides the culminating detail in her engaging reading of 'The Whiteness of the Whale':

> Is it that by its indefiniteness it shadows forth the heartless voids and
> immensities of the universe, and thus stabs from behind with the thought of
> annihilation, when beholding the white depths of the milky way? Or is it, that
> as in essence whiteness is not so much a color as the visible absence of color,

and at the same time the concrete of all colors; is it for these reasons that there is such a dumb blankness, full of meaning, in a wide landscape of snows – a colorless, all-color of atheism from which we shrink? (1986: 295-296)

The most striking phrase, 'the visible absence of color', Seshadri-Crooks reads as a 'simultaneous presence and absence' and suggests that 'Melville's notion of whiteness as the formless and the dangerous essence of visibility is wholly compatible with [her] view of Whiteness as a master signifier' (2000: 58). In addition, it is the power of Melville's rhetorical interrogation of the terror of Whiteness here that is significant – Whiteness is capable of 'stab[bing] from behind' and we 'shrink' from it. Indeed, it is a terror of 'pure and blinding light, which would annihilate and erase difference' (2000: 58). These all-encompassing, everything and nothing, 'voids' and 'immensities', concreteness and 'blankness', 'color-less' and 'all-color' paradoxes of whiteness are the most insidious and tenacious aspects of racial politics in post-apartheid South Africa, where despite an ANC government, and some very real political and social advancements since 1994, it may be argued that the civil norm (or, at the very least, the abiding social aspiration) is still pervasively white, a kind of 'dumb blankness' of inevitable conformity. This phenomenon is not merely a peculiarity of a particularly stubborn white South African community; rather it may be ascribed to the cultural imperialism and sheer egotism of the west.

Conclusion: Plotting a Continuum

As Alfred J. López has rightly observed in his introductory contribution to the recent collection of essays in *Postcolonial Whiteness* (2005), though '[it] would seem a simple enough assumption that the end of colonialism ushers in the end of whiteness, or at least its unrivalled ascendancy [...] the cultural residues of whiteness linger in the postcolonial world as an ideal' (2005: 1). Such an ideal may not always be overt, indeed may even be fiercely resisted, but it is nonetheless a symptom of the cultural practices and mythologies that South Africans (regardless of pigmentation) have come to inherit and pass on.

The following chapters will examine the mythologies that define the white western self in South Africa, especially as she occupies the domesticating spaces of suburbia. The texts under scrutiny will be read to illuminate some aspects of identity and belonging that confront post-apartheid white South Africans generally, and as reflecting the vulnerabilities, deceptions and the constructedness of (post-)colonial 'whiteness'. They will also be read to trace the tenuousness and inevitable sense of conflict and fear that marks the white settler-descendant's relationship to colonised space, and to suggest aspects of residual colonialism in South African suburbia, particularly its tendency to conform to an insular and self-preserving set of values. The residue, in contemporary texts of what Dorothy Driver (1992: 459) has identified in a South African context as white women's complicity in maintaining the ideological position of their settler husbands, is still evident in the literatures produced by white women. This residue and the predictable sense that middle-class, matronly whiteness carries of its own legitimacy, which is reinforced by a concomitant sense of normative neutrality, is ultimately what needs to be deconstructed. Jooste's work, for example, may be read as resisting, as she, arguably, unintentionally reproduces the discourses outlined above. Van Niekerk, however, employs layers of self-ironisation to comment on and acknowledge her own complicity in the discourses that promote and sustain racial hierarchies in South Africa, and each of the other writers featured falls somewhere in between these diametrically opposed positions, sometimes paradoxically.

Summarising contemporary theorisation of whiteness, Wicomb reads 'white [as] an empty signifier, both everything and nothing, [and] that being invisible to itself it cannot acknowledge its existence, [and] it can only articulate itself in terms of the markedness of black, the constant which supplies the meaning of white as norm' (2001: 168). The following analyses of selected white South African women's writing traces manifestations of a particular kind of suburban insularity among white South Africans and tracks the reification of whiteness and the erasure of the processes through which whiteness as a cultural practice comes into being. As Bhabha has pointed out, following Foucault, 'the place of power is always somehow invisible, a tyranny of the transparent' (1998: 21). The most engaged and self-conscious of the writers represented make visible such a tyranny and demonstrate an awareness of the fact that 'in the present state of political and social fluidity, the signifiers are at play' (Steyn 2001: 151).

My study is informed primarily by contemporary contributions to the theorisation of normative western whiteness, with particular reference to Womanhood in sustaining it. Colonial discourse theory, as summarised by Frankenberg, postulates the notion of an 'epistemic violence' that is irrevocably associated with white western European colonial expansion and 'the production of modes of knowing that enabled and rationalised colonial domination from the West [...] produc[ing] ways of conceiving "other" societies and cultures whose legacies endure into the present' (1997: 16). 'Without significant exception', notes Said, 'the universalising discourses of Modern Europe and the United States assume the silence, willing or otherwise, of the non-European world' (1993: 58). This project examines the ways in which white women writers acknowledge or ignore, challenge or co-opt the power of cultural imperialism in the west, and assesses the efficacy of their deconstruction of 'universalising discourses' that promote and sustain it. These writers, who are themselves the products of, and critics of, a legacy of universalising discourses, are thus strategically positioned to offer resistance, and simultaneously, to carry the ideological residue of a legacy that continues to insist on its primacy. How have white women writers negotiated their empowering whiteness and their less empowered womanhood in relation to post-colonial realities? Who amongst them has offered the most powerful challenge to these dynamics that compromise, inhibit and simultaneously empower white South African women? How relevant are these responses in countering the effects of white western hegemony, and how does the genre effect the efficacy and distribution of the ideas uncovered? These questions lead to a final justification for the production of a book investigating literary responses to whiteness by white South African women writers. In 'The Loneliness of Noam Chomsky', Arundhati Roy remarks on the fact that when she first encountered Chomsky's work she was amazed at the sheer volume of evidence he had amassed. 'But now', she writes, 'I understand that the magnitude and intensity of Chomsky's work is a barometer of the magnitude, scope, and relentlessness of the propaganda machine that he's up against' (2004: 63).

'Literature' (and the term is used in its original sense to denote 'all of that which has been written' and not just that which has been canonised in the promotion of western sensibilities) has always provided a fairly reliable barometer of the 'magnitude, scope and relentlessness' of the value system its writers and readers entrench and/or resist. Roy suggests that those of us who resist being slotted into George W. Bush's category – 'You're either with us, or you are with the terrorists' – have work to do that is as tenacious and relentless as Chomsky's is: we need to amass evidence to the contrary, we need to resist the tyranny of binaries (us and them, theory and practice, etc.), the 'tyranny of the transparent' (white is right, west is best), so that in our dissent we 'reinvent civil disobedience' and 'come up with a million ways of being a collective pain in the ass' (2004: 77). This book is one small contribution to that collective goal.

2

Complicity and Cliché in *People Like Ourselves* by Pamela Jooste and *One Tongue Singing* by Susan Mann

> *That I am white, that I share a special genetic and cultural legacy with an identifiable white race who brought us the Bible and planned the Parthenon and raised the Roman Empire, that I am better than other people because I am an American and male and straight and white, that science is white, that objectivity is white, that Christianity is white – that's twisted shit. Whiteness is just some broken-down toxic junk that's been piling up way too long. It's time we all started cleaning out that closet.*
> **Gary Taylor (2005: 360)**

Introduction

'If there's one thing post-apartheid South Africa doesn't lack', writes Fred de Vries in the article 'Singular White Females', published in *This Day*, 'it's bold new women authors' (2004a: 10). Framing the text is a series of pictures representing the 'Distinctive Voices' the article explores – Diane Awerbuck, Patricia Schonstein, Katy Bauer and Jo-Anne Richards, and a series of book covers amongst which are Pamela Jooste's *People Like Ourselves* (2004) and Susan Mann's *One Tongue Singing* (2005). These two books are prime examples of a promoted genre emerging in South Africa, identified by the *Mail & Guardian*'s Robert Kirby as 'post-apartheid weepies' written by 'guilt-ridden white women' (2005a: 23) who have found a niche market in appealing to a premature celebration of new South African rainbow nationhood without having to negotiate the real politics of white normativity. In this chapter I examine two novels in order to gauge the extent to which either might be considered 'bold' (in challenging the mores of white western womanhood) or merely sentimental, the most normative and socially sanctioned values of most white readers unconsciously affirmed. Fiction such as *People Like Ourselves* and *One Tongue Singing* sells, specifically to white middle-class women. What might white South African women learn from these books? How have their realities been depicted? And how, if at all, have the writers negotiated the complex politics of gender, race and belonging in post-apartheid South Africa? In an attempt to answer these and other related questions, the following analysis explores the complicities and attends to the clichés that emerge in each of the novels respectively. The ways in which whiteness as a 'master signifier' operates silently but effectively in the interstices of liberal western discourses is examined, and Frankenberg's 'discursive repertoires' (1993: 290) associated with white normativity are uncovered.

People like Ourselves and People like Them

Before the charge of plagiarism, which will be discussed later, caused a furore amongst South African critics, Pamela Jooste's *People Like Ourselves*, on publication, received more or less consistently favourable reviews. Jennifer Crocker, for example, suggests that Jooste 'has produced a novel of supreme elegance and fine observation' and that 'while [she] remains popular on the book club circuit, it is time she was recognised as one of this country's best serious novelists' (2003: 9). Likewise, Barbara Hollands sees the novel as 'a simple, sometimes unsettling read, which is thought-provoking without being prescriptive or judgemental' (2003: 4). 'Frankly,' writes Sally Kernohan, 'those with a conscience will find it disturbing. But it is an exceptional and absorbing read' (2003: 2). Shirley Kossick sees the novel as 'a colourful, knowing and accomplished work with some penetrating observations about "the way we live now"' (2003: iv). Positive reviews reiterating similar sentiments were written by Margaret von Klemperer (2003: 7), Debbie Derry (2003: 8), Tessa Fairbairn (2003: 12) and Diane de Beer (2003a: 21).

What is initially interesting to note is that every one of these favourable reviews was written by a white English-speaking South African woman. The only seriously negative review, written in Afrikaans, came from Cecile Cilliers in the *Volksblad*, in her challenging question concerning what kind of story *People Like Ourselves* might be:

Wat die leser veral onbevredig laat, is die gebrek aan gerigtheid van die boek. Wat is dit nou eintlik – roman, satire, liefdesverhaal met 'n (onwaarskynlike) gelukkige einde? Dit val tussen al daardie stoele, en daarom – en dis baie jammer – nie 'n boek wat die leser lank bybly nie. (5 May 2003)[37]

This is clearly not a question on the minds of the English-speaking white women reviewers whose identification with the characters in the book appears to have been powerful enough for them to overlook its flaws, this being only one of the most obvious, and one that may at least partially account for the curious back cover statement attributed to the *Cape Times* which hails the book as '[p]erceptive and sensitive and extremely funny': 'perceptive' and 'sensitive' it may be to the average white woman reader, but 'funny' it is not. In fact, most reviewers concur in their acknowledgement of a certain unresolved bleakness that permeates the story. Of all the reviews, though, it is Sally Kernohan's that epitomises the kind of reception the book initially enjoyed, in her summation that 'those with a conscience will find it disturbing'. The question that begs to be asked is who she might have in mind as '*those*' with a conscience or what kind of conscientising experience it provides. Patently, it is white suburban madams that she has in mind, and tellingly it is carried by the universalising plural 'those'. And though the story might 'disturb' the employer of exploited black labour, it does not significantly challenge the power relations that maintain the status quo, as the following analysis of the characters demonstrates.

There is no doubt that Pamela Jooste is well versed in the minutiae of white South African suburban lifestyles. Her portraits of upper-middle-class life in the suburbs of Johannesburg are wholly recognisable and wholly believable, as far as they are hastily sketched. Her error is not in what she depicts, but conversely, in what she *does not* depict when focussing on white family dynamics, and even more problematically, in what she *does* depict when focussing on black South African realities. Jooste may be seen to represent a certain ideological stance from post-apartheid white women writers, which is evident in some of the unexamined assumptions she makes about post-apartheid life in South Africa. My own exploration of her work will attempt to reveal the nature and extent of these assumptions and how they remain unexamined by the author. She is not, like Gordimer, Press and even Krog may be seen to be, able to step back from her own assumptions, instead reading 'flatly' what she encounters.

A significant error of omission is the missing acknowledgement of a reference Jooste used which caused such a furore in the *Sunday Times* and the *Mail & Guardian* early in 2005. Her 'innocent' reading of South Africa is evidenced in her plagiarism, where she sees no problem in merely lifting from another source as if that source were a 'true' representation of South African reality, and this 'truth' is available to all and understood by all. Despite protestations to the contrary (in her claim that the plagiarised passages, having been published in a national newspaper were 'in the public domain' and thus 'susceptible to quotation without acknowledgement' – Jacobson 2005), Jooste knows full well what plagiarism entails: in *People Like Ourselves*, the novel in which these nicked phrases and sentences are to be found, she allows the parenthetical observation that an article had been 'picked up off the wire, [and] reprinted with all proper acknowledgements' (2004: 199). Jooste's own 'picking up' of something without 'proper acknowledgements' involves the verbatim transference of sections of a text (up to 400 words, allegedly) from an article by academic Lindsay Bremner published in the *Sunday Times Lifestyle* magazine, entitled 'Theme Park City' (Celean Jacobson, *Sunday Times*, 3 January 2005). In describing contemporary suburban Johannesburg, whole sentences such as 'Here the fourth of July is celebrated with Elvis lookalikes, Cadillacs and hot dogs laid on by the homeowners' association' (2004: 144), are copied by Jooste straight from Bremner's article. Though Jooste did finally admit to, and apologise for, using the material, her claim that it was inadvertent might be understood as a symptom of the 'flat' reading of complex lived realities that her work represents.

There is nothing equivocal about it: if one 'picks something up off the wire', or copies someone's words from any source, one is morally and legally obliged to acknowledge the author, and both Charlotte Bauer[38] and Robert Kirby[39] are right to have responded to such an act with outrage. The controversy surrounding the incident throws out one major scholarly concern over and above the censure that might accompany any serious consideration of the novel, and that involves suspicion in respect of the novel's originality as a whole. In this regard, it may be argued that it is a text of mass production, containing mass-produced mores for public consumption, and, mass produced literature is generally aimed at a white western middle-class market, and is generally derivative.

White South African readers of *People Like Ourselves* might well experience an uncomfortable sense of *déjà vu* in their recognition of the preoccupations and paranoia that the white middle-class characters experience: their lives are so predictable that they represent nothing that a caricatured, cartoon-type social script in speech bubbles might not accomplish more successfully. And, if anything, this is Jooste's second sin of omission – she does not fill the blanks that even a cursory reading of the novel renders visible. It is important for the present argument to outline some of those blanks, showing the difference between what one may suggest are the experiences and anxieties of the average white woman reader in South Africa and Jooste's representation of these experiences and anxieties. An examination of some of the characters will reveal crucial omissions, of purpose, of motivation, of psychological depth, that other more painfully observed but wholly superficial details of verisimilitude might obscure. The following discussion will focus specifically on two aspects of Jooste's characterisation. The first is her representation of white womanhood, in keeping with the major interest of this study, though the general tenor of its criticism of key female characters might be extended to include all the white characters in this fairly full fictional cast. The second aspect is her depiction of black South African realities.

Jooste's exploration of the dis-ease of whiteness emerges in her portrayal of three key white women characters in the story, namely Julia, Caroline and Rosalie. In each case, she suggests that white women are increasingly alienated in post-apartheid South Africa, and that this alienation manifests itself mentally and physically. Though this reading of white South African middle-class womanhood may be accurate, the following analysis will suggest that white normativity is reinforced rather than challenged. This emerges in relation to the disjunction between what she attempts to do, which is to suggest white alienation, and how she does it, which is by resorting to cliché, and the derivative and perhaps unconscious rehashing of grand narratives.

The central character in the story is Julia: disaffected, perfectionist, privileged housewife on the brink of divorcing her philandering husband, estranged from her only child, whose rebellion is targeted at belittling her mother's sensibilities, obsessed with the loss of her beautiful younger self, in therapy and selling her jewellery to pay for cosmetic surgery, and Mrs Dalloway-like, attempting to reaffirm the significance of her existence by throwing a party (which her husband can ill afford to finance, and which in any case is aimed at publicly humiliating him by inviting his ex-wife). Jooste's 'failure of imagination', charges of plagiarism notwithstanding, is in neglecting to endow Julia with any fully developed psychological life in the manner that Virginia Woolf manages in rescuing the superficial Mrs Dalloway from the unredeemed fate of the Julias of the world. Throughout the novel Julia remains not much more than the string of superlative clichés the above character sketch suggests. Essentially, what brings her to her senses at the end of the novel is her own mortality, having been diagnosed with possible breast cancer (2004: 262), rather than the existential angst that marks Mrs Dalloway's confrontation with her near-death experience lived vicariously through the suicide of her alter ego, Septimus Smith.

However, perhaps Julia is not meant to be a fully developed three-dimensional character with psychological depth. She may be deliberately set up as a stereotype, a cardboard cut-out caricature of white middle-class Johannesburg women, and consequently the novel is more of a satire than a romance. This certainly seems plausible, at least initially. An important example of the kind of stereotyping involved in Jooste's portrayal of Julia, apart from the character sketch already mentioned, is Julia's relationship with Adelaide, her domestic servant. The relationship is typical of suburban madams and their maids. The reader learns that Adelaide is beholden to Julia because a grandchild, a girl, is staying with the servant in the backyard quarters, ubiquitous in white South African suburban homes for 'sleep-in maids', 'in return for which Julia expects at least a greater show of willingness on Adelaide's part' (2004: 11). Part of this 'willingness' is being a silent but watchful bystander during the constant marital tiffs between Julia and Douglas, her unfaithful husband.

Jooste's condemnation of Julia is in the madam's refusal to acknowledge Adelaide's existence except in relation to her own needs and wants. In effect, as Jooste amply demonstrates in numerous anecdotes, the maid does not exist except to witness Julia's existence silently and to serve her dutifully. That Adelaide does have a life of her own is made apparent in the only chapter in the novel given over to the maid's personal problems. The novel consists of chapters, the titles of which are largely the names of the characters whose narrative takes precedence in that particular section, i.e. 'Julia', 'Caroline', 'Douglas', 'Michael', and 'Rosalie' being the most frequently repeated. Jooste's inclusion of Adelaide as a character worthy of at least one chapter may be read in relation to Adrienne Rich's suggestion that guilt-feeling characterises white women's responses to black women (1979: 306), in the sense that the writer's own white guilt may be instrumental in Adelaide's inclusion nominally as a primary character.

On the day before the party a garden service arrives, Mrs Julia Merchant having clearly decided not to buy the flowers herself, bringing multiple bunches of lilies which will float on the surface of the swimming pool during the event. Adelaide has not been given instructions to receive the flowers which are expected only the following day, and while attempting to manage this crisis is unexpectedly visited by her daughter who has come to fetch Tula, the grandchild whom Adelaide is harbouring under duress in the servant's quarters. The scene allows the reader a brief glimpse into the traumas confronting all three of the black female characters (traumas which Jooste appears to have difficulty imagining, an issue that will be examined later), but they are no sooner represented than they are ejected from the story entirely (2004: 264–279). Although it is apparent that Jooste is foregrounding the dysfunctionalities inherent in the domestic dynamic of Madam and Eve in white South African suburbia, the nominal and expendable role that Adelaide is required to play does not effectively challenge the mores governing the relationship. It may be argued that Adelaide disappears into the background as readily for Jooste, the writer, as she does for Julia, the character.

Caroline, Julia's best friend, is a more carefully constituted character, as will be shown, though the string of clichés that emerges in summarising her is almost as long as the one wrapped around Julia. Caroline is another ageing society hostess, who lives in the shadow of her formidable mother-in-law and the mansion she bequeathed to Julia and her husband, Gus Bannerman. As the result of a near fatal car accident, Gus is living out the remainder of his life in a comatose state, in an upstairs room, connected to life by a ventilator and his wife's devoted attention. Caroline's story is dominated by her encounter with servants, nurses and medical care for her comatose husband. Jooste's rendering of Caroline's predicament is sensitive, allowing her both dignity and human frailty, as she watches the edifices of her old South African existence slowly crumbling around her. Though she wields power over the domestic servants and 'runs her life like a railway timetable and nothing seems to upset her' (2004: 221) on one hand, she is haunted by white guilt and the image of a drowned toddler, daughter of a servant, on the other. The superficial control she exhibits in handling the day-to-day responsibilities of running a large establishment and overseeing her black domestic help is undermined by a creeping sense of un-belonging as she begins to notice the plants disappearing from her garden one by one, plants that had 'been there for as long as she could remember, part of the landscape, taken for granted. Then they were gone and nothing but raw earth to show where they'd been' (2004: 218). This constitutes a moment of powerful symbolism in the text. Jooste's image of the barren garden may be read as reflecting the barrenness of post-apartheid whiteness and the centrality of land and land ownership in sustaining white South Africa's sense of belonging.

Caroline's invitation to Julia's party acts as a catalyst in forcing her to end the 'living dead' life of memories she has come to lead in the Bannerman mansion. Indeed, Jooste is clearly using the Bannerman subplot to suggest the demise of white privilege in South Africa. The reader's final image of Caroline is her plotting, with the help of a notified electrical power cut, the death of her cherished but brain-dead husband, which she plans as meticulously and objectively as the dinner menu she imagines negotiating at Julia's party while the Escom power is cut. 'With her old name, old money, good jewellery and good manners' (2004: 298), she is prematurely jettisoned from the story, and what may potentially have been a sensitive rendering of a lonely white woman's painful negotiation of displacement ends in cheap melodrama.

However, it is Rosalie who is by far the most interesting and the most flawed characterisation in the novel. She may be read as showing Jooste's own ambivalences about whiteness, in relation to the uneasiness that is suggested in certain aspects of the portrayal, as the following discussion will show. Rosalie lives alone in London, having returned home after a stint in South Africa in which she becomes embroiled in a failed marriage to Douglas, a fling with Michael, and activist activities, during the ANC freedom struggle, as a result of which she is detained and imprisoned under the State of Emergency in the 1980s. She progresses in the novel from vaguely distracted to distinctly paranoid, and we are finally enlightened in the closing pages that she is suffering from Alzheimer's (2004: 291).

Perhaps what makes Rosalie a more intriguing character than either the predictable Julia or the conventional Caroline is the aura of mystique that is generated in plotting her decline, though it may be argued that the mystique constitutes a vagueness, which marks Jooste's failure to imagine the experiences of a white South African female anti-apartheid activist, having very few specimens to model Rosalie on, not only because Jooste may not have known any personally but because there were in reality only a few white men and women fighting on the other side.[40] The reader knows more about Rosalie's relationships with Douglas and Michael than about her political activities, which is inevitable given the genre and focus of the novel which is essentially 'romantic', but there is not even one significant interaction with a black comrade recounted to lend authenticity to the political role we are asked to believe that she played so valiantly (even Nelson Mandela enquires about her [2004: 118]), and with such traumatic consequences. We witness her growing sense of alienation in a cityscape where only the neighbourhood cats bear witness to her existence ('The cats know her here and that's a good sign, a sign of belonging' [2004: 20]), to the loss of time and sense of self she experiences (2004: 90–92), and finally a total mental breakdown which is manifest in an imagined Other woman occupying her flat (2004: 217). Whereas the implications of this breakdown might well be read as schizophrenia related to the activist's hybrid 'unhomeliness', Jooste does not allow for such a reading, and relies on the safer, hereditary option of Alzheimer's so that the connection between activism and illness, with so much potential for exploring the disease of whiteness, dissipates into a mere plot device.

Jooste has clearly plotted a continuum of increasing displacement in her portrayal of the three white women characters under scrutiny. On the far extreme is Rosalie, former anti-apartheid activist suffering from a severely debilitating mental disorder; in the middle, precariously straddling the line between liberalism and conservatism, between the old South Africa and the new, between madness and sanity, is Caroline; and at the other extreme is Julia, whose measured and sane though clearly resigned response is the last sentence in the book: 'We just have to wait and see', says Julia in response to Douglas's question: 'Where exactly do we go from here' (2004: 336). Though Jooste consciously resists closure and the concomitant and comforting 'happily ever after' clause associated with classic realism and, more recently, pulp fiction, it is nonetheless disquieting to consider the implications of the continuum I have suggested that Jooste deliberately plots: Rosalie is diagnosed with Alzheimer's and institutionalised, Caroline is abandoned on the brink of committing euthanasia, and only Julia, the walking cliché of white madamhood, white wifehood, and white motherhood is allowed, slight as it may be, the possibility of redemption: she is last seen sitting on the terrace with her estranged husband, in an intimate albeit uncertain moment of confession, comfort and reconciliation, which even the threat of breast cancer cannot entirely undo.

Julia, the most 'normal' of the trio, will endure. Her 'normalcy' is her privileged, dysfunctional domesticity, and many white South African women would identify with her in exhibiting the fears and failings of their own domestic realities. As Tania Modleski has noted in her reading of soap operas, a genre not dissimilar to mass-produced fiction:

> It is important to recognise that soap operas serve to affirm the primacy of the family not by presenting an ideal family, but by portraying a family in constant turmoil and appealing to the spectator to be understanding and tolerant of the many evils which go on within that family. (1982: 93)

Julia's life may exhibit the multiple dysfunctionalities of insular white suburbia, and these dysfunctionalities serve to reinforce normalcy as Modleski suggests, but the open-ended ending of the book reaffirms the primacy and normalcy of the family, with Man and Wife coming together in adversity, thus reinforcing the status quo.

In effect, the normativity of all four of the major white characters, Douglas, Julia, Michael and Caroline, despite the magnitude of the crises they each face, is never in dispute, especially given the backdrop of vignettes depicting deviousness against which their normativity is set: in Rosalie's apartment block there are a lapsed Catholic priest and his male lover, as well as a exoticised/eroticised half-naked, fruit-eating Senegalese street performer (2004: 23), all of whom are sketched perfunctorily as sideline entertainment (roadside attractions or circus freaks?) and who function as reminders of 'real' deviance to offset white, heterosexual, patriarchal, middle-class normalness. The marginality of these characters is what reduces them to functioning merely as examples.

If omissions characterise Jooste's portrayal of white women, her characterisation of black South Africans is marked by an uncomfortable and politically insensitive attempt to speak on their behalf, to fill in the blanks as it were in imagining black South African realities, which results in a series of stereotypes that could only have emerged from a white middle-class perspective. One of the ways in which this reduction to stereotype emerges is in relation to the point of view adopted in the narrative. Jooste's use of free indirect speech allows her access to each character's inner thoughts, and although this strategy is relatively unnoteworthy in her depiction of the white characters, it is increasingly uncomfortable in her depiction of black subjectivities.

An example of the possibilities and problems that emerge in Jooste's attempts to flesh out the lives of the servants in suburbia is her depiction of Adelaide's grandchild, the young Tula. There are perhaps many reasons for the relative success of such a characterisation, but arguably the most convincing might be that children are themselves unable to counter such depictions, and adults thus have free range in imagining what children might be thinking, which in a sense has been the rationale for white writers having no qualms about representing black subjectivities. Desiree Lewis has persuasively articulated this tendency in an essay entitled 'The Politics of Feminism in South Africa' (1996: 100–101) by arguing that '[t]he right to interpret black experience has been a white right', and though she is referring specifically to academic and critical practice, her argument might well be extended to include other representational practices:

> The rigid distinction between interpretation and expression [...] plus the discrediting of black interpretation of experience on the one hand and the cultivation of black expression on the other, are an entrenchment of standard racist oppositions – blacks 'express', feel and respond: whites observe, explain and consolidate their normativeness. (1996: 100)

Suburban South Africa provides ample opportunity for white middle-class women to 'observe' at least the most obvious complications in black women's lives, not the least of which is the uncomfortable fact that black women are not exclusively servants, but also daughters, mothers, and grandmothers. Tula has been abandoned by her mother indefinitely and left in the care of her grandmother, Adelaide, and is required to keep quiet and out of Madam's sight. The little girl is therefore left largely on her own and to her own thoughts and fantasies, which Jooste imagines and articulates with some empathy. The contradictory influences in the child's life are manifest: on the one hand her mother has been instrumental in demonstrating a new South African sassiness available to black women who no longer need to be any white woman's servant, and on the other are Mr Malipile (Gladstone) and Adelaide, a submissive older generation of exploited domestic labour, exhibiting the kind of passive servitude that is required in suburbia, a demeanour that Tula witnesses but resists.

A sensitive rendering of the little girl's resistance occurs when her mother comes to fetch her, and she hides in the poolroom in protest against being abandoned for so long. In hiding she watches her confident mother stride through the 'madam's' garden and recalls her mother telling her that 'she'll take [Tula] by the shoulders and shake her bit by bit' if she ever hears her using the word 'madam':

> If that's what she wants then she'll have to get herself ready to be shaken much harder so that the ugly word shakes itself loose and falls right out of her head. They can pick it up off the floor and throw it down from the top of the rubbish chute of the old Ponte City where they used to live, right down to the bottom with all the other rubbish where no-one will ever find it again. (2004: 275)

The word 'madam' is transformed from abstract lexicon into concrete, palpable waste – a physical object that must literally be jettisoned, demonstrating Jooste's awareness of the power of signification in shaping identity and subjectivity, and her recognition of the conscious political effort required to counteract the effects of words. In this moment all three black women are at least partially liberated from the stereotypes other less finely honed aspects of Jooste's representational practice exhibit.

A more problematic characterisation is that of Gladstone, the retired labourer who worked alongside Douglas in his construction business from its early beginnings (2004: 75). For his lifetime service he receives a golden wristwatch and now works in the Merchants' garden, having been put out to pasture, so to speak, where he has an outside room for his use, in exchange for some menial black labour, for which he is supposed to be grateful, as his daughter scathingly remarks (2004: 153). He lives out his retirement working at his part-time gardening job in the suburbs but living at his daughter's house in Soweto. Of all the black characters to make an appearance on the pages of this novel, it is Gladstone's life that is given the most narrative space (four chapters) and this constitutes an enormous imaginative effort on Jooste's part to flesh out the details of a life, that of an old working-class black man, diametrically opposed to her own, as a middle-aged, middle-class white woman.

It is an effort, however, that results in the readers gleaning more about Jooste's positionality in relation to her subject than the subject himself. In all political correctness we are told that his real name is not Gladstone but Mr Malipile, his English name being conferred on him typically by his master who needed a name he could pronounce for his 'boss boy' (2004: 76). Without access to the conceivably more authentic preoccupations of an older black man, Jooste's rendering of his thoughts (which revolve around his stash of money, his aches and pains, and his dream of returning to his hometown) is presented in clipped staccato repetitions and the elementary speech patterns and lack of comprehension that might well be attributed to a child:

> Friday night, end of the week, end of the month and Gladstone in his suit, white shirt, shiny shoes is going home later than usual. Mr M likes him to go back to the township early to avoid the rush, especially on payday but cleaning the river is slow work and Adelaide screaming out the way she did for no reason, giving everyone a shock, didn't make the day any better. (2004: 308)

Jooste's use throughout the novel of a rather unsophisticated adaptation of free indirect discourse, with its characteristic merging of the voices of author and character, provides her with the freedom to manoeuvre her way between multiple perspectives with minimal narrative effort. In the above opening paragraph of the penultimate chapter carrying Gladstone's name as its title, Jooste's heavy-handed use of the technique is apparent: it is almost certainly *her* consciousness that dresses Gladstone in his glad rags. Similarly, it is almost certainly her consciousness, rather than one that might approximate his, that is responsible for refusing him the discernment a) to leave early on payday for the above-mentioned reason or any other, and b) to comprehend what prompts Adelaide's sudden scream. Much of the discourse used to suggest Gladstone's subjectivity is presented in a similar fashion, which despite some deft and sensitive moments, has the effect of reducing him to one-dimensionality, reminiscent of American minstrelsy.[41]

One potential moment of empathetic imagining is in relation to his disorientation in trying to fathom geographic name changes, in having to keep on reminding himself that what was once Louis Trichardt is now Makhado:

> No one has any idea where they are any more with all the name changes.
> Mr M will say that too and perhaps when he says it he speaks for all his generation and says more than he knows. (2004: 309)

Gladstone's yearning to return home (to Louis Trichardt, alias Makhado) poignantly and necessarily remains unfulfilled, partly because it is a place that no longer exists, except in his memories. One could comment on the implausibility of the strong identification between 'boss' and 'boss boy', but the gesture, flawed as it may be, nonetheless functions to create empathy. It is plot development, however (the suspension of disbelief, and the creation of suspension), which ultimately dictates Gladstone's depiction in the text: Julia's party has meant that he will have to evacuate his room for a day in order to make way for the waiters, which means having to move his savings which he stores under the mattress. It has also meant that he has had to take orders from Julia rather than Douglas, hence his cleaning up of the river and straining his old body in the process. On his way back to Soweto, with his cash supply strapped around his torso, he has a heart attack, but some kind nurse from Baragwanath rescues him and gives his money to the matron for safe-keeping. Perhaps, if the characterisation of Gladstone had been more believable, this new South African good news conclusion might be more believable too. This is not to suggest that there are no good Samaritans in Soweto, but to highlight the stereotypicality of the ones to make an appearance in this lily-white story: they are either domestic workers or nurses. Only teachers are missing in the troika of types that white South Africans have conventionally accommodated as 'good' black people.

The most seriously flawed attempt at representing black subjectivities in the novel is Jooste's portrayal of Regina, the 'maid' who works for Caroline. Regina is summoned to the Madam's study to hear the rules pertaining to black labour in the household: she may have one day per week off, she may not exchange days with other staff, she may not ask for advances on her salary and she may never have any black man come anywhere near the house, all conditions typical of white suburban expectations of black labour. Indeed, as Cuckoo reminds her, she 'isn't interested in husbands, boyfriends or babies. If there is anything like that going on it must stay in the township where it belongs, she doesn't even want to know about it' (2004: 184). Jooste accurately portrays the inhumanity that characterises the white suburban madam's response to her black domestic help, especially insofar as black women are expected to have no life at all beyond the high walls and locked gates of their employers' suburban estates.

But, crucially, it is when Jooste tries to imagine Regina's existence outside of the servants' quarters that she blunders into embarrassing western stereotypes, ones which Sander Gilman has identified as central in a taxonomy of being that emerged in nineteenth-century European literature and iconography, and which is still residual in the western imaginary, positing the black woman as an essentially sexualised being (1986: 248). Regina, when she goes back to 'the township […] can put on her red dress […and] walk down the street in high heels. She can feel her bum move from side to side, nice and smooth as she walks and if that gets a whistle that's all right too' (2004: 185). Though the focaliser in this account of her personal life is clearly meant to be Regina, it is a white gaze that (un-)dresses her, and uncovers her 'primitive' and 'unbridled sexuality' (Gilman 1985: 248). If black women are not reduced to the sum of their body parts and their inarticulate 'kekkeling'[42] under the white gaze, as they 'walk down the street, showing [their] bum[s], letting [their] breasts point in any direction [they] like […], laughing [their] laughs as loud as [they] like' (2004: 186), they are perceived as breeding vessels,[43] as demonstrated in Jooste's follow-up image of Regina's 'other' life when the author imagines the character thinking that she

> would like to lie in the hot dark and drink beer, and maybe make another baby and why not? She's not old and she's strong, she likes the feel of life taking root in her womb. If she could be mother of all the new world she would do it.
> (2004: 187)

The 'Mother Africa' figure lurking in this description, coupled with the implication of 'hot dark' moral lasciviousness, not to mention Douglas, the bridegroom's rapacious gaze (2004: 187), arguably constitutes one of the most dangerous and one of the most concealed brands of racism, couched as it is in the seemingly innocuous and thus overlooked genre of popular white women's fiction.

The charges of plagiarism Jooste has faced might be read in relation to the reader's experience of the novel, and the extent to which the entire narrative seems, in the end, derivative; second-hand; plagiarised inadvertently; operating as it does well within the confines of the stereotypically probable and according to the dictates of mechanical plot development, which is an undisputed requirement of mass-produced fiction. Like the ubiquitous soap opera, pulp fiction such as *People Like*

Ourselves is mass-produced and thus 'recognisable by its *similarity* to other products of its kind' as Christine Gledhill (2002: 352–353; emphasis in original) argues:

> Within the ideology of mass culture this use of 'convention' [...] takes on an inherently conservative connotation, its main function being to reinforce normative meanings and values.

In conversation with two journalists, Alan Swerdlow and Margaret von Klemperer, Jooste has discussed the implications of the book's title. In response to Swerdlow she attempts to include all characters in the plural pronoun in noting the 'cross-section of the population' represented in 'people like ourselves', but goes on to suggest that behind the 'big houses and big cars, and all the obvious accoutrements of opulence [...] were just frightened, rather small, little people – and very spiritually impoverished sometimes' (1 June 2003). Von Klemperer reports that when asked who she was writing for Jooste said, 'At the beginning, I didn't know, but now I suppose it is basically white middle-class South Africans who buy books. People like myself' (2003: 7). The readership Jooste has in mind, in her acknowledgement of the demographic as 'basically' white, may have their consciences pricked as Sally Kernohan has suggested in her review, but the story reinforces rather than challenges their world-view: the black characters remain 'basically' physical presences, either sexualised or stupid, or both, as in the case of Tula's soap opera star mother, and the white protagonists, Julia and Douglas, sitting on the terrace of their opulent home, may indeed be 'spiritually impoverished', but they remain materially and culturally enriched, their white privilege and assumptions threatened but intact. *People Like Ourselves* is *really* about 'people like ourselves' and *for* 'people like ourselves'. Except that the plural inevitably incorporates exclusively white selves, and it would be no surprise if black readers did not recognise people like themselves at all on the pages of this book, except in the stereotypes and clichés that they already know are in circulation in white South African images of them.

One Rainbow, One Nation, One Tongue Singing

Susan Mann's *One Tongue Singing*, first published by Secker and Warburg in 2004 and subsequently by Vintage in 2005, has been dubbed '*Disgrace*-lite', and reviewers have commented on the similarities of character and plot in the two novels: both contain an ageing male artist/academic who gropes young female students, and both negotiate the violent sexual assault of a single white woman living in rural South Africa (Rosenthal 2004: 5; De Vries 2004b: 28; Swerdlow 15 February 2004).

Though these elements may indeed be regarded as derivative, it is a relief to note Susan Mann's carefully listed acknowledgements at the end of the tale, protecting her from charges of plagiarism. The story is nonetheless filled with the stereotypes that are the necessary ingredients of plot-driven, best-selling narratives, and thus not particularly 'original' in the politics of identity it explores. More finely wrought than *People Like Ourselves*, more structurally coherent and more courageous in its feminist challenge to gender norms, *One Tongue Singing* offers the reader of women's fiction a vision of the violence that is often an underlying precept of the sexual 'romance' in a heterosexual economy of being, and as Jane Rosenthal has noted, '[d]espite the lurching between penny novelette and passages of clearly didactic purpose, it proves to be worth reading this novel through to the end' (2004: 5). However, it may be argued that both Jooste and Mann, in their representational practice, rely too heavily on cliché to express their opposition to apartheid, and inadvertently allow whiteness to emerge as normative, as the following analysis of Mann's contribution to post-apartheid literature will demonstrate.

In stark contrast to Rosenthal's fairly scathing review of the novel is André Brink's, in which it is described as 'story-telling at its best', as 'superb', and as 'deceptively low-key but brilliant' (2004: 18). The front cover quotation from Brink claims that it is '[s]ensitive and sharp and charged with authentic passion [...] a book that sings in a tongue of liquid fire'. Fiery praise indeed, and predictable, emanating as it does from Mann's tutor in the Creative Writing course she completed at the University of Cape Town, but whether it may be regarded a fair assessment of the novel is another story. The *Guardian* review printed on the back cover of the book, however, provides another curious response to the book which takes cognisance of all its preoccupations – race, class and gender:

> Strong on characterisation, *One Tongue Singing* is an incisive and emotive reminder that power in human relationships always manages to transcend colour, gender, wealth or class. (2005: back cover)

This proves to be an even stranger summation of the novel than Brink's fiery praise, because, as the following analysis will show, the novel appears to demonstrate the exact opposite: that 'power in human relationships' *never* 'manages to transcend colour, gender, wealth or class'. In fact, the single most far-reaching and climactic event narrated in the novel is the rape and murder of a middle-class white woman by a man whose identity, though deliberately left undisclosed, is almost certainly a coloured labourer, based on the narrative hints and cues the texts delivers. Amongst these hints and cues are a multitude of stereotypes relating to gender, race, class and language which need to be tracked, at the risk of resorting to plot summary.

Camille Pascal, a nurse and unwed mother, leaves her homeland, France, with her father and her daughter to settle in South Africa after a love affair with the child's father ends abruptly. The three foreigners settle in the parochial Stellenbosch wine-farming district in a cottage sold to them by a wine farmer, where they lead a quiet life, keeping largely to themselves, though uneasily aware of the exploited and oppressed coloured community of farm labourers and the new settlement of shack-dwelling blacks who occupy the territories adjacent to the farm. The first part of the scene is thus set for the judgemental juxtapositions of cosmopolitan French whiteness and parochial South African whiteness, of European liberal largesse and 'settler'[44] conservatism. The elevation of a liberal European civility may be read in relation to what Lévinas has termed 'ontological imperialism', which has been instrumental in maintaining the privilege of western philosophy and its tendency to 'neutralise' and 'encompass' difference in 'its long history of desire for Unity and the One' (1969: 21). This, he suggests, denotes an egotism that is characteristic of Eurocentrism. Such elevation of European whiteness is evident in other aspects of Mann's characterisation. For example, the lack of medical facilities prompts Camille to set up a practice, with the help of an Italian doctor (predictably not a South African), which she runs from home, dispensing medication, '[j]ust the basics: contraceptives, painkillers, antiseptics and some antibiotics' (2005: 135), to the underprivileged other races during the height of apartheid. The second part of the scene is thus set for the inevitable: vulnerable white woman at the mercy of rapacious drunken coloured men and/or even darker more threatening black men.

Four possible suspects for the murder of Camille Pascal emerge as the narrative unfolds. The crime committed is the culminating act and the list of suspects deliberately points to the uncertainty of the rapist-murderer's identity. The first is a drunk coloured man 'in torn overalls' whom Camille finds attempting to sexually harass her daughter, Zara (2005: 150–151) and whom she threatens with a rock. The second is the white wine farmer, Mr Hermann Smit, who sold the land to the Pascals and who offers her a lift home after a *Wynboerevereniging*[45] which Camille attends to convince the wine farmers to assist her financially with the clinic she intends establishing. As they walk towards the car, Mr Smit makes a pass at her (a fumbling hand touching her breast), to which she responds 'spin[ning] like a whip, the *thwack* of her hand cutting through the night' (2005: 157). In addition to this unwelcome advance, further suspicion might be engendered when the reader is informed that

Mr Smit has offspring amongst the coloured labourers (2005: 195). The third is one of two black men who arrive at the clinic asking for work and food. When Camille disappears into the kitchen to make them sandwiches, one of them enters the house, but she is saved by the sound of a car arriving, as the following qualification implies: 'The tall man looks towards the source of the sound, before taking his sandwich and walking out' (2005: 167). The fourth and final suspect is the sangoma who treated one of Camille's black patients and who may have been angry that Camille had intervened and prescribed western treatment (2005: 226). It is Camille's father who provides the most revealing response to the 'list' of suspects when he is questioned by the police, and coerced into blaming the 'savage bunch' of 'natives':

> You know, Inspector, I have not lived here that long. But this much I do know: in this country it could have been anybody. Nobody of any colour, shape or creed seems to escape the dry brain rot here. A psychopath would be quite comfortable in any environment you choose. Yes, it could have been one of the labourers, blind drunk and violent after a night's drinking. Or one of the black people, erupting out of a mire of repression. Or the witch doctor, angry with her for interfering with his power. Or one of you! It could have been one of you, the white people of this place. After all, nobody seems to sin quite as expertly as you Calvinists. Pah! (2005: 226)

Although the old man is right to identify a psychopathology inherent in South African race relations, and to include in his conjecture the sweep of pathologies engendered by exploitation and repression, one cannot help registering the possibility that in the tenor and trajectory of his response to the police inquiry, his inclusion of the white man is merely insulting rather than accusatory. In effect, the list, as verbalised by Mr Pascal, moves from most to least likely, or from 'real' to rhetorical, as the following textual 'facts' concerning the suspect reveals: firstly, the reader is made more aware of alcohol abuse and the ensuing violence amongst the coloured labourers than of any other pathology related to 'race'. It emerges prominently in the subplot that introduces Blom, Zara Pascal's coloured friend whose mother, Leah, is regularly beaten up after drinking binges by her husband, Goiya (2005: 61) and, in one instance, is almost killed by him (2005: 74). This alcohol-induced violence prompts Camille to make enquiries about the *dopstelsel*[46] which 'keeps [the workers] quiet, "dronk", and dependent' (2005: 82, 94). In addition, as has already been established, it is a drunken coloured man who is asking Zara to show him her '*broekies*'[47] when Camille arrives to rescue her daughter from sexual abuse.

The only clue the reader is given pertaining to the identity of the rapist-murderer is that there is a 'funny smell. Sour […]' (2005: 224) in the room when Zara enters and witnesses the killing of her mother. It is as likely as any other explanation that the sour smell is stale alcohol, as registered from the point of view of a child. Cumulatively, these narrative clues are impossible to dismiss, rendering Mann's alleged intention (which she, or at least her publisher on her behalf, conceivably endorses, having afforded it book cover status) to demonstrate that 'power in human relations always manages to transcend colour' effectively unaccomplished, in regard to the abiding stereotype of the coloured man in South Africa: that he is a cowardly incomplete man, unable to stand up to the oppressor, and thus a drunken woman-abuser, always caught with his pants down (2005: 76, 224), prone to bouts of alcohol-induced violence, wife-battering, child-molestation, and therefore, by implication, rape and murder. Such stereotyping reflects Frankenberg's notion of the 'discursive repertoires' (1993: 290) available to white middle-class women, repertoires that carry traces of colonial attitudes (1993: 17). This aspect of the story thus belies the blurb's assessment of what the novel has achieved because though the perpetrator of the heinous crime 'could have been anybody' (2005: 226), given the amount of stereotypical detail in evidence, it is more likely to have been a coloured man than any other character-type depicted, and thus the novel firmly entrenches, rather than challenges, the race, class and gender dynamics governing relations of power in this country. It may be argued that Mann's depiction of this scenario is meant to reflect the political and social realities of the apartheid era, given that the incident takes place in an earlier temporality than the 'current narrative', which plots the development of Camille's daughter. Such a reading, however, would have to examine Mann's negotiation of subsequent scenarios and the attendant characterisations, which do not convince the reader that power in South African relationships manages to transcend race, gender, class, wealth or even culture.

Susan Mann has clearly struggled to negotiate the dynamics of interracial politics in South Africa in her reliance on cliché to carry her condemnation of the rape and murder of Camille. What is arguably just as problematic is the writer's general disapproval of white South Africans, but white Afrikaans-speaking South Africans in particular. With the exception of the young Pieter, who defies his conservative *boere* parents by maintaining his friendship with Blom and Zara despite multiple beatings, and who studies Engineering rather than Agriculture, to make matters worse, there is not an Afrikaner in the story who is sympathetically rendered. Jane Rosenthal's review rightly targets this aspect of the novel. 'Afrikaner bashing', she writes, 'is such a tired old cow, dragged once again from the *sloot*'[48] (2004: 5). They are depicted as boorish, ill-educated, inarticulate and unaccommodating of difference. First there is Mrs Smit, with her 'clipped colonial accent', 'her white blouse stiffly starched' and her 'gold-rimmed bifocals' (2005: 79), whose advice to Camille is to stay away from the coloureds because they are 'a violent lot' who 'drink too much' (2005: 80). Then there is Mrs Smit's husband, his 'skin flushed, his small eyes darting to and from her body and face' (2005: 81), whom we have already encountered, in a moment narrated later in the text, groping Camille's breast. Next is Zara's teacher at Valley Land Junior Primary 'with the beetle-shaped body and a nose for delinquency' (2005: 48). Mrs Meijer with her 'baguette-shaped arms' and 'vein-spattered nose' (2005: 50) is the consummate *boere tannie*,[49] whose Calvinist wrath ensures that Zara's experience of the white public school system in South Africa is short-lived. And finally, there are the boers themselves who congregate once a month to discuss community affairs, and who are described as 'large-boned men' with 'powerful frames' and 'strong jaws' made for Afrikaans, a 'masculine' language '[h]andcrafted for the people by the people' (2005: 155). This catalogue of quotations suggests the extent of Mann's representation of the Afrikaans community depicted in the novel. In each case, the Afrikaner remains irredeemably stereotyped, with the presence of each character serving merely as a backdrop to suggest white racist mentality and a colonial backwardness which throws into pretty relief the French gentility of the Pascals. Babb's plotting of a hierarchy in an American historical development of cultural/racial politics in which 'English is the preferred form of white' (1998: 33) may be extended to suggest that such an elevation of European civility is the preferred form of white. In this regard, one cannot overlook the implication that the author considers European whiteness as untainted and normative, and that it is Afrikaans-speaking white South Africans who must bear the full responsibility for apartheid, whilst their English-speaking counterparts remain relatively exempt.

English-speaking white characters in *One Tongue Singing* are, however, not entirely excepted from the stereotyping evident in Mann's heavy-handed representation of Afrikanerdom, though the two main characters, Jake Coleman and his wife Maria, in the narrative that alternates with the Camille Pascal story, are fleshed out sufficiently to allow them at least some substance and authenticity. The narrative that features Jake and Maria is set between ten and fifteen years ahead of the Camille Pascal murder story and commences with the arrival of Zara Pascal at the Jake Coleman International School of Fine Art. The old South Africa has been eradicated in this temporality, at least officially, and the new one is struggling to be born, but, as the text amply demonstrates, not much has changed to challenge white English-speaking South Africans out of their insularity and liberal self-congratulating self-absorption.

Jake, like Douglas in *People Like Ourselves*, is cheating on his wife, a phenomenon that appears to be a characteristic feature in emerging fiction for white women, as Fred de Vries has pointed out in his suggestion that in many of the novels he encountered in preparation for his article 'Singular White Females', '[t]he South African [white] man is portrayed unflatteringly [being, as he is] macho, adulterous, materialistic and emotionally immature' (2004a: 10). On one level, Mann (and Jooste) may be accommodated for such depictions, writing as they are against a history of western literary representations of gender 'norms' that posit Woman as overtly sexual, superficial and emotionally unstable, and Man as the mature, responsible, rational proprietor of wily femininity. On another level, however, such portrayals do nothing to alleviate the anxiousness around masculinity that is inevitably heightened as a result of a too easy reliance on the abiding stereotype of masculine sexual excess. Though Jake is the villain of the story, it is clearly intentionally ironic that it is he and the dirty, scavenging art critic, Frank Rosen, who offer the most acerbic take on white South African society. It is Jake who comments on the bourgeois notion of romantic and monogamous love, labelling it a 'rather irritating, middle-class, female preoccupation' and the 'meagre product of a supreme lack of imagination':

> The demise of a mind small enough to be hemmed in by garden fences, corporate success stories and fifteen days' leave per annum [...] And in this country, the scenario would usually come complete with razor-wire trimmings and two corpulent, gas-filled Staffordshire bull terriers. (2005: 6)

Apart from the cleverly (and accurately) constructed image of white suburban South Africa, which is powerfully indicting, and which recurs several times in variation in white women's writing under scrutiny in this study, the author's intentional irony here includes the fact that it is Jake who will fall romantically and dangerously in love (with his student, Zara) and is himself thus guilty of perpetuating the 'rather irritating, middle-class, female preoccupation' he condemns. Likewise, it is the disreputable Frank Rosen, with his 'nicotine-stained teeth' (2005: 184) who in addressing his cat comments that 'the nouveaux riches have inherited the earth. And art – or no, wait, *creativity* – is replacing tennis parties as the favoured hobby of this little troop of bored bourgeois plutocrats' (2005: 185). Perhaps André Brink is right to suggest that Mann has purposefully and ironically given the 'truest words' to the most unlikeable characters in order to demonstrate that 'nothing can simply be taken at face value, that everything is loaded with multiple meanings and possibilities and alternatives' (2004: 18), but it is equally probable that any real critique of social mores is effectively neutralised, emanating as it does from such clearly unpopular sources.

What is interesting to note is that Mann specifically targets white South African men, whereas her portrayal of the Frenchman 'Pappi' Pascal, the Hungarian potter, Mátyás, and the Italian doctor who assists Camille in establishing a clinic, is marked by a very real admiration for their cosmopolitan civility. This is perhaps the most damaging and reductionist aspect of Mann's treatment of white masculinity, because for as long at it remains popular 'to whip the [other] tired old cow' (Rosenthal 2004: 5) by means of white South African male bashing, and simultaneously elevating the gentility of European white masculinity, one runs the risk of reifying white masculinity by default. Clearly, the beachcombing Italian Doctor Belotti, in addition to being the requisite 'tall, dark, handsome stranger' of romantic fiction, with his 'sleek silver 1972 Mercedes sports car' (2005: 137) and his ability to exhibit 'grave concern one moment, and undiluted flirtation the next' (2005: 135), also epitomises western normativity in relation specifically to his profession: it is Dr Luca Belotti who has to undo the work of African traditional sangoma superstition (2005: 169) by amputating the leg of a black woman who had stupidly, the narrative suggests, relied on traditional healing rather than western medicine. And though it is not within the scope of this study to assess the relative efficacy of either African or western healing practices, this particular subplot lays the foundation for a dangerous binary that the narrative allows, even condones. Indeed, Mann's rendering of the black woman's response when Camille tells her that her foot will have to be 'cut off' is shot through with the same overt zoological stereotyping of black subjectivities as Pamela Jooste's is:

> '*Hawu!*' She says. 'Oh my God.' She rolls her eyes, the whites veined and creamy. The other two women shake their scarved heads like chorus members in a Greek tragedy, making clicking sounds of disapproval. (2005: 169)

Clearly, too, Mátyás, Zara's father, who operates on the fringes of the art-collecting in-crowd of Capetonian high society, is a foil against which Jake Coleman's artistic failure and sexual excess is amplified. Though both men have been adulterous, Mátyás's life is rendered as tragic (2005: 234) whereas Jake Coleman is the butt-end of a bad joke: at the end of the story he is pictured having coffee with Maria and whining about being alone and wanting his good old reliable wife back while simultaneously harbouring thoughts about the new secretary he has appointed, while Maria is groping inside her bag for the 'single round-the-world ticket on the QE2' (2005: 243). In effect, the narrative suggests, European forms of adultery are somehow superior – less deceitful, more romantic – to the white South African equivalent. The colonial cringe is almost palpable and once again Mann's attempt to suggest that 'power in human relations always manages to transcend colour, gender, wealth or class' has patently not succeeded.

The white women characters in this story do not fare much better than the men, though Maria's predicament garners more sympathy than that of any other white women in the story, at least partly because she is awarded more narrative space that any other, but also because it is her story with whom the intended readers of such novels will most powerfully identify, being as she is middle-aged, middle-class, English-speaking and, to add extra identification value, on the receiving end of marital infidelity. Curiously, though, it is Jake who is the focaliser more often than not in sections dealing with Maria's life, so that the reader comes to know her from Jake's perspective more readily than from her own. Indeed, so completely is she depicted in relation to Jake alone that it comes as something of a surprise at the end of the story that she takes such bold initiative to leave, touching 'like a secret caress' (2005: 243) the cover of the travel brochure containing her 'ticket out', though this desire may arguably be read as a celebratory gesture towards women needing an escape from bourgeois/patriarchal entrapment. However, from the first page, Maria is depicted as not much more than a vaguely disconcerting physical presence, which problematises the feminist politics that Mann is engaging. Jake, waking in the middle of the night, finds her next to him:

> Maria's ample form engulfs his space. Monopolises the cotton sheets. Her arm slops heavily over the edge of the bed and a thin line of saliva trickles from the corner of her mouth onto the crumpled cotton pillowcase (2005: 5).

Details of verisimilitude notwithstanding, it could only be the combination of what might be considered a 'typical male' such as Jake, with the helping hand of a very critical amanuensis, that could have spent quite as much lavish verbal energy depicting the magnitude of Maria's physicality. Jake's secretary is also all body: 'Outwardly, she has a powerful womanly confidence. She knows the difference shoes with a heel make to the swing of her gait' (2005: 41). Zara, too, the female student Jake seduces, as Jane Rosenthal has observed, seems 'a little wooden' (2004: 5) under the gaze that zooms in on 'the smooth arch of her foot [… the] gentle curve of her shoulder [...] the outlined arc of a breast' and her 'savage impenetrability' (2005: 43), (the 'savage' part of which manifests itself in her clawing and biting Jake!).

While it might well have been Mann's intention to accentuate such details to reinforce Jake's crass objectification of women, no such explanation can be visited upon the author's representation of the other female protagonist, Camille, in the parallel narrative, who is also the object of a 'sexualising' gaze. The 'authorial' gaze here appears to be compromised because the focalising and authorial perspectives are at odds with each other. One could argue in defence of either interpretation, that is, Mann is fully aware of the implications of the male gaze, or, that she is, albeit perhaps unconsciously, reproducing it. But the representation of Camille militates against the former reading. Apart from being 'an annoying [and unconvincing] foreign do-gooder' (Rosenthal 2004: 5), she is, like 'Pappi', Mátyás and Dr Belotti, a good white person because she is a foreign white person, or so the narrative appears to demonstrate. She is defined in opposition to South African women and Afrikaans-speaking women in particular: 'She does not look like the people who live here. Perhaps it is this that offends them. She does not perm her hair, nor set it in rollers, and her clothes are not always functional or sensible. She is definitely thinner than most of the women here too' (2005: 116–117). Once again, Mann's colonial cringe is blatant. From her long neatly coiffed to look uncoiffed hair down to her 'strappy high heels' (2005: 117), even her name, which is reminiscent of a brand of French perfume, (and including her romantic liaison with a handsome Italian doctor), Camille Pascal remains a cardboard cut-out, a paper doll upon which Mann hangs current fashions, both sartorial and behavioural, and ultimately she seems rather a flimsy but appropriately commodified representative of all that is best in the west. Fred de Vries is right to suggest that Camille is just one of many 'cliché-karakters' (clichéd characters) in the book (2004b: 28). Perhaps the responses of both De Vries and Jane Rosenthal may be attributed to the discrepancy between the abundance of physical detail provided in 'fleshing out' the characters, and the rather scant attention given to other aspects of their characterisation.

But it is the pretentious Juanita le Grange who epitomises Mann's derision of a certain recognisable type of white woman to have emerged in post-apartheid South Africa. The type is the English-speaking product of a privileged and liberal background who needs people to know that 'she has a PhD, [...] that she is a communist, [...] that she married a man who died in "the struggle"', and who is 'quoted as saying, "I hate capitalism but there's nothing wrong with capital", in *Style* magazine' (2005: 69). Mann's disdain for the type is possibly shared by many of her readers, but the caricature cameo role the character is called upon to play is not adequate in demonstrating the ubiquity and resilience of this brand of white privileged normativity. Indeed, Maria might conceivably be just such a type, but she gets away with it. So might many of the readers of the book, but the character's 'gloved paw', 'fat little body' and 'peroxided very short hair' (2005: 69) might allow readers the false self-congratulatory comfort of not recognising themselves in her depiction.

It is the younger generation of South Africans depicted in the novel, however, having experienced something of post-apartheid racial integration, who are invested with the writer's attempt to move beyond stereotype and her hopes for a truly liberated new South Africa. Blom learns, as a result of her interaction with Zara, that she can be a 'fairy' and a 'friend' (2005: 59) to the white child, and not, as the internalisation of racial shaming has convinced the young coloured girl, a 'Hotnot' (2005: 13), '[b]rown, like mud' (2005: 25), but it is when she is older, having returned from a relative in the Karoo (2005: 124) and upon being invited to a party in Cape Town with Pieter and his university friends, that Mann's celebration of integration is entertained. At the party, Pieter, for the first time, feels part of the social group, rather than an outsider (2005: 177), and his acceptance hinges on his partner:

> As the evening progresses, classmates he has never spoken to wander over to him and chat. At first he cannot understand it. Why all of a sudden? They've had all year to befriend him, why now? But after catching a few of their stolen glances at Blom, he starts to understand and a strange warm feeling creeps through him. (2005: 182)

The narrative does not reveal whether it is Blom's beauty or colour that engenders the sudden interest and the stolen glances, but one cannot overlook the implication of tokenism, which in the predictably 'white' version of 'integration', manifests itself as conciliatory assimilation, in which the group of white student engineers (with names like Piet and Jaco) clearly enjoy the novelty of a conservative *boereseun*[50] dating a young coloured woman. But mere gesture aside, any real potential to pursue the possibility of a mixed-race relationship is almost immediately undone by Mann in her authorial manipulation of a subplot that reveals Blom's parentage and makes her Pieter's half-sister (2005: 195). Clearly for the writer, miscegenation is as difficult to negotiate as incest is.

Ultimately, it is left to the young Zara, sensitive artist with cosmopolitan sensibilities, to voice Mann's critique of whiteness. For the exhibition of student work that Jake is holding, Zara paints her first self-portrait. Entitled *Innocence*, the portrait depicts Zara with 'her eyes closed' and '[b]lack blood drip[ping] from her mouth' (2005: 199). When Jake suggests that the portrait signifies the 'satanic' rather than 'innocence', her response is:

> Innocence is black, not white [...] White is a negation. It is not a colour, only a reflection. It does not exist. Within black, there is every colour. What you call innocence is simply a state of unknowing. Naivety. What I call innocence embraces all of life's colours, and celebrates it. (2005: 199)

Relevant and challenging as this definition of whiteness may be in switching the terms of the moral binaries governing the signification of good and evil, it does seem to be oddly misplaced: the black blood dripping from the subject's mouth much more readily signifies the character's psychic pain – the narrative reveals that she witnesses the murder of her mother – which leaves little room for 'innocence' or a celebration of it. If this is Mann's philosophical critique of whiteness, it seems strangely ineffectual, competing as it does with these other more likely interpretations of the portrait.

Conclusion

In *People Like Ourselves* by Pamela Jooste and *One Tongue Singing* by Susan Mann, the assumptions of universal white normativity emerge in the interstices of liberal discourse. Though both writers confront and challenge official narratives of racial inequality, they simultaneously emerge as products of an insular middle-class frame of reference that privileges a worldly (read western) cosmopolitan largesse: in the case of Jooste, by allowing the most normal (and wealthy) couple to survive, albeit less comfortably, the political transition their generation has had to face; and in the case of Mann, by elevating the gentility of European whiteness as exemplary in comparison to the more plebeian and dubious parochialism of South African whiteness.

In addition, both writers are wholly reliant on stereotypes to carry testimonies of apartheid atrocities without paying due attention to the ways in which those stereotypes advance apartheid thinking beyond the backdrop they are intended to provide for plot-driven narratives, and into the lives and psyches of the readers. Jooste's representations of black South Africans, and in particular her imaginative entry into the subjectivities of working-class black men and women, are fraught with white western preconceptions of black realities, and Mann's unintended caricature of the weak, drunken coloured man who is always caught with his pants down is charged with the paranoia emanating from colonial tropes of the dark lascivious other. Representations such as these have been so wholly discredited that it is no wonder that the only place still left for them to thrive and multiply in is the pulp of pulp fiction, where plot counts more than politics.

Adrienne Rich's notion of 'white solipsism' (1979: 306) and bell hooks's notion of 'bourgeois decorum' (1994: 180) are evident in both Pamela Jooste's and Susan Mann's 'post-apartheid weepies' in the sense that whiteness disappears into valorising neutrality. Rich's argument that guilt-feeling paralyses white women and 'paralysis can become a convenient means of remaining passive and instrumental' is precisely the manner in which the representational practices of these writers act as a form of hegemonic social control. And their representations reinforce Seshadri-Crooks's reading of whiteness 'as a master signifier' (2000: 58) in the inadvertent and completely unconscious duplicities that this analysis has uncovered. These representative writers of bestselling fiction have attempted to write confessional and reconciliatory post-apartheid fictions that explore the damaging inequalities of the past, but in the very process of doing so, some of the most dangerously concealed assumptions emerge despite themselves, resulting in a whitewashing of the racial dynamics that their target market, 'people like ourselves', need most urgently to negotiate.

Nancy Armstrong's view of white western middle-class women as reinforcing and perpetuating class hierarchies is relevant in negotiating this brand of popular fiction, but race hierarchies are just as unconsciously perpetuated as class hierarchies are. The favourable reviews written predominantly by white women at least partially suggest that these representative readers have already unconsciously assimilated the universality principle in operation in the two novels, a universality that shores up white normativity against the backdrop of black deviance.

3

The Metamorphosis of the Sole/Soul: Shades of Whiteness in Antjie Krog's *A Change of Tongue*

> *All families invent their parents and children, give each of them a history, character, fate, and even a language.*
> **Edward Said (2000: 400)**

Introduction

A Change of Tongue (2003) received mixed reviews when it was published, reviews that grapple with an uncertainty at the heart of the book. In most cases, though, the reviewers blame the structure rather than the content for what may be read as an obfuscatory quality that characterises the project: '*A Change of Tongue* is te veel boeke wat in een boek saamgevat is',[51] writes the journalist in *Insig* (2003: 69). Graeme Bloch suggests that the book 'drags on a bit' and that the 'transition' (and by this he means the political transition) 'has been too short' and is thus 'too uncertain, and is still too close to produce the [sic] great book' (*The Bookshelf* 2 November 2003). And Anton van Niekerk's ambivalence is marked: 'Krog se boek maak 'n mens moedeloos en deurmekaar – in die eerste plek omdat jy nie goed verstaan hoekom dit 'n boek is nie! Nogtans is dit een van die merkwaardigste intellektuele prestasies van ons tyd'[52] (2003: 24). Collectively, these responses suggest a discomfort that may well be misdirected, in the sense that the form might reflect the content which is shot through with an ambivalence that remains unresolved, as the following analysis will demonstrate.

Guilt, the white woman's burden, permeates the narrative, but if Margaret Atwood's 'Four Victim Positions' (1996: 37–39) were invoked to assess Krog's achievement in *A Change of Tongue*, one might be tempted to agree with Anton van

66 ■ White Women Writing White

Niekerk's final recommendation, that it is 'one of the most remarkable intellectual achievements of our time' in relation to the demonstrative ways in which the writer negotiates her own white complicities and works towards being a creative non-victim of gendered oppression, but more poignantly, a creative non-perpetrator of racial prejudice. However, Atwood's plotting of national motifs, to which I have added a white South African category (that of belonging), suggests that the transformation from white 'right'[53] to white un-belonging is one that may not have been effectively negotiated in *A Change of Tongue*.

In the following analysis of the book, Krog's experimentation with genre and other kinds of categorisation will be examined in order to account for the mixed reviews quoted above. In addition, this chapter will explore the narrative perspective and its engagement with a post-apartheid crisis in white identity and in Afrikanerdom, paying specific attention to the notion of a monolithic whiteness versus 'shades' of whiteness. In this regard, the aim is to analyse Krog's responses to the encounters she experiences with members of her own community and extended family, as well as the encounters she has with black South Africans, in order to map her understanding of what post-apartheid whiteness might represent and how it might be transformed. Such a mapping demonstrates the ambivalences that emerge in the interstices of Krog's painful grappling with her growing sense of un-belonging.

Unsettling Generic (and Other) Boundaries

Whereas *Country of My Skull* (1998) emerged out of Antjie Krog's participation as a journalist covering the Truth and Reconciliation proceedings and consists mostly of the collected stories of individual trauma inflicted by the apartheid regime, which are overlaid with her own responses to these graphic details, *A Change of Tongue* (2003) is more autobiographical and personal than the earlier work, more searching in its negotiation of the complexities and paradoxes confronting white identities in relation to a newly acquired sense of unhomeliness in a space that was reserved exclusively for whites as home. It is also less comfortably indicting of the regime responsible for the atrocities, and more willing to confront the continued force of whiteness as a cultural construct. The author seems to have deliberately resisted the label 'autobiography': the inside cover blurb refers to it only as a 'full-length work' and as a 'brave book', although as a series of 'voyages of *personal discovery*' (my emphasis) it is obviously autobiographical to a large extent.[54] Part of Krog's project is to unsettle the category 'autobiography' in the same way as she unsettles the categories 'white' and 'Afrikaner', and to this end she points on several occasions to the constructedness of generic classification and to the obvious ways in which all narrative, including non-fictional writing, is always already autobiographical *and* fictional. Though some readers may find such experimentation disconcerting, it nonetheless carries the potential for unsettling normative prescriptions.

Antjie Krog's profession as a poet and a journalist for much of her adult life has stood her in good stead to bear witness to the notion that the personal is always political and that the tension maintained between them is achieved 'precisely through the understanding of identity as multiple and even self-contradictory' (De Lauretis 1998: 10). The multiple narratives that she records in *A Change of Tongue* (2003) may be conceived of as a collection of personal (at times even poetical) responses to the politically charged experiences that she is forced to negotiate in her role as observer and recorder of media stories, which in the last decade have necessarily been devoted largely to the growing pains of a fledgling democracy. One of the most sensitive political/personal difficulties the writer must have confronted was to publish this book in English initially. The manuscript was written in Afrikaans, translated into English and the first publication appeared in English as *A Change of Tongue* in 2003. The Afrikaans edition appeared only in 2005.[55] Though it may be argued that her decision to publish in English first stems from her recognition that she will draw a wider readership both here and abroad (2003: 270–271), there may be the added implication that she is specifically addressing white English-speaking South Africans, and international readers, on behalf of Afrikaners. The other possible implication is articulated by Bhabha in 'Signs Taken for Wonders' in relation to the power of the English book as signifier[56] (1986: 174), in which case the sense of betrayal that she feels in abandoning her mother tongue is even more complicated. Krog's awareness of these arguments and counter-arguments comes to a head in Part Four of the text, entitled 'A Translation', in which she grapples with her decision to write in English, and in which she perceives English to have become 'the door to the Father' (2003: 270), by which she might mean a neocolonial force threatening to erase cultural difference in this country under the umbrella term of 'whiteness'. *A Change of Tongue* is thus, amongst other things, a story about language.

In *Country of My Skull*, Krog offers her own manifesto on authorship and it is to this text that one needs to return in order to understand her sense of the relationship between fact and fiction, truth and lies. When one of her colleagues, Patrick, reads her version of what transpired at a radio team workshop set up to deal with the trauma of journalists covering the hearings, he suggests that she is stretching the truth. The conversation that ensues (2002: 170–171) suggests a number of crucial issues regarding narrativisation.[57] In what is ostensibly a factual account of a workshop, a version of which Krog prepares for her radio listeners, she admits to lying in order to uncover a deeper truth, and she also argues that there is no one universal Truth, but multiple and often conflicting truths, and that her truth is just that: *hers*, at a specific moment in her life, and thus subject to revision by herself and others. She also suggests in the conversation that it is not the myriad *facts* that constitute the authenticity and verisimilitude of a narrative, but the way in which those facts are recorded, how they cohere, and how they affect and are interpreted by the tellers and recipients of the tale. This in itself prepares the reader for the revisions one encounters in *A Change of Tongue*.

Krog thus rejects the categories that have governed and to some extent continue to govern the act of writing, whether that act is performed in the name of journalism, autobiography, translation or poetry. Interestingly, both *Country of My Skull* and *A Change of Tongue* are likely to be found in bookshops and libraries catalogued either under South African non-fiction, or under general history, which further demonstrates the ongoing effects of conventional generic classification against which Krog writes. The major writerly admission that the conversation recorded in *Country of My Skull* calls up, however, is that Krog not only invents characters who live alongside 'real' people in her work but she also sees herself as a character in her own text, and invents some of the situations she 'experiences', not the least of which is the affair she supposedly has. An alternative reading of this is that she did, in reality, have an affair, and 'fictionalises' it to protect herself and her family. Either way, for Krog to insert such a 'fictionalised' incident could not have been easy. Marital affairs may arguably reflect the deepest kind of personal/public betrayal which ordinary adults might have to confront for the obvious reason that marriage is a *social* contract as well as a *personal* relationship. The testimonies of Afrikaner atrocities recorded during the TRC hearings may well have been experienced as betrayal, in the sense that Krog would have had to face her own complicity as an Afrikaner, so that the personal and the political, or the private and the public, are shown by Krog to be not only inseparable but a false dualism in the first place. And Krog obliquely accepts the blame for her own treacherousness in what amounts to a personal and public declaration of duplicity in her fictionalised account of 'the truth'.

Readers of *Country of My Skull* will thus be familiar with Krog's postmodern propensity to cut and paste, invent and record, and blur the boundaries between past and present, truth and fiction, and other tenuous binaries. It is important to note that this strategy has not always met with approval, particularly in relation to victims of gross human rights violations whose call for the Truth would not be likely to entertain such blurring of the boundaries between truth and fiction. Fiona Ross (1998: 2) summarises the debate engendered by Krog's tampering with the facts in *Country of My Skull*, and her appropriation of pain in retelling it. Ross suggests that such criticisms, though valid, might best be countered by acknowledging the 'slipperiness' of truth. She notes that the 'tension between truth and not quite truth' is one that the Truth and Reconciliation Commission itself could profitably have incorporated in the sense that the merely factual might 'oversimplify [or] reduce pain to a cipher', whereas narrative, with its capacity to incorporate the dialectic of truth and lies, personalises human tragedy.

A Change of Tongue deploys similar authorial strategies in blurring the boundaries between fact and fiction and one of the reader's tasks is unravelling the focalising perspectives recorded in the book. Clearly, the experiencing and narrating subject is Antjie Krog, the woman, the Afrikaner, the journalist, the poet and the writer, who uses the first person for her strongly autobiographical narrative. The text is marked, however, by a powerful metatextual self-consciousness with the narrator casting herself in the third person in the several interpolated mini-chapters in which she recalls her youth, and at other critical moments in a more contemporaneous temporality. It may thus be argued that Krog sets herself up as the protagonist in the book and quite consciously plays various parts in order to stage crucial debates along the road to self-discovery (Nelson Mandela's autobiography, *Long Walk to Freedom*, is a central intertext and the image of a 'change of tongue' invoked in her title is central to understanding the process).

There are a number of possible readings of this strategy. In a sense Krog is deliberately adopting a certain persona from which she, as a writer, remains at a distance, and this slipperiness signals a split self which may characterise a new and growing sense of white South African displacement. But equally plausible is the alternative reading that it is when Krog records aspects of her experience that are the most painful to negotiate that she resorts to the third person, a possibility examined later in this chapter. In addition, it may be argued that Krog exhibits the denials that normativity depends on. But perhaps the fairest reading is the most complex one, which includes elements of both displacement and normativity, as the following analysis will attempt to demonstrate.

The first signalling of Krog's unsettling generic boundaries (as well as person/public ones) is her response to the interpolated essay written by her mother, Dot Serfontein, for the Afrikaans women's magazine *Sarie*. She accuses her mother of lying because the essay she reads in the magazine differs in significant detail from the way Antjie remembers the incident, which revolves around a family trip to Cape Town. Dot Serfontein's response to the young Krog (this interaction occurs in one of the many sub-chapters that deal with her past) signifies a seminal moment in the writer's experience: 'If you feel that I'm twisting things, you can write your own story and correct it' (2003: 82), she tells her daughter. This is precisely what Krog does in *A Change of Tongue*. She rewrites her own writerly life, as well as her mother's, allowing their versions of the story to speak to one another across an ideological and generational divide, and thus effects a kind of personal and public reconciliation between, and transformation of the terms mother and daughter, fact and fiction, past and present. In the final pages of the text, Krog once again points to the confines of generic classification, and once again with direct reference to her mother. Her brother relates a conversation he had had with their mother about her decision to give up writing fiction and to write personal essays, which she claims is a result of a need to escape the ever-present 'other' world of television and newspapers and become intimate with one's 'own' world. Krog, in an aside, reiterates her 'view that everything which has been translated into language has already become fiction' (2003: 362). Perhaps Krog's major project, then, is to revisit and revise, challenge and celebrate her 'mother tongue' in all of the contradictory and connotative resonances of the phrase. *A Change of Tongue* is a book not only about language and translation but also about writing, and about 'thinking back through our mothers' in Virginia Woolf's formulation.[58]

Metamorphosis of the Sole/Soul: De-/Reconstructing White Identity

Krog's unsettling of generic categories anticipates her unsettling of cultural/racial categories. To this end she examines the notion of home and belonging. 'Home' is figured predominantly in relation to the space she occupied in her childhood, a farm near Kroonstad; and it is this area which is consistently the most featured geographic space in a text that covers great distances both within and beyond the borders of South Africa. A rural town historically servicing a farming community, Kroonstad is a heartland of Afrikanerdom, and what Krog meticulously plots is the changing (or unchanging) attitudes and responses of those who have remained there (family, friends and acquaintances) since 1994 and the birth of a new nation.

The main questions she tries to answer, by asking the same question in many ways and in response to multiple perspectives, is how her people have survived transition, whether indeed they have transformed, and what in fact transformation might mean. And the question of transformation hinges on the ultimate question the book poses, and that is whether there is a place for the white person in post-apartheid South Africa, whether white people can ever truly belong in a country which their predecessors colonised, amongst people whom their predecessors exploited and abused, and in a country where the effects of that historical relationship have not been erased. The book cover and title confirm the necessity of white transformation as Krog's abiding preoccupation: in Afrikaans, a flatfish or 'sole' is called a 'tongvis' (tongue fish), and on the front and back covers respectively are the head and tail of a sole, so that the sole is represented in its entirety but one has literally to turn the book over on its back and upside down to see the whole picture. The last page of the text contains only a picture, of the sole, in black and white and in relief. Quoting from *The Aquarist's Encyclopaedia*, Krog records the most salient features of the flatfish or sole:

> 'The chief characteristic of flatfishes like the sole is that one flank really functions as the underside of the fish ... The juvenile fish are built perfectly normally and have to go through certain kinds of *transformation* and *metamorphosis* [her emphasis] before the function of the flank is determined. At the same time this is happening, other forms of morphological asymmetry take place. The eye of the underside migrates to the other flank, which will now function as the upper side. The mouth becomes oblique, the nasal and the gill openings are removed to a different position, various skull bones develop asymmetrically, and on the upper side a dark pigmentation develops.' (2003: 128)

What Krog has found in this aquatic oddity is the perfect image to account for a necessary change: of tongue, of voice, of being, of identity, that white South Africa must negotiate. Krog repeats the phrases: 'The mouth becomes oblique, the skull changes, the upper side turns dark' (2003: 129), thus highlighting the most salient and significant changes she has in mind for white South Africa. Another feature, however, of the sole and one omitted from the extract quoted, is its propensity to camouflage itself under the soft sand on the ocean bed in order to conceal its predatory intentions, and there may therefore be an additional, though not necessarily intentional, implication in the analogy: that white power secures itself by seeming not to be there at all. Krog apparently wants the reader to take from the analogy only the idea of *metamorphosis*, that white South African 'tongues' or voices have been loud and dominant enough, and that now is the time for a repositioning of that capacity, from one of centrality to an obliqueness, an off-centredness; that white South African skulls, or minds, need to change shape; that whiteness itself needs to be metamorphosed away. The tangible, and excruciatingly altered (though beautiful) physical form of the fish is invoked to emphasise figuratively the enormity, the miraculousness, but most significantly the *possibility* of effecting change: these are not superficial adjustments or realignments, but fundamental reconfigurations dictated by the surroundings to which the creature must adapt. The juvenile sole fish is 'normal' in appearance but nature requires its reconfiguration for survival. So, too, Krog's analogy, by extension, suggests that the white South African must relinquish her/his claim to normativity, and adapt to new surroundings. This requires work at the level of Chomskian[59] 'deep structure'. The same image appears in Krog's collection of poems translated in English, *Down to My Last Skin*, and prefigures her appreciation of the metaphorical potential of the image. In a poem entitled 'transparency of the sole' (2000a: 40–41), translated by Denis Hirson, she conceives of her children as 'these fish of mine in their four-string flotilla' who must endure the transformation from childhood to adulthood, the mingling of Krog and Samuel (or Afrikaans and English), the reconfiguration of their genetic encoding, and in the process become adapted to a life 'between sand and stone'.

The sole may indeed be biologically and genetically programmed to adapt, but what of the social and political programming of which we are products as 'citizens' of the world? Antjie Krog scrupulously and bravely plots her own responses to such conditioning and measures her progress carefully (though not necessarily accurately) against white and black responses, both at 'home' and abroad, in her personal and her public life. The remainder of this examination of her journey will thus follow that trajectory and entail an attempt to locate the moments in which her certainties are challenged, her very tongue and physiology figuratively reconfigured, in order to examine the implications of her endeavour to belong or to adapt in a space (exemplified as Kroonstad) which she sees as part of her very 'soul' but from which she feels increasingly estranged.

Kroonstad: Middle-class White Normativity
Krog's introductory vignette is clearly chosen for the typicality it suggests in depicting the ordinary activities that continue to occur in ordinary small-town

South African life. The place is Kroonstad, a representative enough South African 'dorp'; the narrative temporality more or less concurrent with the first few months after the first democratic election; the occasion a sporting activity – and, indeed, the true colours of South Africans of all hues emerge in and around the sports arena. Krog is visiting her hometown and spends a morning at a schools' athletic meeting, one of the obvious occasions in which ordinary Afrikaans-speaking white South Africans learn the social script for playing the part of ordinary white Afrikaner South Africans. So what has changed besides the growing numbers of black children participating in the sporting event? In assessing the level of integration, she interviews a few of the locals, two of whom are white men. Clearly, Krog's selection of these 'sample' responses right at the start of the book signals her intention to condemn an untransformed whiteness, and in doing so to position herself in opposition to such responses, and though it is important to plot her critique of whiteness, it is equally important to interrogate the moments in which she fails to take cognisance of her own position, one which initially seems unambiguous. Her first encounter is with an anonymous man in a tracksuit, a father, predictably a farmer, who, from the detailed account he offers of the transition facing white schools, is clearly a regular attendant in support of his 'podgy' (2003: 17) son's sporting progress, and perhaps chosen to represent an ordinary middle-aged, middle-class white man. This specimen appears to be adapting, though with some difficulty, and there is a certain wholesome honesty in his matter-of-fact, certainly amusing, at times bemused regaling of the logistical and interpersonal communication crises that have been battled, though not always won, on and off the athletics field. The possibility of transformation peeps through the chinks in his hard 'boere' armour, especially when he recounts the story of how he celebrated the victories of his son and his 'chief tractor driver's son' (2003: 16), but it soon becomes apparent that transformation for him means the successful assimilation of black children (and their parents) into a white world, rather than any real negotiation of another world. This is signalled in response to the first question posed by Krog. She asks why everyone is so happy, and the farmer responds: 'The blacks are happy because it is a black kid beating the whites. The whites are happy because the winning black kid is from a white school and was trained by them' (2003: 13). Though the response of the blacks might be understandably victorious, the response of the whites suggests that it is ultimately a hollow victory since credit goes to the power of white superior training rather than to the talent of the black child. A far more crass response is given when Krog phones the second white man, a top athletics trainer in Kroonstad, and asks him why eighty per cent of the winning athletes are white. His reply provides a prime example of a certain kind of 'whitespeak'[60] endemic to South Africa, and one which Krog clearly finds abhorrent:

> 'You can ask the people of the town: I am not racist. They will tell you, no one had more enthusiasm for the new dispensation than me. But I will tell you straight: laziness is a terrible thing. If laziness is in your blood, nobody can do anything about it. When the blacks were still angry and wanted what we had, it was better, because they wanted everything ... But once they were sitting there in our places, they found that all these things were actually a lot of work. An athlete, you have to train in your spare time. You have to drive him to sporting events over weekends in your own car, with your own money and without overtime pay. You have to attend coaching courses in your holidays ... That is what sport is. Free dedication of teachers to their communities. The success of the athlete is the reward. *Nou ja*. These people, that they don't like.' (2003: 17)

Starting with the predictable disclaimer from which he launches into spectacular racist rhetoric, the speaker represents the standard and most recognisable dis-ease of whiteness. It manifests itself in numerous ways: a) In his unwavering conviction that laziness is a genetically encoded flaw – it is in the blood; b) and that, by implication, whites are a superior race because laziness is not in their blood; c) that blacks, in the new 'dispensation' have made a sorry mess of things because of their inherent laziness; d) that it is completely normal to have one's own vehicle, and the spare cash to fill the tank and drive one's students to sporting events; e) that this bespeaks 'dedication to the community' way beyond the call of duty; f) and that the morals, mores and values of this imagined community which encourages its members to display their dedicated superiority, are Truths beyond question, universal, irreproachable and eternal.

Fanon still has the most commanding response to this kind of rhetoric in his insistence on the power of colonial vocabulary and its effect on (previously) colonised peoples. Though both Bhabha and Chow have examined the limitations of a pessimistic Fanonian intractability in its insistence on a version of oedipal envy that can only ever be experienced as lack,[61] Fanon's recognition of the trauma of the recently decolonised is nonetheless pertinent: in the Manichean world of apartheid (of which the athletics trainer is a product), 'the settler paint[ed] the native as a sort of quintessence of evil [...] insensible to ethics [...] represent[ing] not only the absence of values, but also the negation of values' (1963: 32). The colonial language in which this image of the native is articulated is filled with the usual zoological tropes and the charge of innate laziness. But what the 'settler', or in this case, his descendant interprets as laziness, Fanon suggests is more akin to a defiant insolence:

> As soon as the native begins to pull on his moorings, and to cause anxiety to the settler, he is handed over to the well-meaning souls who in cultural congresses point out to him the specificity and wealth of Western values. But every time Western values are mentioned they produce in the native a sort of stiffening or muscular lock-jaw. (1963: 33)

Krog's athletics trainer (at the helm of well-meaning cultural congress) accurately identifies the energy of envy emanating from the (previously) colonised, but misrecognises as laziness the powerful rejection of western values in the gesture of refusal that Fanon calls 'muscular lock-jaw'.

Shades of Whiteness

Though Krog demonstrates a profound awareness of the constructedness of whiteness in her portrayal of her own community, her own family and her own responses, a significant part of her project is to suggest that whiteness is not a monolithic category, that indeed there are shades of whiteness, and that Afrikaners have been persecuted at the hands of the English in much the same way as blacks have been persecuted at the hands of white South Africans, and in the same way that one group of blacks (or whites) persecutes another. This she does in the cleverly constructed and powerfully postmodern Part Two of the text, entitled 'A Hard Drive', by juxtaposing extracts from her mother's history of Boer War atrocities with extracts from her own collection of journalistic entries on the war in Rwanda. She points out that the Hutus and the Tutsis 'speak the same language, share the same culture and religion. In South Africa, it would be like the AmaPondo killing the Thembu' (2003: 148); or like a Brit killing a Boer. Though Brit and Boer do not share a language, they certainly share a settler legacy that insulates them from the uncomfortable presence of more markedly different others. The ten pages of alternating verbatim (though broken) reportage on one hand effectively exposes the senselessness of war, any war, but on other hand involves an attempt on Krog's behalf to insert traumatised Afrikaner history into the mainstream of English (South African) literary history, and in so doing to suggest that there are shades of whiteness that have been rendered invisible as a result of the cultural chauvinism (and amnesia) of the English, and the purported solo culpability of the Boer.

An additional effect of the juxtaposed war reports is to emphasise her view that there is '[no] easy walk between perception and truth in this country' (2003: 27), which echoes Nelson Mandela's autobiography *Long Walk to Freedom*,[62] and, of course, refers back to the title of Part Two: 'A Hard Drive', with its intentional play on words (a hard drive being that vulnerable memory component of a computer prone to 'crashing' as well as a phrase suggesting the tough navigation of a journey). The 'hard drive' metaphor is also employed to equate Krog's experience of losing important information when the hard drive on her computer crashed, and the effects of the stroke she subsequently experienced (2003: 120). The image seems to suggest the difficulty but also the necessity of remembering accurately, and the tendency in human beings to remember selectively, hence her conscious *selection* of the documents to highlight the process of *recording*, or committing to memory and in so doing to negotiate the distance between truth and perception.

Perception, like perspective, or Truth, for that matter, is a convention, socially learned, the parameters of which are disseminated most efficiently through language, as has been amply demonstrated in poststructuralist theory. Binarisms such as 'barbarian' versus 'gentile' or 'perpetrator' versus 'victim' carry our perceptions, as Serfontein's record of Colonel Thring's story clearly illustrates. When a wounded British officer asks where the Boers are and Colonel Thring points them out, the officer says, 'No, no, you don't understand me – I mean the wild, savage Boers, the people they say look like the orang-utans' (2003: 150). Directly after the computerised gobbledygook which serves as a 'break in transmission' and highlights Krog's textual production and reproduction, the reader is transported into the middle of a late-night discussion amongst the journalists enlisted to report on the civil war in Rwanda: 'we explore the question of how the victim can become the perpetrator'. Fanon's four psychological consequences of racism are invoked, from 'intense intra-psychic pain', through the internalisation of impotence, or self- and family-abuse, to 'the psychological double bind', and finally, the 'killing rage'. The question that Krog appears to be asking is where white South Africans, particularly Afrikaners, find themselves on Fanon's continuum, though it constitutes an equation Fanon would not necessarily have supported, given his reading of a racially constituted Manichean divide. The following observations need to be read in the light of this problematic.

It may be argued that Krog's very detailed record of Fanon's account of the pathologies incurred in racist societies suggests that she is interested in plotting the position of the Afrikaner against this outline, particularly in sandwiching the

Fanonian account between Boer War and Rwandan 'footage'. There is thus some evidence to suggest that Krog's use of Fanon here provides a warning to her people that, having internalised the 'racist' messages as expressed by the wounded British soldier, and having subsequently turned perpetrator, they now find themselves discredited and marginalised in what may well be the dangerous beginning stages of experiencing 'intense intra-psychic pain', in which case one cannot help hearing the other implicit warning aimed at black South Africans: that at some point the victim turns perpetrator.

So the white Afrikaner is victim, perpetrator and victim again in this reading of Krog's inclusion of Fanon, initially cast as inferior and 'savage' by the English, capable of rampant racism by turns, and psychologically wounded by having now become the 'persecuted or despised group' (2003: 150) responsible for apartheid, by another turn, and as such possibly experiencing a 'psychological double bind' though of a different kind to the one experienced by Fanon's oppressed group.[63] The white Afrikaner version manifests itself as being caught between newly empowered black governance on the one hand and English 'neutrality' and normativity on the other, and, as such, both victim and perpetrator simultaneously. This makes the Afrikaner angry and simultaneously ineffectual.

The psychological double bind is effectively demonstrated in Krog's characterisation of her cousin, Peet. The first glimpse we are given of Peet is when he is surrounded by his family on the farm they visit for a meal. Here the 'talk is peppered with expressions of ruin – the wheels coming off, grinding to a halt, *in sy moer in*, going to pieces, unravelling, *opgefok*.[64] An overwhelming sense of being hounded, deprived and on the edges of chaos rises amidst the aromatic vapours of food' (2003: 21). Krog's rendition of this moment suggests that she is well aware of the paradoxes upon which the white version of the psychological double bind hinges. These people appear blissfully unaware of the privilege and sheer excess of their laden plates, and clearly the newly elected largely black government which is held responsible for things falling to pieces has made little impact on the attitudes and standard of living enjoyed by Peet's extended family. His response falls somewhere between Ouma Hannie's (who is waiting for the day when the Afrikaner is brought back to power) and Rina's (Peet's wife, who acknowledges that there is plenty of 'reborn racism' in the community). His attempt to be neutral (2003: 23) renders him ineffectual, and like the half-built medieval castle they see abandoned in the empty Free State landscape, he becomes a figure in the text of the utterly alienated, broken white man. As Krog stares at this Gothic edifice, half built and abandoned by some rich white man gone bankrupt, she makes a remark that might well be transferred to describe Peet, or at least the people and their abandoned white dreams that Peet represents:

> Several pasts roam across our skin in shades of stone and setting sun. I feel at once touched and repulsed by this place draped in the smell of uprooted visions of grandeur and unanchored, wild expectations. (2003: 25)

Because of its placement and foregrounding in the second chapter of the book, this image remains a haunting symbol throughout the text of European displacement. This is one of the moments in which, sole-like, Krog maintains her silence: she cannot come to Peet's rescue, and '[s]ilence grows firmly in [her] mouth'. That Peet has become an empty shell or crumbling edifice of a previous era is illustrated in two ways. Directly following the description of the castle, Peet and Rina relate the story of how their dog attacked one of their black labourers. Rina lay on top of the labourer to protect him from the vicious attack, and Peet arrives home purely by chance while the dog is savaging the labourer who is lying underneath his wife's body, both of them bespattered with his infectious blood. This is truly a spectacle that would send the average 'sane' white South African man right over the edge as Krog well knows, containing as it does multiple taboos, the least of which is 'the woman on top' aberration of the missionary position. His response is telling:

> I was so furious, I thought I was going to lose my mind – this kind of stupid, naïve caring for someone who is nothing more than a bloody half-drunk, half-retarded, Aids-infested little swaggerer. I wanted to murder him. With her I've given up. She has always been utterly clueless when it comes to blacks. (2003: 27)

This reaction to the incident is as absurdly misplaced as the castle is, and though Peet is powerless, his deeply entrenched racial hatred surfaces in the string of dehumanising invectives hurled at this man whose conduct has resulted in Peet's failure to protect his wife, and thus his failure to play the role expected of him as a man. We hear later in the book that Rina did not contract the virus from all the spilt black blood, but it may be small consolation for Peet, whose white masculinity has been rendered obsolete. Once again, Krog relinquishes, at least symbolically, her *authori*tative right to speak: 'That evening', she says, 'I sit with my notebook, but later I put it away again' (2003: 27). Peet's frustrated response to this incident reflects one strand of a general pattern discernable in representative white responses examined in this study: an inability to let go of narratives of the past that continue to rely on an 'Us/Them' dialectic. It may be argued that there are no shades of white in such responses, only a monolithic white anger.

The second incident in which Peet has to confront the hollow, disintegrating edifice of his national/cultural identity is in relating army stories to Krog one night. He confesses that it was in the army, during the height of apartheid, killing 'terrorists' on the Namibian border under the guidance of the heroic and legendary Colonel Jan Groenewald, that he felt 'more alive, more proud, more brave, more real than ever before in his life – or after' (2003: 214). Now he has to confront the magnitude of the lie sustaining his sense of self worth, the shame of which is etched on his body: Krog notes that 'whereas his hands always seemed rather stodgy and childish to [her] when [they] were younger, they have transformed their potential for cruelty into a clumsy vulnerability' and that, as she holds him to comfort him, '[h]e feels as if he's made only of sad, heavy flesh'. And indeed there is nothing left to say: 'The moment that defined him has now betrayed him' (2003: 214).

Of Krog's extended family, it is possibly Peet's wife, Rina, who provides, at least at first glance, a progressive and challenging counter-response to Peet, who appears to be caught in an impossible victim/perpetrator position. Rina recognises and articulates the dis-ease of Afrikanerdom, and the necessity of giving up the exclusiveness of such an identification. It is not surprising that it emanates from a white woman, rather than a white man, for the obvious reason that she has less to lose in relinquishing her position in the hierarchy. However, it may be argued that it is not an articulation uncontaminated by certain characteristically white assumptions. She sends Krog an e-mail from London where she is visiting her cousin, Katrien.[65] Given that this is represented as a personal correspondence, and not a public manifesto, the dubious generalisations around Afrikaner identity may be forgiven. However, Rina has used some curious analogies to suggest Afrikaner assimilation in the New South Africa, each of which suggests a masking, an act, the playing of a part, rather than a genuine attempt to transform. The athletics trainer whose discourse has already been examined is surely proof that 'mean-whiskered bullies' have not miraculously transformed themselves into 'arse-kissing poodles' except superficially and quite transparently so, in the deployment of the 'I am not a racist BUT…' disclaimer characteristic of 'whitespeak'. Similarly, that Rina's children go to 'mixed' schools and read about Bongi and Thandi rather than Jack and Jill is hardly an accurate measure of the Afrikaner's successful assimilation into the New South Africa, neither is learning to pronounce words in an African language nor making oneself scarce. Firstly, because 'mixed' or 'Model C' schools are historically 'whites-only' schools which, in the new dispensation, have assimilated black students. Secondly, because global media practices, and the centrality of America in managing these practices, has meant that Ken and Barbie will remain far more universally recognisable couples than Bongi and Thandi. Thirdly, because learning to click is merely paying lip service to multilingualism, and finally because making oneself 'scarce' only succeeds in concealing a source of power that the new government has not managed to override – white money and white global cultural wealth. In effect, the Afrikaner may not *be successfully assimilated*, but may more readily *assimilate* difference. Assimilation, as contemporary studies in whiteness have shown, requires the 'coconut-isation' of the former native, rather than the Africanisation of the former settler.

Krog's return mail suggests that she too has witnessed the tragic disempowerment of the white male, turned poodle with his tail between his legs. She tells Rina it was clear who the South African men were amongst the white men she witnessed disembarking from international flights at the Cape Town airport. Resorting to generalisation, she notes:

> The white men walking off with big, self-assured strides, hailing taxis with broad gestures and loud voices, are from America and Europe. In South Africa, white men have not walked like that for a long time now. Head down humbly on the chest, shoulders drawn in to avoid attracting attention, ego wilted, he slips into the parking area before you have seen him. (2003: 72)

This image of white South African men needs to be read in relation to a poem from *Kleur kom nooit alleen nie* (2000b) in which she expresses exasperation at the sheer ego of the typical white (Afrikaans-speaking) South African man: 'ai tog!'[66] (2000b: 47) registers her feminist response to masculine prescriptions emanating from a 'male vanity wat die laaste woord spreek oor die voorwaardes van hulle hoort'.[67] This poem suggests that there may be a hint of glee in Krog's observation of the disempowerment of the white male, especially his capacity to continue dictating what people ought to be doing (in a 'taal gestroop van die grammatika van menslikheid en berou'),[68] while manoeuvring his way out of any responsibility by offering his services at the 'nuwe barcounter van identities'.[69] Krog is clearly not convinced that white South African men have been defeated, and her response to Rina may therefore be read as a small victory for women, but not much more.

Defining Whiteness: Negotiating and Mediating Black Reponses

Krog thus needs to look elsewhere for answers as to what whiteness might mean in a post-apartheid context, and turns away from her own family and community in order to engage alternative responses, and in particular, she explores the power of naming in conveying perceptions. A question she poses consistently throughout the text is what 'whiteness' might mean to those who are not white. Clearly those who are white have little to offer, except their sense of loss combined with an impossible sense of their own normativity, as is evident in Joep Joubert's comments, for example, or in Rina's notion of assimilation. In a flashback to her youth, Krog remembers the slaughtering of an Afrikander ox, and a discussion she has with Eveline and some other black female farm labourers who were helping with the cutting up of the meat. The young Krog asks Eveline what the Sesotho word '*makgoa*' means, knowing full well that it means 'whites'. While Eveline remains 'somewhat respectful', offering only that it means 'those on whom we spit when we see them', one of the younger women says the word means 'Baboons', and tenders the explanation that 'baboons always look over their shoulders, because they look one way but walk the other way, because they do nothing, they just check out, check out, check out – the whole day' (2003: 85–86). In this definition, two significant features emerge: namely, the surveillance and 'baaskap' assumed by the settler, always 'checking out', which, in an ironic reversal is interpreted by the black farm labourers as inherent laziness, and in another twist, the reversal of the zoological terms reserved by the settler to mark the condition of the native.[70] Further definitions of whiteness from a black perspective are offered by Professor Mayekiso whom Krog interviews on her trip to New York to cover Nelson Mandela's address to the United Nations in 1995. Mayekiso tells Krog that 'Xhosa and Zulu were among the first black languages that named whites in Southern Africa' (2003: 184). He points out that although at first the names were merely descriptive of the strangers' appearance and behaviour, for example, 'They-whose-hair-washes-down-from-their heads' or, more worryingly, 'They-who-point-with-sticks-from-which-fire-and-lightening-burst', the naming soon incorporated an attitude that indigenous people came to associate with whiteness: 'They-who-speak-to-others-as-if-they-were-bundles-of-washing' or, increasingly disturbing, the '[l]atecomers – who-soil-the-water-as-they-grab-everything-for-themselves'. In addition, Mayekiso quotes an extract from a poem by S.E.K. Mqhayi, the 'Shakespeare of African languages' whom Krog admits she had never heard of: 'you whites/you-who-are-not-able-to-share-anything/the English, the Germans, the Boers' (2003: 185). These attitudes bespeak the sense of superiority and entitlement characteristic of imperialist/colonialist sensibilities, regardless of the Dutch or English origins of the group. Towards the end of the book, as Krog relates the African poets' pilgrimage to Timbuktu, the group is reminded that the Swahili word for whites is 'They-who-surround-you-with-questions' (2003: 297), interrogation being a colonialist strategy to figure out whether the natives were friendly or not, and how much plundering of natural resources could be effected. In these definitions, it may be argued, there is a very real sense that whiteness *is* monolithic, or at least experienced as such, contrary to Krog's attempt to suggest that there are shades of whiteness evident in the continuing effects of historical relationship between Brit and Boer. This is just one manifestation of a contradiction which suggests an unresolved ambivalence at the heart of Krog's project.

In her interrogation of whiteness, Krog engages a number of black friends and colleagues, and from the earliest encounters recorded in the book she shows an awareness of her role as mediator in recording, selecting and assessing these responses. The first of these encounters occurs when she visits the new mayor of Kroonstad, Mr Lebona, and fires a series of questions at him about poor delivery and possible corruption in local government. Krog admits, in this moment, that it is difficult for her to ask these questions and that she is struggling 'to find a way of making him understand that [she is] on his side' (2003: 53).

Krog may be experiencing the lingering residue of ineffectual and burdensome white guilt, the kind that manifests itself in post-apartheid South Africa when the liberal intellectual demands answers but is defensively self-conscious of the privileged position from which the demand derives. This awkwardness is expressed in her acknowledgement that '[it] is hard to find a legitimate space to criticise from, but it seems harder still for him not to feel victimised by it' (2003: 54). She need not have worried about offending the mayor, it turns out, because his detailed account of the insurmountable difficulties he faces in an attempt to appease both township residents and residential whites suggests that feelings of victimisation have transmuted and are now beginning to take the shape of something far less familiar and thus more threatening to white South Africans: he regards Krog's precious 'white-informed' point of view with 'something like pity' (2003: 55). Krog, however, continues to mediate the responses she is given in interviews with people from previously disadvantaged communities, at times demonstrating a profound awareness of white presumption, and at other times taking it upon herself to defend her whiteness quite vociferously.

Negotiating Whiteness: The 'Universal Sanctity of Whiteness'
In conversation with Sheridan (a black friend and former colleague with whom she taught music and marched against the apartheid regime), Krog asks how Kroonstad is faring a decade into democracy. Sheridan says that nothing much has changed: 'The whites still have everything and the blacks still have nothing' (2003: 117). When quizzed he suggests that the changes that have happened are largely superficial, and that they have occurred where it does not really count:

> On television black men are suddenly drinking whisky, black women are doing their own laundry. In Kroonstad, a black man wears the mayor's chain, there are black children in white schools. But these things don't matter. As soon as black people take control of something, that thing loses its power. *Sjoep!* Suddenly the power is gone, and you look around and see that the whites have twisted things here and there, and the power is with them. It is somewhere else again.

Krog responds by citing black corruption as opposed to white hegemony as the primary factor in making sense of post-apartheid power relations. It is in this mode that racism operates effectively. It reinforces the problem of disentangling class and race in the sense that the economy (and capitalist consumerism) is the place of concealed power. This may be read in relation to David Wellman's argument that racism is a scheme that 'systematically provides economic, political, psychological, and social advantages for whites at the expense of Blacks and other people of color' (1977: 37). Thus, white power resides in multiple institutional practices, and a few black faces in local government and in television advertising amounts to not much more than window-dressing, whilst poorly educated working-class township people remain as disempowered as ever. Following Wellman, Sandra Harding suggests that institutionalised relations (of race, gender, class and sexuality) are not 'caused by prejudice – by individual bad attitudes and false beliefs', though these of course are not to be condoned and do not help matters. Individual prejudice is simply a symptom rather than a cause, and Harding suggests that we pay due attention to institutional rather than the individualistic dynamics to uncover the ways in which 'an individual may be well informed about, and not at all hostile toward, people of colour, women, the poor, or gays and lesbians – that is, he or she can have the proper *mental* characteristics that constitute lack of prejudice – and nevertheless continually and effectively support beliefs and practices that maintain economic, political, and social inequality' (1995: 122). In Krog's book, Sheridan reiterates this phenomenon.

When Krog's own liberal humanist tolerance for difference and rainbow nationhood is expressed, Sheridan suggests that the Mandela/Tutu vision of the New South Africa was too idealised to have lasted:

> 'It is only now that we've woken up and realised that you don't take the whites out of power so easily. Their white skins protect them everywhere in the world. If you touch a white person it has international repercussions. And that is what I resent most. We are not dealing with real fellow citizens here. *Whites have the universal sanctity of their white skin.*' (2003: 118, my emphasis)

In response to this, Krog demonstrates her reticence in acknowledging the 'universal sanctity' of whiteness, by getting up to leave. However, she does not do so, and this may indicate that she may be posing in this moment for the benefit of her (white) readership: she wants her reader to endure the uncomfortable moment with her, thereby enabling her to teach the lesson more effectively. In a sense, she may be read to be consciously and purposefully exhibiting the allegiances of the well-informed, unprejudiced individual that Harding suggests is never overtly racist, but who is nonetheless very much a product of the universalising assumptions that whiteness continues to embody.

During this encounter with Sheridan, Krog initially appears to be unambiguously offended, but when Sheridan quotes Njabulo Ndebele whom he identifies as Krog's hero, and whose articulation of the sanctity of whiteness is powerful, Krog's reactions suggest uneasy ambivalence:

> The white body is inviolable, and that inviolability is in direct proportion to the global vulnerability of the black body. This leads me to think that if South African whiteness is a beneficiary of the protectiveness assured by international whiteness, it has an opportunity to write a new chapter in world history. It will have to come out from under the umbrella and repudiate it. Putting itself at risk, it will have to declare that it is home now, sharing in the vulnerability of other compatriot bodies. South African whiteness will have to declare that its dignity in inseparable from the dignity of black bodies. (Ndebele in Krog 2003: 118)

Krog's prior response to Sheridan is to pick up her bag in readiness to leave, but having listened to him quoting Ndebele, and particularly in having transcribed verbatim a sizeable portion of Ndebele's recorded response to whiteness, it may be argued that she is acknowledging the challenge to her as a writer in contributing to what Ndebele conceives of as a new chapter in world history. Momentarily unable to rise to the challenge, she resorts to white defensiveness in suggesting that Sheridan wants to put her into a 'convenient "white box"' and thus avoid confronting what she calls 'the complexities of good and bad whites, and good and bad blacks' (2003: 119). It is interesting to note here that what Ndebele articulates as the violence of the bodily experience of racism appears not to have been heard by Krog whose language suggests the 'discomfort' of being marked by labels as opposed to Ndebele's words which depict a more painful vulnerability inscribed on the body – an embodiment of racial markings. The differing responses emerge in the very lexicons employed by each of the writers, the most telling verbal cues perhaps being Ndebele's choice of bodily *complexion*[71] as dominant signifier, and Krog's highlighting of *complexities*. These words move respectively from concrete to abstract, or from lived to imagined. Clearly Krog's position in this rejoinder, whether she is conscious of it or not, is that of the liberal white in anti-racist debates. A position, Alistair Bonnet suggests, that allows 'white people […] the luxury of being passive observers … of knowing that 'their' 'racial' identity might be reviled or lambasted but never made slippery, torn open or, indeed, abolished' (1997: 177–178). This is not to suggest that Ndebele stands accused of essentialising racial categorisation but to indicate his experience of the *effects* of such categorisation.

The conversation ends abruptly after Sheridan praises Zimbabwean president, Robert Mugabe, for real redistribution of wealth and land and suggests that in South Africa 'we are being squeezed like lice between the fingers of America and Europe' (2003: 119). Krog's very next, and very telling statement is: 'There's not much left to be said.' This represents a familiar deadlock in black and white relations in this country. It is an impasse that *cannot* be readily overcome in the face of continued white privilege, and one that Krog herself does not effectively negotiate in this vignette: after the meeting with Sheridan she sees hundreds of disintegrating school desks and chairs in the parking lot of the Education Department, and her sense of anger is palpable in the description that ensues. But Ndebele's challenge to white South Africans is indirectly revisited in the very next scene narrated in the book. It is primarily the proximity and therefore the deliberate juxtaposition of these scenes that suggests the possibility of such a reading. On her return to the farm, Joep Joubert, the new manager, drives her off to witness something. What he shows her is one of the black women working in the field with a new bright pink hat on her head, and Krog perhaps hears the echo of her earlier anger and despair in Joep's summation of the woman and her pink hat. He says:

she bought a bloody fucking hat with half her money [child-support grant]. And she's working in the fields with it! And I can promise you, she will have a child every year as long as she can keep herself in money. These are the people that we are sharing the country with! *Transformation!* You don't understand the half of it. (2003: 120)

This encounter constitutes a painful turning point for Krog in her negotiation of difference, and in the mediatory role she has been playing in recording and interpreting black responses. For Krog it was a pile of unused desks, for Joep a pink hat that signified inalienable difference, but it is ultimately the writer who recognises the bitter sound of racist and sexist sentiment in Joep's comments, and perhaps recalls an echo of the white exasperation in her own response to Sheridan and the abandoned desks. Her countering description of the woman confirms the probability:

I clasp my lame left hand to me as he drives me back. I think about the woman – how her face glowed as if light was collecting on her skin underneath the pink hat. How, while we were looking, she raised one hand softly, as if she were touching something very special, and pulled the hat forward on her brow.

Here Krog feels the brokenness of post-apartheid South Africa physically, in the hand that was affected by a stroke, and perhaps figuratively in the lameness she experiences in the face of such injustice, but more significantly, in the poignancy (the complexions) she reads into the scene. Her frustration has been eclipsed by a mightier, more dangerous brand, and it is replaced with something akin to shared human suffering: she feels the pain of the woman labourer who has been so ruthlessly dehumanised in Joep's image of her, and Krog responds by validating this other woman's existence in gentler words, and in doing so, perhaps indirectly, rises to Ndebele's call for white South Africans to write a new chapter in world history, one that counters the impression created by Joep Joubert that *his* version of the story unfolding before them is the right (white) one.

Negotiating Whiteness: Becoming White

Krog's frustrated response to the abandoned desks after her encounter with Sheridan is counteracted in her recollection of Deborah Matshoba's testimony at the Truth and Reconciliation Commission. In narrating this scene that emerges as a result of a follow-up interview with Deborah, Krog demonstrates not outrage at being labelled white but outrage at what white people have done in the name of their whiteness. After a hard-drive crash, she is able to salvage some of an interview conducted during her reportage of the TRC, an extract of which is fittingly used to end Part Two of the book, entitled 'A Hard Drive' and consisting largely of reportage on the war in Rwanda and the earlier twentieth-century Boer War. Deborah, having experienced torture and solitary confinement at the hands of the apartheid security police, is a traumatised black woman, who displays all the symptoms of a torture victim – 'depression, anxiety, sexual dysfunction, irritability, physical illness' (2003: 156). Krog asks her: 'What is it in whites that will make [her] say: that is why [she doesn't] want to live in a country with them?' (2003: 157). Her response confronts an aspect of South African whiteness that needs to be scrutinised:

> 'Things like – and I'm just mentioning a few – they don't know that we only started having a democratic vote, a democratic government in 1994. Oh really! Were you oppressed? You were arrested? We didn't know that! You couldn't get a management position? You were in jail? What for? They don't know that they used to put the National Party in power. That is irritating, very, very irritating.'

This brand of assumed innocence is a symptom of the insularity and normativity associated with whiteness. Such 'innocence' may stem from the fact that most middle-class white South Africans have not needed to develop an awareness of anything outside their frame of reference, since it is their frame of reference that is supposedly universal, educated, liberal and thus beyond reproach. It is an 'innocence' born out of a seemingly benign indifference amongst younger generation white[72] South Africans whose other pat response is that they had nothing to do with apartheid, and should therefore not be obliged to carry the burden of white guilt. It is also an 'innocence' that constitutes a crass dismissal of the magnitude of the struggle for freedom in South Africa and the ways in which white people have benefited and continue to benefit from the 'universal sanctity of whiteness'.

When Krog asks Deborah why she chooses to live in a racist white suburb with its 'burglar bars, and guard dogs', she says that having fought so hard for freedom she will now live wherever she wants to because she *can*, and that her neighbours need to seek acceptance from her, and if they do not seek acceptance 'they might as well go and live in Canada' (2003: 157). Many white South Africans do in fact choose to leave the country rather than forego the narratives that promote a sense of superiority and entitlement, as Melissa Steyn (2001: 276) has pointed out, but those who have stayed are often guilty of an insularity that relieves them from actively seeking acceptance. Krog is not convinced that the acceptance Deborah seeks has come easily, or at all, and interviews one of Deborah's AWB (Afrikaner Weerstandsbeweging) neighbours. Bokkie, on hearing that Deborah was a 'terrorist', says simply that 'she has changed'. And this constitutes a recognisable, even typical, white response in this country: the expectation that black people in general ought to change their ways, become whiter, while they expect of themselves nothing more than the odd gesture of multiculturalism in the exoticisation of 'tribal' traditions – Bokkie's last anecdote revolves around her daughter's borrowing traditional wear from Deborah to attend a corporate cultural day (2003: 158).

Deborah has not changed, at least not in the sense that Bokkie imagines, namely, that because she lives in a predominantly white suburban space she has been 'civilised'. Bokkie appears to have interpreted economic upliftment (Deborah has a pool in her backyard) as a measure of her transformation, but the debate around race versus class is explored by Krog in the next encounter in which she mediates black responses.

Negotiating Whiteness: Race, Class and Belonging

This is an exemplary debate that takes place 'in one of the most obscenely expensive shopping malls in the country' (2003: 273) during the 2002 South African Conference on Racism when Krog is reunited with two former colleagues, Ghangha and Mamukwa, from her teaching and activist days in Kroonstad. A version of this scene is recorded in *Country of My Skull*, and it is intriguing to compare the two scenes in order to examine Krog's changing responses to the same debate. In the earlier text, the names of the characters taking part in the debate are Mamogele and Eddy (2002: 287), both identified as former colleagues from the same period in Krog's life, but much of the debate is omitted. For example, in the later version Ghangha tells Krog that she is now living in Bloemfontein in a formerly white suburb and suggests that initially she was 'held accountable for every single thing a black person did':

> If a black man rapes a child or steals a million, the neighbours or my colleagues want me to explain. And if I want to know why it is I never ask *them* to explain when a white farmer shoots a black baby – is it perhaps because I know them well enough? – then they're quick with this ubuntu thing: blacks stick together because of ubuntu, you know? And I can tell you, nothing pisses me off more than whites pretending to understand or even care about African concepts like ubuntu. (2003: 272)

Ghangha's experience of 'integration' once again suggests the universalising normalcy of white responses. But it is Krog's knee-jerk response to this experience that is of greater significance, a response that is heard more and more frequently in liberal white anti-racist rhetoric and one that is recorded more or less verbatim in the earlier text:

> *Why has race become the only debate? [...] Nobody talks about class, or human rights, accountability, how to prevent abuses, how much of the past is already part of the present, collective guilt, moral choices, the definition of 'perpetrators' – the only thing we hear is race, race, race.* As if my identity is 'white', and I'm not allowed to be more than that! (2003: 272) (*2002: 287*)[73]

Clearly, the catalogue of satellite debates that Krog introduces is *not*, strictly speaking, alternate to race and this is the obvious flaw in the argument. Clearly, too, her position has not shifted significantly since writing the earlier version of this encounter. Equally apparent, however, is that the list of alternatives from class through to the definition of perpetrators is arguably almost exactly the list a reader would recognise as constituting Krog's entire project in writing *A Change of Tongue*, though the final product, ironically, is ultimately and explicitly about race. Krog's preoccupation with race, and in particular with whiteness, is evident throughout her oeuvre, and most notably in her most recent collections of poems: *Down to My Last Skin* (2000a), and *Kleur kom nooit alleen nie* (2000b). The first section of the poem, 'ná grond-invasions in Zimbabwe'[74] from the latter collection (2000b: 45), poses a set of fiercely asked questions which suggest her exasperation at being labelled white.

Krog's exasperated rejoinder in response to Ghangha is even more overt than in the bleak images of black and white that appear in this poem. In both cases she seems unable to move beyond race, though she is simultaneously and painfully negotiating the impossibility of divorcing racial dynamics from the other pressing debates she engages. Echoes of this exasperation also appear in *Country of My Skull*, where she expresses a similar bitter acknowledgment that no debates in South Africa come *sans* racial implications: her reading of the then Deputy-President Thabo Mbeki's thoughts on reconciliation (that it is only possible if whites take responsibility for apartheid and ask for forgiveness) is that this is a political line that 'freezes the debate in tones of black and white and gives no guidance on how the individual can move forward' (2002: 58).

It may therefore be argued that rather than simply staging a debate, or as she puts it, 'a lively discussion' (2003: 273) for the sake of exposing the faulty logic in 'white' thinking for the reader, she may be exhibiting a very real reticence, which comes across as defensiveness, in negotiating whiteness as a distinct and persisting racial category. It may be argued that Krog needs to resuscitate the categories 'individualism' and 'humanism' in the face of strong evidence that these western constructs have lost much of their credibility as a result of rampant neocolonial and global exploitation of humanity.[75] Indeed, as Robert Young's critical reading of Fanon's espousal of a new humanism suggests, whenever universal, 'human(ist)' ideas are circulated, it is almost always accompanied by a 'mask[ing] over [of] the assimilation of the human itself with European values' (2004: 161). Krog's next line of attack, omitted from the first version, is the centrality of class in negotiating racial dynamics and suggests that highlighting race at the expense of other debates is strategic in black politics:

> Let me tell you why we only hear about race. The new black elite hates it when the debate turns from race to class. They will keep the race issue spinning, so that their greedy hands can grab more and more, until they have it all. They need whites as a serviceable Other. As long as a few whites are still living on a farm or two, no matter how modestly, no matter how strongly they identify with Africa and all that shit, the black elite will cry race, they'll send in the poor to do the dirty work and afterwards they'll throw them to the wolves. (2003: 273)

Krog does have a point – one that has already been adequately theorised by Fanon in his identification of the post-liberation black bourgeois in newly appointed positions of power, who replicate colonial oppressions, having learnt well from the master what to desire and how to acquire it. Ghangha's counter-argument, however, is difficult to dispute, in her suggestion that 'whites are in complete denial' and borne out in Krog's curiously inaccurate generalisation concerning 'a few whites' living on 'a farm or two' who might 'identify with Africa and all that shit'. Firstly, land redistribution has not progressed satisfactorily, as statistics indicate, and secondly, to refer only to farmers, whom we know are experiencing less support than that to which they were previously accustomed, and to omit middle-class urban dwellers, is to miss the major constituency of representative white South Africans. In addition, her reference to an identification with Africa 'and all that shit' suggests a very real sense of uneasiness, embarrassment even. After all, what might such identifying with Africa mean? Does it entail identifying with the continent, the climate, the landscape, the people or all of the above? One response might be that it is largely an identification with the land, but this emerges only later in the book, and consequently later in this discussion, but a serviceable example of how this identification emerges is in Krog's preoccupation throughout the book with the family farm which is sold, and to which she is forced to return when she visits Kroonstad in the capacity of something like a '*bywoner*',[76] residing not in the family homestead but in the adjoining bungalow. Krog once again exhibits a desire to rely on the notion of the individual as opposed to negotiating the cultural/racial group out of which that sense of autonomy arises. Indeed, she says as much in her response to Ghangha who argues that '[w]hites can never know what it is to be black' (2003: 274):

> Race is the only thing about yourself you cannot change. I can change my perspective, my words, my thinking, my body language, but not my skin. So if you have a problem with me because I'm white, I'm trapped. There is no room for change. Race moves the debate from moral questions – how are you acting? – to narrow, nationalist ones – what colour are you? what group do you belong to? (2003: 274)

Her response suggests that *A Change of Tongue* attempts to demonstrate that it is possible but extremely difficult to change one's perspective, one's words, one's thinking and one's body language – and of all the categories, it may be argued, 'body language' is the hardest for Krog to change, being as it is, the most unconscious manifestation of an attitude. The discomfort that emerges through body language is evident in Krog's scatological preoccupations throughout the book, a point discussed later in this chapter. So far, in the text Krog has wrestled with all of these categories to a lesser or greater extent, and in the section entitled 'A Translation' she wrestles specifically with words and, in this moment, the word 'race' appears open to conflicting definitions: Krog is ironically and dangerously close to essentialising and biologising the concept in her attempt to argue *against* using pigmentation as the primary indicator of a person's worth and is reminded by Ghangha that whiteness is *not* a matter of skin colour:

> 'white' is a mindset, an outlook. Whiteness is pervasive: it's not only the way you walk and gesticulate, in your words and thoughts, it is also to do with confidence, with where you start from. With exclusion. With the assumption that your way of running a country is the best, that your definition of a town, what you need to be happy in a town, to call it your town, is the only one.

It is this aura of assumption and exclusion that is the most difficult to define or identify in ordinary everyday interactions, and it is in these unconscious, seemingly trivial gestures that white normativity is most effectively camouflaged.

That Krog chooses to record the same debate, though in variation in two consecutive books, suggests two likely explanations: that she recognises that it is a debate that is necessarily ongoing and must continue to be re-articulated, revisited and recycled, a point she makes in summing up her response to the Truth and Reconciliation Commission at the end of *Country of My Skull*, where she acknowledges that though the TRC did not exactly succeed in all it set out to achieve, it at least made 'a new relationship possible. But the cycle will have to be repeated many times for this new relationship to be lasting' (2002: 292). Furthermore, that she herself is living proof of the difficulty facing white South Africans of engaging in a debate in which white racial identity is under such intense scrutiny, and in danger of being torn apart. The second version is much fuller and more nuanced than the first, intimating perhaps that Krog has thought through these black and white responses more fully. Indeed, Krog's second rendition contains a lively banter lacking in the first, noticeable specifically when she records her own reaction to being labelled a 'kangaroo'. If she is going to have to live with labels signifying her outsider, exotic status as a white woman in Africa, she'd rather be a 'eucalyptus tree' than 'a bloody kangaroo hopping around the Free State':

> From elsewhere, but impossible to imagine the South African landscape without it. Small towns, farms, railway lines, forests, windbreaks. The eucalyptus towers over many memories. It is used in mines, in pole fences, furniture. It is a handy tree. Tenacious. *'n Windskerm*. It's true that nothing will grow under it, that it consumes more water than other trees, but it has turtle doves in its leaves and sheep in its shade. And where it is desolate it grows. And it gives great honey. (2003: 275)

Krog's rambling free association here intimates more perhaps than she intended because it presents such a recognisably colonising image of Africa which the turtle doves and pastoral sheep and great honey do not manage to override. And the eucalyptus tree towers over *her* memories, which are culturally specific. Humorous reflections of self and community aside, though, the outcome of both versions is fairly bleak: Krog appears to abandon the moment to uncertainty, leaving the reader to draw her own conclusions, and perhaps predictably, those conclusions will be directly related to the skin colour (or at least its concomitant identification) of the reader. In the first version Mamagele tells her that only when she 'can remove [herself] from under that big umbrella of whiteness, and live the black life of risk, will [she] become one of [them]' (2002: 288), whereupon Krog sits with 'a mouth full of teeth'. In the later version, when Mamukwa suggests that whites may never really be 'acceptable', Krog admits to being 'a bit stuck' (2003: 274). In effect, in both instances, she does not know how to respond to black solidarity and black resentment, which are *responses* to white entitlement.

At the end of both versions Krog confesses that what she really wants to hear from her black friends is that as a white person in post-apartheid South Africa she 'belongs', but she senses that the moment is not opportune, and in both versions she walks off with Mamogele/Mamukwa, together but apart: 'We walk slowly back to the hotel – window shopping. The past bleeding softly between us' (2002: 289), 'We walk slowly back to the hotel, window-shopping. The future already unfolding in different ways between us' (2003: 275). Whereas at the end of *Country of My Skull*, Krog believes it is a bloody past that separates the two women, towards the end of *A Change of Tongue*, she seems to believe it is the future that will continue to come between them, a future perhaps in which a racist past continues to lurk, one in which the white woman feels that she does not belong, and one in which the black woman feels for the first time that she does belong. The very phrasing of the revised final sentence is fraught with ambiguity: read positively, it may mean that the future, though 'differently' experienced or interpreted by the two women, is at least shared 'between them'. Read negatively, it may suggest that the future, containing all of the unresolved trauma of the past, will always come 'between' them, keeping them apart, and the latter is arguably the more credible reading, given Krog's attempted parting comment to the two black women, the one which remains incomplete: 'But I want to...' (2002: 289; 2003: 275). [Belong] remains unsaid and unanswered, unsayable and unanswerable, and perhaps exemplifies a growing white South African sense of 'unhomeliness'.

In an essay entitled 'The World and the Home', Bhabha describes the 'unhomely' as the shock of discovering that where you are is no longer home and marks its emergence in that 'unhomely moment [that] relates the traumatic ambivalences of a personal psychic history to the wider disjunctions of political existence' (1992: 144). Bhabha is referring to the experience of non-western subjectivities in this moment, and uses Toni Morrison's *Beloved*, and Nadine Gordimer's *My Son's Story* to examine the ways in which each of the houses or 'homes' (124 Bluestone Road and a house in a 'grey' suburb in Cape Town, respectively) throws out what he calls 'freak displacements', a phrase he co-opts from Gordimer's novel, which he sums up as 'the profound divisions of an enslaved or apartheid society – negrification, denigration, classification, violence, incarceration' (1992: 145).

It is only when white South Africans truly begin to feel the effects of being forcibly displaced themselves, and to acknowledge the possibility that such a sense of displacement is the inevitable outcome of a colonising western history for most of the world's population, which is a condition that is neither new nor avoidable, that a less conspicuous, more uncomfortable, and necessarily more uncertain space might become available for them to inhabit. Whereas the condition of experience for most colonised people is always a sense of 'freak displacement', for the white western subject living in South Africa it is a relatively new sensation, since white subjectivity has not only *not* been tainted by 'negrification, denigration, classification' but it has also 'naturally' benefited from the privileges that such processes inculcate. In a sense Krog's incomplete appeal to 'belong' may conceivably be read as an indication of her awakening sense of a white post-colonial 'freak displacement', as is suggested in the poem 'ai tog!' (2000b: 47) from *Kleur kom nooit alleen nie*: having catalogued her challenge to the prescriptions she associates with normative social/cultural identification, the poem ends with her proclamation of dissociation in suggesting that 'mens hoort by haar wat daagliks woordeloos/nuwe wolle by die mat vleg'.[77] This constitutes a powerful rejection of patriarchal prescriptions, and an alternative identification with the woman worker. But it is an identification lacking in Krog's stifled appeal to belong in *A Change of Tongue*, so that the transformative potential contained in the earlier poetic image remains unrealised in the latter encounter. That the appeal is addressed to black South Africans may suggest an unconscious western will to entitlement, but that it is a *stifled* appeal and that it appears in a book addressed predominantly to white South Africans suggests Krog's recognition of her own assumptions.

Redefining Whiteness: Working with Words
If Krog appears to have reached an impasse in her discussions with the two black women with whom she is reunited at the South African Conference on Racism, she makes a relatively significant breakthrough in the struggle with words that she experiences in translating into Afrikaans Nelson Mandela's autobiography, *Long Walk to Freedom*. It is here, at the level of working with words (rather than with people), that her most valuable negotiation of white displacement occurs, though whether or not it is wholly effective is questionable.

In her interviews with black people Krog has recorded the multiple words used to describe white people in African languages from the merely descriptive through to the most disparaging, but it is the self-proclaimed designation 'Afrikaner' that causes the most difficulty when thrown out of an English text into an Afrikaans one. She discovers that in the autobiography, 'African' appears to be a central concept for Mandela, but in translation 'African' and 'Afrikaan' are not easily rendered without the political innuendos of black and white versions of nationalism vying for supremacy. Indeed, as she points out, 'African' might be translated most accurately into 'Afrikaan', but with the omission only of the 's' at the end, it is a word already appropriated by European settlers of mainly Dutch descent to represent their own colonising identity, so that when she uses the designation there is a necessary slippage in meaning, resulting in ambiguity, and a grammatical awkwardness that Afrikaans readers would find difficult adjusting to.

Krog refuses to use the Afrikaans colloquial '*Afrika man*' to describe a black person, which, though it might solve the problem of ambiguity and grammatical clumsiness, does little to address the more sensitive political appropriation of 'African' to designate white settlers. It is in response to the difficulty of translating Mandela's sense of the concept 'African' that Krog realises the significance of his explicit insistence on having the book translated into Afrikaans:

> He is using this request, with his usual instinct for power relationships, to force Afrikaans to make room for all the people of the continent. He is forcing Afrikaners to go back to the roots of the word they took so exclusively for themselves, to share it with others, to transform the language of apartheid into a language of coming together, to rid it of the vocabulary of power and retribution. (2003: 279)

Though it is obviously hugely enriching to have the heroic figure of Nelson Mandela as iconic reminder, to black and white South Africans, of transformation and reconciliation, it may also be argued that there is something bordering on entitlement (albeit unconscious) that prompts Krog's perception of 'making room for' and 'sharing' the designation 'African'. Her sense of accommodating multiculturalism brings to mind Bhabha's scepticism of liberalism's all too easy notion of equality in his reminder that '[p]rejudicial knowledge, racist or sexist, does not pertain to the ethical or logical "reflectiveness" of the Cartesian subject' (2002: 55), but unconsciously manifests itself in a myriad invisible assumptions.

Like her image of the eucalyptus tree, fraught with images of a colonising history, her notion of shared equality does not take due cognisance of the disjunctions that might render such a position(ality) untenable from a black perspective. One might easily reroute a single word's meaning, but not so easily the string of associated words, images and realities that orbit around it. Thus, it may be argued that Krog's liberal tolerance and her presumption of equal respect is untimely, and simultaneously renders her comfortable white 'Observer' status invisible. That said, the attempt to 'resignify' in translation the concept 'African' remains one of Krog's most powerful gestures in the politics of identity that she confronts in *A Change of Tongue*.

Scatological and Eschatological Preoccupations: Latrines and Doctrines
If the sole is the abiding reconciliatory and transformational image in the text, then defecation and excrement are the abiding images blocking the passage to transformation. Indeed, Krog's preoccupation with excrement is not confined to *A Change of Tongue*. In *Down to My Last Skin* there is a poem entitled 'toilet poem' (2000a: 54), which offers a graphic description of urinating 'into a toilet bowl heaped halfway up/with at least four different colours of shit'. In addition, there is a poem entitled 'verskrikking'[78] (2000b: 93) in *Kleur kom nooit alleen nie* which offers a poetic rendition of an incident described in the book (discussed further on in this section). Earlier in this chapter I suggested that of all the categories Krog examines in her negotiation of identity, including her 'perspective' and her 'words', it is her 'body language' that she finds the most difficult to modify because it is the most unconscious manifestation of a response. The book contains such a laborious examination of the scatological that one might even be tempted to label it scatomancy, such is Krog's effort to divine something from people's toilet habits.

There are five sections devoted to the minutiae of sewerage in the book, the first three consisting of extracts from her mother's writing and dealing with the switch from pit latrines or 'long-drops' to the 'water closet' (WC) sanitation model in small-town South Africa at the beginning of the twentieth century (2003: 45–45, 50–52, 121–123). Krog anticipates critical attention to this curious aspect of the book in an avowal of her interest in the subject when reading an extract of her mother's essays to her husband:

> For some reason I've been seized by this morbid scatological interest here in Kroonstad [...] Preoccupation with excrement. How we deal with what the body has purged, the rubbish cast aside after transformation, the outward signs of internal change, or something to that effect. (2003: 121)

Though this interpretation or confession of her preoccupation is certainly self-reflectively convincing and in keeping with the central theme of transformation, it does appear somewhat dismissive of serious critical attention, particularly in the disclaiming clause 'or something to that effect'. And it would suffice as an explanation for the inclusion of the multiple stories relating to excrement and the disposal thereof were it not for the very personal account of a scatological incident described in the latter half of the book, which covers Krog's poetic pilgrimage to Timbuktu.

As the single representative South African poet in a group of African poets, Krog feels particularly estranged on this trip. Perhaps more so than on any other occasion narrated in the book, she feels the heaviness of 'dragging the corpse of white skin and Afrikaner tongue behind [her]' (2003: 169) while travelling into what may be described as the mythological heart of Africa, with no other white person in sight for three weeks. The entire narrative of this journey (Part Five: 'A Journey') is marked by Krog's sense of utter alienation, and one of the ways in which this manifests itself is in her preoccupation with physical discomfort. Indeed, the account of the trip leaves the reader with very little sense of the places she visits, apart from the lack of sanitation, the squalor, the financial squabbles and the logistical obstacles in getting from one place to another. Even her travelling companions constitute little more than a backdrop to the story of Krog's difficulties with strange food, the consumption of it, the digestion of it and finally, after pages of constipation, the expurging of it (2003: 320).

Had it not been for this extended and explicit account of taking a shit, one might be tempted to agree with Krog's rationale for the inclusion of her sewerage stories, that they are in some obscure, figurative way about 'transformation'. But a Freudian reading of anal retention would not be amiss in the sense that the preoccupation may be read as regressive rather than transformative. After an initial titter, which is more or less involuntary when confronted with such bathroom humour, the reader is left feeling cheated because a journey such as Krog has undertaken, with so much potential for reconciliation and transformation and all the other idealistic abstractions she has been known scrupulously to unpack and examine, dissipates in a preoccupation with bodily emissions (and intellectual omissions). When one reads her summarising of the trip, 'that she wants to be nowhere else but here, wants to be from nowhere else but here, this continent that fills her with so much anguish and love – this black battered but lovely heart' (2003: 333), one cannot help registering it as mere gesture, or idealisation, given the magnitude of personal discomfort recorded prior to this declaration of identification with Africa. There is a sense that Krog *yearns* to belong, apparent in the very choice and repetition of the word 'want', but despite her best intentions, she has failed to do so.

If there is, however, any sense of real transformation in this section of the book, it is on an aesthetic level, and not, once again, in her relationship with black people. Her rendition of poetic moments shared on the trip is passionate, and her descriptions of the African landscape are magnificently evocative of her powerful identification with the continent, with its natural wonders (the water, the animals, the firmament),[79] but all these elements fail to make up for her apparent inability to identify with the people in whose presence she feels so ill at ease, except in her *wanting them to accept her*. What is interesting to note in this regard is the implication of psychological regression as opposed to social transformation not only in terms of the scatological but also in relation to the narrative perspective from which such 'purging' is delivered. It has already been noted that Krog deploys the third person at crucial moments in the book, most noticeably in the mini-chapters in Part One, 'A Town', in which she records pivotal experiences in her childhood and adolescence.[80] There are only two other occasions in the book in which she switches from first to third person: a few sections of Part Four, 'A Translation', in which she struggles with the translation (and transformation) of her mother tongue in grappling with the concepts in Nelson Mandela's autobiography, and the whole of Part Five, 'A Journey'. The question of what it is that these moments delivered in the third person have in common is significant. One answer might be that it is when Krog is at her most vulnerable, when she is undergoing some kind of personal and radical transformation, that she resorts to a less personal and thus less threatening authorial perspective. The less sympathetic answer might be that in these moments she regresses, and regression is necessarily at odds with transformation.

Though it may be argued that Krog's preoccupation with excrement, particularly in relation to the journey she undertakes, is used as a powerful metaphor to emphasise her difficulty in coming to terms with Africa, and her success in purging herself (of preconceptions, of white guilt), such a reading is difficult to sustain in the face of evidence throughout her oeuvre of an abiding obsession with defecation. 'Verskrikking' (2000b: 93), for example, describes the same incident as recorded in 'A Journey' (2003: 320), the title of which ('Horror') echoes Kurtz's 'The Horror! The Horror!' (1988: 68) from Conrad's *Heart of Darkness*, and the echoing of the incident and its associations suggest an impasse rather than a breakthrough. In addition, the poem 'ai tog!', discussed earlier, makes use of the scatological explicitly in relation to race, with the images of humanity divided into 'drolwit en pisswart' (2000b: 47).[81]

The incident described is thus not simply an isolated and shocking moment that is used exclusively to suggest, figuratively, Krog's battle with transformation and purging. Rather it is one that recurs in variation and the alternate implications of regression cannot be overlooked.

In Krog's earlier response to Ghangha (2003: 274) she noted that it was possible to change her 'perspective', her 'words', her 'thinking', and her 'body language', and I suggested that of all the categories it is body language that is the most resistant to change. In *Country of My Skull* she admits as much in relation to her interactions with the white and black participants in the TRC hearings respectively:

> I cannot read the body codes of black people. It is as simple as that. When I interview Boraine or any of the white Commissioners I *know* when they cannot tell me the truth [...] But when I interview the black Commissioners I am at a loss. (2002: 234)

This telling admission may be productively used to read the scatological implications of *A Change of Tongue* and other works, in the sense that at the level of non-verbal, unconscious communication, the body signifies what the rational mind represses. Krog's 'body language' thus suggests something in excess of her own justification for the inclusion of the scatological (2003: 121), in addition to emphasising the gulf between black and white responses.

A Conclusion

Krog appears not to have journeyed much further from the liberal insights she recorded in *Country of My Skull*, except perhaps in that the earlier work is marked by a sense of hope that reconciliation is at least possible, whilst the latter work is marked by a sense of resignation and disillusionment. The final section of the book entitled 'An End' (as opposed to the conventional 'The End') consists of three seemingly unrelated chapters that operate as codas to the book. The indefinite article 'an' resists the teleology of narrative closure, and in her acknowledgment that there is more than one ending, Krog's authorial manifesto that there is more than one truth is reinforced. Chapter One of Part Three takes us to the former apartheid homeland of the Transkei, now incorporated in the Eastern Cape, and culminates in Krog's visit to a hospital serving the poorest black communities of South Africa. Here she encounters such enormous suffering that any traces of hope in the transformative potential of South Africa are suddenly and more or less irrevocably erased. Dr Kabir shows her the new wing of the rural hospital built to accommodate the growing numbers of HIV/Aids patients, and on walking the length of this 'death row', she ends the chapter with a series of unanswered but fiercely asked questions:

> And I breathe, in order not to suffocate in shame. I want to blame. I want to pluck someone from somewhere and shake them for answers. What has happened to us? Where are all the dreams we had for ourselves? What happened to the desire to change, to release ourselves into more caring lives? Where are we? Have we forgotten so soon what we wanted to be?
>
> How could we ever become that, how could we become whole, when parts of what we are die every day into silently stacked away brooms of bones? (2003: 354)

A question that emerges is who 'we' might be whom she incorporates in her sweeping inquisition, especially given that 'what we wanted to be', as has already been established in relation to a town like Kroonstad, may be different for a black population and for a white one. But perhaps she cannot ask those questions for the same reason that she felt uncomfortable asking the newly appointed black mayor of Kroonstad about poor delivery and charges of corruption – that it is hard to find 'a legitimate space to criticise from' (2003: 54), because there is 'no easy walk between perception and truth in this country' (2003: 27). Having failed to make sense of the country's woefully inadequate response to the HIV/Aids pandemic as it manifests itself in rural Transkei, Krog closes that chapter, as it were, and opens the next on a lighter, perhaps more resigned note.

Chapter Two takes the reader back to the beginning of the book in Krog's return to Kroonstad, where she interviews another male resident – Oom Pieta, her mother's philosophical cousin, who knows all about sewerage disposal in Kroonstad in the New South Africa. In this, the last of the book's mini essays on faeces, Krog exposes the lies that circulate amongst whites, lies that maintain the divide between black and white residents. In quoting Kroonstad hearsay she asks Oom Pieta whether there is truth in the rumour that there is any difference between the excrement of white people and the excrement of black people (2003: 359–360). Oom Pieta manages to dispel some of the more vicious rumours, and to suggest practical ways to improve sanitation for all people. The transformation of nourishment into waste, and the transformation of waste into nourishment are at the heart of this discussion, with the vital ingredients being recyclable water and soft, expensive biodegradable paper. A fine lesson, quirkily and unflinchingly told, but this final foray into the scatological seems merely excessive as opposed to exemplary.

In Chapter Three, the final chapter of the book, Krog returns once again to Kroonstad to attend the funeral of her father. That the book ends with the death of the white father figure is clearly significant. Though her father has not been an overt presence in the book, at least not in the same way as her mother has, he represents the old South Africa, and his going represents the possibility of a new start for his descendants:

> We stand here forlornly [at the graveside], your children, lost in a landscape in which we so often feel we no longer belong. A landscape we are bleeding from, generation after generation. You could not safeguard a place for us here. You leave us bereft, unfamiliar with sharing. (2003: 364)

This poignant farewell to her father constitutes the possibility of a new beginning for Krog, one in which she might learn to accept the dis-ease of not belonging not as temporary but as terminal, and one in which she might learn that the desire to belong may not be fulfilled in her lifetime or even in the lifetimes of her descendants.

But despite the writer having exposed the doctrines and beliefs that justified white settlerhood and belonging as fictions, the narrative itself, perhaps superfluously of the writer's authorial control, seems to suggest that much more eschatological purging needs to be done to expel the final traces of white right from the social systems in South Africa.

Conclusion

In this chapter I have offered an ambivalent reading of *A Change of Tongue*, one that has shown how astutely Antjie Krog has blurred the boundaries between fact and fiction, truth and lies, the personal and the political, and how in doing so she has challenged the assurance of the categorical and classifiable in her call for transformation, particularly in relation to fixed racial classification and the prejudice it engenders. I have also shown that the personal reconciliation between Krog and her mother enacted in the book constitutes a political act of feminist recovery, as well as a means to insert traumatised Afrikaner history into mainstream English literature. But the analysis has also illustrated that although Krog very powerfully and personally engages with the politics of whiteness in post-apartheid South Africa, there is some evidence to suggest that she herself may not always be conscious of the ways in which her explorations reflect a continued, though perhaps increasingly uncomfortable, hegemonic white privilege in her responses to post-apartheid South Africa. Despite her searing indictment of conservative white (Afrikaner) attitudes and her astute apprehension of a current crisis of whiteness which is marked by a sense of white displacement, her project is nonetheless often undercut by her own perhaps unexamined assumptions. In this regard, Krog's longing to belong has been examined, and it has been suggested that this longing is expressed more readily in relation to land or geography than it is in relation to people, and though Krog recognises this phenomenon as perennial to Afrikaner settlerhood ('I have land therefore I am' [2003: 76]), she herself is unable to move beyond such an identification. In addition, Krog's exploration of the victim/perpetrator dialectic in her inclusion of Afrikaner history has been acknowledged, as has her courageous confrontation with the self-proclaiming innocence of English-speaking white South Africans. Also acknowledged is the possible political strategy involved in her decision to publish this book in English originally, in the sense that it may have been addressed specifically to those who have not taken the step that Krog has, in confronting her own complicity and attempting to move beyond it. However, my analysis of her interactions with black people demonstrates that it is not Afrikanerdom that is at stake here but a monolithic whiteness, an 'optic white' that washes out the cultural detail, so that her attempt to suggest that there are shades of whiteness is in the end unsuccessful. In referring to Krog's battle with words, and translating them, it has been suggested that she is aware of the power of language in moulding our perceptions, and that her rescuing of the Afrikaans word 'Afrikaner' from its colonising prerogative constitutes a powerful gesture towards a painful renegotiation of her cultural identity. Her interrogation of language, however, does not appear to have effectively incorporated body language, and it is her very body that at times betrays her, in symptomatically expressing what her conscious, rational mind cannot. Ultimately there remains a sense, having turned the book upside down and on its back to see the 'soul' of it in its entirety, that Krog may have accurately identified and defined the elements of radical transformation, but she may not always have managed the kind of reconfiguration and transmutation that she recommends for white South Africans generally.

4

The Wise Fool in the Queen's Court: 'Unfair' Commentary on White Western Womanhood in Marianne Thamm's *Fairlady* Columns

> *I come to you dressed in a pair of tights, one leg green, one leg purple (and my bum does not look big). On my feet are black, knee-high goblin boots with pointy, coiling toes. I'm wearing a Marianne Fassleresque chartreuse jacket with a ruffled collar frothing at the neck. On my head is a brown monk's cowl with two huge donkey's ears and a tinkling bell. In my right hand is a fool's staff, with an inflated meerkat bladder affixed to the top. It makes a flthop, flthop sound when I wave it around.*
> **Marianne Thamm (March 2005: 12)**

> *[A] statement which, [...] from a wise man's mouth, might be a capital offence, coming from a fool gives rise to incredible delight [voluptatem]. Veracity [...] has a certain authentic power of giving pleasure [delectandi], if nothing offensive goes with it: but this the gods have granted only to fools.*
> **J.M. Coetzee's rendition of Moria's speech**
> from *The Praise of Folly* (1996: 94)

Introduction

Marianne Thamm's *Fairlady* columns, entitled 'Unfair Comment', may arguably represent a certain new left liberal and progressive image of white western womanhood. Whereas initially the columns were situated at the back of the magazine, they have in the last three years been repositioned and now appear directly after the editorial page. Regular readers of *Fairlady* often make the comment that the first article they read when opening the magazine is Thamm's column. They also often suggest that Thamm is always entertaining, mostly controversial and that they do not always agree with the opinions she expresses.[82] These aspects of the column's placement and reception signal the necessity of examining Thamm's role as columnist for *Fairlady* in relation to the self-representation of the magazine. A possibility that emerges is that Thamm's role reflects an uneasy duality that *Fairlady* has battled to overcome as it vacillates between promoting an ideal of western femininity on the one hand and progressive social and political engagement on the other. Thamm's ambivalence becomes evident in that although she criticises white western mores as they are evident in South Africa, she herself can be shown to be a product of some of those very mores she presumes to criticise. This is indicative of a kind of post-apartheid white writing extant in the popular media at this time. It does not examine its own assumptions carefully and runs the risk of repeating certain normative, 'universal' ideas that reify a white western frame of reference, albeit from a liberal and progressive point of view. In order to explore all of the controversial ramifications of the columnist's representational practice, the following discussion is divided into several subsections which attempt to situate the writer in relation to the reproductivity of white western mores. The first section deals specifically with *Fairlady*, its self-image and readership, which is followed by a section exploring Thamm's role as the Wise Fool in the Queen's Court. The potentialities of a dissident and critical reading of normativity are then examined in an analysis of Thamm's strategies in challenging the insularity of white middle-class womanhood. This is followed by a reading of Thamm's focus on race, which manifests the ambivalences that emerge when normativity is at odds with multiculturalism, and the chapter culminates in a reading of the potentialities and difficulties that are apparent in Thamm's strategic duplicity in which she precariously negotiates the narratives and counter-narratives that continue to promote black and white positions. Thamm's published collection of articles entitled *Mental Floss* (2002) and selected columns from *Fairlady* from 2003 to 2005 will provide the material for analysis.

Conversations with Women
Fairlady, one of white South Africa's most popular[83] women's magazines, marked its forty years of existence in April 2005 with a glossy bumper edition celebrating its history and continued relevance. Despite the numerous attempts in this publication to claim that the magazine has always been a socially and politically engaged one, there is ample evidence in any of the close to 500 editions to suggest the contrary. Like all magazines of its type, *Fairlady* targets an audience that accepts, may

even demand, homogeneous and stereotypical images of western, middle-class womanhood, and it has done so using three basic ingredients of western capitalism's will to conspicuous consumption: fashion, food and celebrity glitz.

There are just two articles in the Fortieth Anniversary Edition that offer a serious challenge to the magazine's own celebratory self-representation. These are by two fairly recent 'interloping'[84] regular columnists, namely Mike Behr (April 2005: 106, 108, 109) and Marianne Thamm (April 2005: 30). And though Behr is right to suggest that the magazine has predominantly spoken *for* rather than *to* men 'often as if they were not in the room' (106), which he considers strange given the fact that the magazine 'has boasted a significantly high male readership', what he ignores is that the magazine is *about* women, written *for* them, and addressed *to* them exclusively, and directly *as a result of* patriarchal control of norms dictating women's identity. But like the conduct books produced in nineteenth-century Europe, the popular woman's magazine produces and maintains the bourgeois image of womanhood that western societies have traditionally condoned and demanded. If *Fairlady* does indeed boast a high male readership (no statistics are offered) it may have something to do with the general approval amongst white men for the 'discipline and punish' regime of bodily obsessions that the magazine promotes, and this is precisely what Marianne Thamm confronts and challenges. As I shall show, her primary method of challenging these stereotypical representations is in demonstrating the constructedness and performativity of gender and race.

In the same anniversary issue it is Thamm, in her regular 'Unfair Comment' column, who offers the most challenging response to the magazine industry for perpetuating gender stereotypes. As *Fairlady*'s monthly columnist, her piece entitled 'You've Come A Long Way ... Maybe' recognises the power of branding in the advertising practice of creating catchy taglines. She recalls the tagline for a cigarette brand, Virginia Slims, aimed at women consumers in the United States during the sixties. The slogan for this advertisement campaign, 'You've come a long way, baby', was, as Thamm points out, meant to be an ironic comment on the achievements of the western women's liberation movement that saw its second wave emerging in the late sixties and early seventies of the twentieth century, the idea presumably being that women now had choices previously denied them (the choice to be a sexual object and to partake of habits conventionally or traditionally considered unfeminine).

What Thamm is drawing attention to implicitly is the tagline that has been used to sell the product the reader has in front of her – the magazine she is holding, which has also 'come a long way'. The initial tagline (or, more formally, the 'mission statement') of *Fairlady* was 'The Woman You Want To Be', which when it became politically incorrect to continue to promote an unreachable ideal of femininity was converted to 'The Woman You Are'. This did not do much to alleviate the problem since the magazine continued to promote an unreachable ideal of femininity regardless. The magazine's next attempt at inclusiveness and heterogeneity, as well as its attempt to suggest that a woman is more than the sum total of her body parts and her domestic serviceability, was the final variation of this tagline: '*All* The Woman You Are' (my emphasis). More recently the editorial team, having no doubt taken cognisance of the unfortunate implications of such *all*-encompassing prescriptive tagging, has opted for the motto: 'Conversations with Women', which, like the epithet 'You've Come a Long Way, Baby' is meant to be a progressive affirmation of a woman's right to speak and be heard above the din of masculine prescriptions, and though there does appear to be a change in perspective with the anniversary edition,[85] Thamm suggests that:

> More than a quarter of a century of feminism may have changed some of the structures in society, but it has made little difference to the interior lives of many women, who remain prisoners of culture, tradition, religion and media. In some way, women's magazines must also carry the blame, for just as they tried to liberate women, so they have also enslaved them. (April 2005: 30)

The use of the qualifying clause, 'In some way', suggests something about Thamm's relationship with the magazine and its ethos and introduces the most important aspect of this chapter's engagement with her work. Clearly, Thamm's is a voice in opposition to the general 'conversations' with women that are enacted on the pages of *Fairlady*, and clearly too she has been *allowed*, encouraged even, to pursue such an 'unfair', oppositional stance. But how unfair and oppositional is she, and why would a publication which she suggests is partly responsible for promoting the gender stereotypes that continue to govern women's self-image and their conversations, accommodate Thamm's diatribes which are at times directed against the very magazine they are printed in? A question that may arise at that juncture is why I have chosen the columnist rather than the magazine itself as the more appropriate material for a productive examination of whiteness and middle-class womanhood, and one that is anticipated in my foregrounding, in this introductory discussion, the centrality of *Fairlady*'s image, readership and self-representation. One answer might be that Thamm's role reflects the ambiguities of self-representation that the magazine continues to negotiate. Another answer may be that it suits *Fairlady* to offer dissidence because it makes the magazine look *avant garde* and open to opposition. Yet another might be that Thamm's dissidence is one of the most interesting examples in contemporary women's writing of the ambivalence *and* the normativity of whiteness.

In order to explore Thamm's role as columnist for *Fairlady*, it may be useful to begin with the obvious fact that though the magazine has patently struggled to formulate a politically correct tagline, it has not had such a problem with its name, *Fairlady* – one word that contains two of the most loaded lexical units in the English language.[86] Obviously, the name derives from an earlier twentieth-century Broadway musical, *My Fair Lady* (1959), which is the frivolous adaptation of George Bernard Shaw's stage play, *Pygmalion* (1913), in which an English professor takes on the responsibility of educating a cockney flower seller, thus preparing her for a role in the upper classes of British society.[87] Predictably, having educated her, the crusty old professor falls in love with her and marries her. This age-old plot has been reinterpreted countless times, for example in the Hollywood blockbuster *Pretty Woman* (1990), the moral of which is: learn the cultural cues in the Arnoldian tradition of 'the best that has been thought and said in the world',[88] be pretty (or 'fair'), and eminently trainable, and you will be rewarded with the newly bestowed designation, 'lady', and on the arm of the espoused 'gentleman'. Apparently, the magazine, despite protestations to the contrary,[89] at some level must still subscribe to this philosophy, given that the name has never been in jeopardy. Marianne Thamm fiercely challenges 'fair lady'/'pretty woman' notions of white western middle-class femininity, particularly in relation to the age-old courtly figure of the Fool whom she emulates, but at times her critique is sabotaged by a) self-censorship, and b) an unguarded universalism that residually and inadvertently propagates Mathew Arnold's 'culture and civilisation' tradition.

The Court Jester: In Praise of Folly

Traditionally, the court jester is given licence by the king to criticise the court, as long as the 'Fool' couches his critique in cryptic humour, so that the king's authority is not undermined publicly. This places the jester in somewhat of a compromised position: he is given licence to criticise, but only on condition that he also entertains, and on condition that he knows well where the boundaries are in relation to the licence bestowed upon him. In an informative discussion on the implications of the impossible duplicity that the role entails, J.M. Coetzee has pointed out in relation to Desiderius Erasmus's *The Praise of Folly* (1509) that the Fool traditionally 'claims licence to criticise all and sundry without reprisal, since his madness defines him as not fully a person and therefore not a political being with political desires and ambitions' (1996: 84). Coetzee's reading of Erasmus, which invokes Foucault's attempt to write an 'archaeology of madness' and Lacan's attempt to engage the unconscious, points to the impossibility of the position of the Fool in relation to official rivalries in the 'court' (or the political terrain contested), and in relation to the paradox of speaking of madness from within reason. He suggests that Erasmus 'exposes the dynamics of rivalry', and that 'Folly [is] at her most canny and deft in side-stepping its violent imperatives' (1996: 84–85). The character of Folly, or Moria, in Erasmus's play is a woman, '*propagatrix*', representing the '"little" phallus', not the 'transcendental signifier [the Big Phallus] but a *thing* of sport, of free play, of carefree dissemination rather than patrilinearity' (1996: 96).

Marianne Thamm has identified on at least one occasion with the role of the Fool, and may to some extent be considered a latter-day Moria, in what Coetzee has conceived of as the character's 'jocoserious abnegation of big-phallus status' (1996: 103): in a piece entitled 'Royal Male' (March 2005: 12) she refers to herself as 'the court jester' and indeed dresses up quite elaborately to play the part (quoted as the first epigraph to this chapter), but it is a role, arguably, that she plays quite consistently in her capacity as columnist for *Fairlady*. There are two equally likely rationales for this proposition, the first of which is related to gender and the second to class and race. As a writer, Thamm is a self-proclaimed feminist, but the other identification which she only cryptically hints at in her columns is lesbian. The traditional jester is a eunuch, or a 'female male', castrated and thus sexually neutered and safe. In addition, he is oxymoronically designated a Wise Fool, which Coetzee's reading of Erasmus posits as an impossible ambivalence. Given that the 'royal harem' in which Thamm is the officially appointed jester is a best-selling women's magazine, it would be safe for her to proclaim her feminist affiliation, but too dangerous to flaunt her sexual orientation, which would be considered aberrant in a publication devoted almost entirely to reinforcing white middle-class heterosexual feminine normativity. She is thus in the similarly precarious outcast position of the court jester – her 'deviance' is tolerated as long as she remains entertaining, and provided her self-censorship continues to uphold the boundaries of social propriety. Despite these constraints, or perhaps because of them, Thamm manages quite tenaciously to expose some of the most universalising, insular and self-preserving assumptions that *Fairlady* and its readers subscribe to, as will be demonstrated in an analysis of selected columns. In this regard, she is interestingly positioned, and exhibits one of the most powerfully effectual manifestations of the ambivalence I have identified as characterising white women's writing in post-apartheid South Africa. As officially sanctioned jester, she is allowed to be dissident in her opinions, a licence she uses to full advantage, ironically by being 'ballsy' and measured (wise) rather than emasculated and frivolous (foolish), thus reversing the gender prerequisites governing the eunuch's position, but, perhaps contradictorily, maintaining the dissident power of the Wise Fool. And it is in this sense that she reincarnates Moria of Erasmus's work. But the role allows the reader the same licence as the king and court enjoy: she may agree with Thamm's pronouncements and congratulate herself on her liberal humanism on the one hand, or she may dismiss the writer's criticism on the other, and congratulate herself on her normativity in the face of such foolish 'aberrance'.[90] Thus, it may be argued, (sexual) difference is entertained but the (heterosexual) status quo is not seriously challenged.

It is, however, Thamm's white, middle-class representativeness that makes up for less normative aspects of her personality as a columnist, at least as far as her readership is concerned. As she has rightly recognised in an unofficial interview (14 July 2005),[91] she is probably more readily accommodated as the voice of dissent because at least it is dissent from within the ranks of whiteness, rather than from a black person whose oppositional stance might be much more alienating to negotiate than a white woman with 'suspicious' sexual proclivities. Furthermore, were a reader to catch herself disapproving of Thamm's sentiments for 'moral' reasons, she might be tempted to proffer the kind of largesse that white western subjectivity readily entertains as liberal and accommodating. Thamm's double bind is, as a result, more troublesome, more contradictory, and more interestingly and perhaps consciously duplicitous than, for example, Antjie Krog's is. Whereas Krog uses testimony and 'personal' discovery to witness to the anxiousness around white post-apartheid unbelonging, Thamm uses playful conceit to ridicule aspects of white normativity, thus unsettling its claim to naturalness.

In addition to Coetzee's reading of the Fool's role, Mikhail Bakhtin's exploration of the Wise Fool, as interpreted by Dale Bauer in 'Gender in Bakhtin's Carnival' (1997: 716), provides a frame of reference to investigate Thamm's unsettling of normativity. Bauer suggests that the Bakhtinian Fool 'serves to defamiliarise the conventions which have been adopted as "natural"' and that the carnival offers the participants momentary escape from the prescriptions of social living. It is an occurrence which 'suspends discipline – the terror, reverence, piety, and etiquette which contribute to the maintenance of the social order' (1997: 717) and the Fool resists 'convention, using the threat of the inconclusive, open-ended possibilities of the carnival, to retain subversive force in the social arena'. A question that arises from Bauer's discussion of the carnivalesque is whether Thamm harnesses the subversive potential of the Fool to write against the prescriptions that produce conformity and whether she defamiliarises the feminine conventions that are naturalised in *Fairlady*.

In the following analysis of selected columns, Thamm's role as court jester will be examined to assess the extent to which Thamm's dissidence has merely been co-opted by popular culture, thus neutralising her critique, or the extent to which, as a consequence of her consciously and conspicuously inhabiting the uncomfortable space *Fairlady* offers her, she destabilises and interrupts the official 'Conversations with Women' which the magazine encourages and promotes, and, in doing so, writes against the transcendental signifier of the phallus. A related question is whether her political power as a feminist lesbian writer has been diluted, in her reticence to discuss her sexual orientation, which in turn invites the question of whether her white western normativity is the overriding feature in accounting for the relative success she has achieved.[92] It may be argued that a productive tension is maintained between these opposing responses, one which only intermittently and interstitially manifests itself as residual white right. In this sense, the commodification of Thamm makes her product (the column) a text of popular culture,[93] which is simultaneously marked by resistance and incorporation, or, figuratively, by goblin boots and ruffled collars.

Goblin Boots and Ruffled Collars: On the Possibilities of Duplicity

The purpose of this subsection is to gauge the potential in Thamm's journalistic practice for a sustained critique of white western normativity. Two strategies are identified, the first being her negotiation of popular culture and the second her negotiation of the performativity of gender. The following discussion is thus aimed at exploring the potential of such strategies in deconstructing *all* social and cultural categorisation, including race, which is covered in the following subsection, though the focus here is implicitly on whiteness as a global affiliation which informs white South African social mores.

The first of the columnist's trademark strategies is to tap into popular culture (as a white western global media-generated phenomenon), and from this familiar space, to launch an attack on the predictable sensibilities that are imbricated in such artefacts. A representative example of this approach, which illustrates the freedoms and limitations characteristic of her self-censoring though simultaneously forthright social commentary, is to be found in a piece entitled 'Duh, Duh, Duh, Duh' (February 2005: 12) in which she takes on one of the most ubiquitous products of consumer culture: 'the banal soporific charms of McMusic', a brand of easy listening, middle-of-the-road, largely retro music that is currently popular, produced by the likes of Katie Melua, Josh Groban and Michael Bublé.

This is no doubt a viable target to attack, but more significantly it is Thamm's negotiation of the terrain that is cleverly duplicitous and manifests itself in three overlapping strategies. Firstly, she uses the subject matter to underpin the pervasiveness of the global media industry (that promotes a white western frame of reference) by quoting chunks of the most familiar and inane lyrics, and thus calling attention to the market this brand of 'nice' music attracts: 'gainfully employed, unconcerned, disengaged people [who] feel safe and all warm and fuzzy inside'. Of course, she could be referring to just about anybody here, but in South Africa, and particularly in Cape Town (where Thamm lives), the catalogue readily invites an association with middle-class, western whiteness, which includes the readership of *Fairlady*. Simultaneously, she invites the reader's self-congratulatory sense of superiority by calling up 'universally' known, largely American (oppositional) social commentators in the music industry, from Bob Dylan to Eminem, in order to suggest the apolitical apathy of the insular middle-class, middle-of-the-road, easy-listening music currently popular. And finally, she hints at alternative identifications by mentioning Rod Stewart, whom, in an aside, she notes 'is looking more and more like an old Camps Bay lesbian'; by invoking the movie soundtrack, *Amandla! A Revolution in Four-Part Harmony*; and by allowing Johannes Kerkorrel the last word.[94] Thus, Thamm berates, cajoles and subtly undermines white western normativity, all within the space of a single page.[95]

An earlier example of this strategy appears in the column entitled 'The More Things Change' (2002: 81–83). Thamm's subversion of white normativity once again manifests itself in a number of interrelated ways. Her topic this time is herself, and the particularly intimate and conversational tone Thamm adopts in this column allows her to destabilise the official 'Conversations with Women' in *Fairlady*. The reader is invited to picture the columnist lying in the bath and perusing the latest issue of her 'favourite magazine, which is *FAIRLADY* of course' (2002: 81). Here already the subversive potential emerges: given Thamm's (albeit later) public proclamations about the damaging stereotypes perpetuated in women's magazines (April 2005:

30), and coupled with the disclaiming phrase 'of course', the statement is clearly meant to be ironic. In commenting on the photographs of herself accompanying the columns, Thamm then introduces a 'volley of intelligent social banter' on the subject of hair, a subject she well knows is a standard conversational piece in a magazine aimed at women. Cleverly though, she mocks the reader by suggesting the opposite: 'Oh, don't tell me you don't want to talk about hair', she chides, and promptly sets about subverting all of the race and gender norms that are signified in hairstyles. First she confesses that in 'the soft-focus, rear-view mirror in [her] own mind' she has been trying 'to cultivate a certain look' which she describes as a 'sort of cross between Joanna Lumley and Jim Morrison'. The image deliberately unsettles normative conversations about hair in its transvestism, in addition to which Thamm hints at the performativity of gender in her framing of the image. Next she satirically exposes the extent to which hair continues to operate as a racial signifier by noting that 'white folk don't look good with Afros, to say nothing about dreadlocks' (2002: 82). But it is outside of the column in an editorial aside that she makes her most subversive remark. In response to her rather sharp criticism of *Pop Idol*'s Will Young's rendition of Jim Morrison's 'Light My Fire', Thamm's postscript reads: 'A few weeks later Will came out and I forgave him everything' (2002: 83). What is interesting to note is that Thamm's confessional identification with the pop idol's 'coming out' is clearly not something she feels is safe to proclaim from within the space afforded to her as *Fairlady* columnist, but, as professional writer in her own publication, she is freer to negotiate the identification. Self-censorship, in this case, is overt, though in a sense overcome.

A more controversial manifestation of Thamm's subversions, and one which foregrounds the second of Thamm's characteristic strategies, namely, to expose the performativity of gender, appears in a piece entitled 'I Do, I Don't' (July 2004: 14).[96] In this column she takes on the subject of marriage and wedding ceremonies in 'real' life and in 'reality TV' in the form of *The Wedding Show* (the South African version aired on SABC3 in 2004). She thus purposefully draws attention to the cultural artifice that marriage is, and simultaneously problematises the distinction between the 'marriage' and 'the wedding', and at the same time points to the romantic lie that conceals the economic motivation for marriage. Once again, the target is fair game, but it is Thamm's negotiation of the politics surrounding marriage and sexuality that is strategically duplicitous. Rather than simply slipping in the odd reference to queerness and unsettling normative assumptions like she does in the 'Duh' column (February 2005: 12) discussed above, here Thamm launches her attack by quoting a joke from *The New Yorker* about 'gay marriage', in which a clearly conventional couple considers the topical subject. 'The husband [...] says, "Gays and Lesbians getting married – haven't they suffered enough?"' It is Thamm's response to this indictment of both marriage as an institution and the exclusion of homosexual people from such social institutions, however, that proves to be more interesting: 'Listen', she confides, 'it was only going to be a matter of time before queer people began demanding the right to participate in the only camp straight ritual known to humankind.' Here Thamm is demonstrating Judith Butler's theory of gender performativity in which it is suggested that 'all gender is like drag' and that '"imitation" is at the heart of the *heterosexual* project and its gender binarisms. Indeed, that drag is not a secondary imitation that presupposes a prior and original gender, but that hegemonic heterosexuality is itself a 'constant and repeated effort to imitate its own idealizations' (1993: 125, emphasis in original).

Thamm's unsettling of gender norms not only anticipates her unsettling of cultural and racial norms but actively and subversively highlights the ways in which all identifications imitate an idealisation. Her depiction of the ways in which heterosexual women respond to the wedding ritual reinforces the enactment of femininity: they act like 'divas, wear dramatic, outrageously expensive dresses and way too much make-up without having to answer to anyone' (February 2005: 12). Furthermore, she introduces the 'nature versus nurture' debate by invoking the 'rational' theory of sexual 'deviance' being genetically encoded, in noting the gene's manifestation in well-known heterosexual men: 'David Beckham, Jamie Oliver, Michael Mol and Will Smith', thus using the very scientific discourse responsible for homophobic discrimination to implicate straight people. At this point she says, 'But we're straying' (February 2005: 12). The plural pronoun strategically includes the reader in this 'deviant', 'straying' aside, and reinforces Butler's claim that 'drag is subversive, [and that it] disputes heterosexuality's claim on naturalness and originality' (1993: 125). Such a strategy is powerful in its implicit capacity to unsettle claims on the ordinary, 'natural', normal way of being human.

Thamm's foregrounding of queer responses does not end there, however. In one final covert moment she wrests the shaming inflicted on gay couples entrenched in the phrase 'the love that dares not speak its name',[97] and redirects it to qualify something much more 'normal' and 'shameless': 'that thing that dare not speak its name – a D.I.V.O.R.C.E.' (February 2005: 12). In doing so, she destabilises the normativity of officially sanctioned heterosexual unions by exposing the shame involved in buying into the fairy-tale wedding that will, as statistics have amply demonstrated, in all likelihood end in the divorce court. Though Thamm never explicitly negotiates her sexual orientation in her columns (she has admitted to being criticised for this choice[98]), and may thus stand accused of self-censorship, in moments such as this she does not need to: her positionality in relation to the double standards she uncovers is both patently transgressive and powerfully indicting. Indeed, Jonathan Dollimore's definition of a 'transgressive aesthetic' may usefully be deployed to gauge Thamm's practice: she uses subterfuge (a survival strategy) as a weapon of attack (1991: 310).

One Purple Leg, One Green Leg: On 'Colour' in Thamm's Columns
Having suggested the performative nature of gendered identity as a 'constant and repeated effort to imitate its own idealizations' (Butler 1993: 125) in columns such as 'I Do, I Don't' (July 2004), Thamm, not surprisingly, uses similar strategies to suggest the performativity of race. Christine Sleeter has defined whiteness in South Africa as 'ravenous materialism, competitive individualism, and a way of living characterised by putting acquisition of possessions ahead of humanity'. She suggests that 'one does not need to be of European descent to participate in such a way of living' but that it is 'a way of living that people of European descent constructed and sell, and one that we are persistently socialised to identify with and support' (in Ingram 2005: 270). In 'Trying for White' (September 2003: 12), Thamm uncovers aspects of Sleeter's definition of whiteness. This column consists of an open letter to Happy Sindane, the young boy who claimed to have been white, mentioned in the introductory of Chapter One, whom she advises on a few cultural cues that are necessary in playing the role of a white subjectivity. In doing so she exposes the performativity of whiteness. Despite lurching into a dubious generalisation by suggesting that 'it is not everyday [that] someone aspires to be white', her declaration that 'there is no such thing as "white pride"' points towards the performativity of race by invoking 'black pride' or Black Consciousness as political affiliations constructed to counter discourses of white supremacy. In addition, the anomalous notion of 'white pride' effectively marks whiteness as an unmarked marker.

Thamm's definition of whiteness, for the benefit ostensibly of Happy Sindane but primarily for the predominantly white readers of *Fairlady*, begins with her recognition of the consumerist acquisition of material goods, which is compulsory in white suburbia, in her suggestion that the only time white people 'come together is when we form an opposition party, have to erect a boom in our suburb or organise a 24-hour bicycle patrol'. The first in this catalogue of 'communal' white behaviours points to the insularity of middle-class sociopolitical tendencies in its propensity to support the largely white, pseudoliberal Democratic Alliance (DA) then under the leadership of Tony Leon, and the last two indicate the paranoid protectiveness of goods accumulated. Secondly, her definition includes the cultural imperialism and chauvinism of whiteness in her suggestion that Happy will be expected to communicate in either English or Afrikaans because white South Africans 'cannot speak any of the other nine official languages', in addition to which she suggests that there 'is no such thing as "white culture"' in South Africa, a condition she attributes to white South Africans 'look[ing] to the West for cultural guidance'. Thamm's definition is extended to acknowledge the paradoxes upon which white identity is built in her summation of an 'intrinsically pessimistic mien' which permeates white society in noting that '[f]or some reason we have come to expect the worst when we've enjoyed only the best' (2002: 17).

But it is Thamm's final 'questionnaire' that offers the most powerful recognition of whiteness as normative. If Happy's answer to all four propositions is affirmative, she writes, he will be 'well on [his] way to becoming an average white South African' (September 2003: 12):

1. This letter pisses you off because it raises the issue of 'race' and you think it's all nonsense that belongs in the past.
2. You think affirmative action is 'reverse discrimination'.
3. You are beginning to warm to Patricia Lewis or Candice Hillebrand.
4. You sometimes mistake 'Shosholoza' for the national anthem.

Expressing agreement with all four of the above statements suggests the most resistant and pervasive attitudes that shore up white hegemony: the first and second articulating a defensiveness that is endemic to white middle-class insularity, the third and fourth articulating the values and appropriations of popular culture, respectively. Patricia Lewis and Candice Hillebrand are both 'blond bombshell, showbiz babes' whose successes have little to do with talent and everything to do with the ubiquitous and impossible Barbie ideal of 'fair lady'-hood generated in the western media industry. 'Shosholoza', though originally a wistful working-class song sung by black migrant miners who call for the train ('stimela') to take them back home,[99] is more readily recognised in contemporary South Africa as the victory anthem sung typically at national rugby matches, by predominantly white fans. From black working-class protest to the celebration of middle-class leisure and white masculine prowess, the appropriation is total.

'To Be or Not To Be – PC' (2002: 99–102) provides another interesting example of Thamm's critique of white normativity and of her attempt to make whiteness visible. It features an unsolicited remark on an aeroplane from a white South African woman returning, presumably on holiday, to South Africa from 'exile' in the United States, a remark that Thamm suggests is 'the verbal equivalent of a burst sewerage pipe' (2002: 99), and one which elicits one of Thamm's harshest indictments of her 'fellow white South Africans' (2002: 101). The woman's remark addressed to Thamm is familiarly and conspiratorially racist: peering out of the window on the plane's stopover in Johannesburg, she says, 'Well, here it is. Madibaland, ha, ha. God, I'm glad I left this place [...] they're all savages and bloody criminals' (2002: 100). In an essay entitled 'The American Celebration of Whiteness', Judy Scales-Trent examines these conspiratorial whispers between white Americans, which are informed by an assumption of a shared and universal normativity. She notes invariably 'when someone thinks [because she is] white that he is therefore safe to say anything racist he wants' in what she sees as a moment of white people's celebration of 'their whiteness, and their privilege, and their power' (1999: 56). The woman on the plane whom Thamm angrily refers to as a 'megaphone', a 'blabbermouth' and 'idiot wind' makes just such an assumption, and Thamm notes that she is 'seldom offended by conversations with people of colour'. 'It is white people', she suggests, 'who generally assume a fellow honky will share their point of view' (2002: 101). In doing so, she calls for a continued vigilance that contemporary usages of the term 'PC' have been guilty of rejecting as 'passé' (2002: 100).

As has been suggested in the introductory chapter of this book, whiteness as a construct meaning privilege and cultural superiority is something of a global phenomenon. It may be argued that South African white identity is reified and reinforced by the universal sanctity of whiteness afforded by global media practices.[100] In 'The Coalition of the Brainless' (October 2004: 16), Thamm continues her assault on white sensibilities that are characteristically assuming and simultaneously ignorant. Her target this time is the Hollywood movie industry and related western media practices which fortify general western attitudes towards Africa, attitudes 'informed' by massive ignorance. First, she explores the 'tacky 2003 little Hollywood epic called *Beyond Borders*', not only for the predictably crass way in which 'first world' countries patronise 'third world'[101] countries that the movie exhibits in the service of promoting the impossible ideal of romantic love, but for its co-opting of a nominal 'mixed heritage'[102] American actor, Angelina Jolie, to ventriloquise the solipsistic rhetoric that the United States is notorious for: 'I was really moved by [Namibia]', Jolie is reported to have stated in an interview, misidentifying the country providing the setting for the film, which was Liberia. Thamm's vitriol is well directed: 'Clearly [Jolie] hadn't absorbed very much even after making the film. Namibia, Sschmamibia; Ivory Coast, Syrupy Toast. It's all the same to me', says Thamm, mimicking the insular and self-congratulating sentiments socially scripted into American imperialism. Then, she takes on the BBC documentary version of disseminating western value systems in her mimicking of a travel programme in which the hosts gush over the tourist attractions in South Africa, backed by music from Senegal and Uganda, a mistake that Thamm notes is 'about [as] appropriate as using traditional Moldavian music to accompany a travel programme exploring the thrills of Cornwall'. Finally, she calls up the ubiquitous TV talk show as yet another vehicle for the dissemination of western normative values. In this case she does not even have to mention the name of the ventriloquising host, except metonymically, so globally recognisable is the persona: 'the one with the big heart, a weight problem and a messianic complex'. Thamm notes that the introductory images of Oprah Winfrey's South African tour (2004) depict the Masai people of East Africa. She concludes by suggesting that 'there is something quite smug, parochial and myopic about England and America at present', the smugness emanating from a sense of superiority, the parochialism emanating from the insularity that is a concomitant of self-righteousness, and the myopia a residual affliction of imperialism, it might be argued. Another example of such attitudes appears in the column 'Twist in my Sobriety' (2002: 78–80). Thamm co-opts the phrase from Tanita Tikaram's 1980s hit for the purpose of exposing the kinds of transfiguration that Antjie Krog calls for in *A Change of Tongue*. She does so by (re-)interpreting the phrase as denoting 'an event, person or realisation – that shifts your understanding and perception of things' (2002: 78). After providing an entertaining and neutral example of such a revelatory 'twist', she offers one that demonstrates the ignorance which is at least partially responsible for white self-righteousness. This she does by drawing the column to its conclusion with an acknowledgement of her own ignorance in respect of Africa and her resolve to change that. She offers the following statistic and its 'twisting' effect:

> 'Between 1996 and 2000 there were 147 elections in Africa, all of them certified "free and fair" by international observers.' Now that not only shifted a couch but snapped back the roller blinds and opened a window as well. (2002: 80)

It takes curiosity and resolve to tweak the mindsets responsible for myopic propriety, and Thamm shows the way in a column such as this one.

'Welcome to the Matrix' (July 2003: 12) is written in response to the South African equivalent of the media-generated lifestyle norms that account for American and English smugness, parochialism and myopia. In *Playing in the Dark* Toni Morrison suggests that what she is attempting to do is 'to avert the critical gaze from the racial object to the racial subject, from the described and imagined to the describers and imaginers, from the serving to the served' (1992: 90). This proves to be a useful frame of reference in considering Thamm's project in this column, which features the glitzy magazine programme on SABC television called *Top Billing*. Having quoted A.A. Gill's suggestion that what is really interesting in the world of television journalism is '[n]ot what we see of the oppressed, but what the oppressed see of us', Thamm cleverly hints at the pathologies engendered by consumerism in making the reader picture her standing up at 'an AA or Gambler's Anonymous meeting and saying: "Hello, my name is Marianne and I watch *Top Billing*"', and at the excesses that the 'big, brash, bling-bling' lifestyle promotes. But the most powerful aspect of her redirecting the gaze is in her imaginary reinvention of the show:

> *Bottom Billing* with [hosts, Bassie and Michael] traipsing around an informal settlement looking for the chicest shack. 'And here we have Mrs Hashe's home, made entirely of Pam Golding "For Sale" signs. After the break, we return and ask the neighbour for a cup of sugar.' (July 2003: 12)

Here Thamm admits that she 'jests' when she ought not to, but her imaginative attempt to see what things look like 'from the other side' results in an image that remains a stark reminder of the paradoxes and excesses upon which white South African privilege is premised: from the oxymoronic 'chicest shack' to the richest southern African estate agent having the 'sign' of her financial power quite literally displaced to assemble the makeshift homes in shanty town, the picture is a haunting one.

Christian National Education is the subject of 'Ignorance was Bliss' (2002: 14–16), a system that produced most adult white South Africans over thirty, sentencing them in all likelihood to 'a life of drudgery, conformity and tax-paying' (2002: 14), and though Thamm offers a tongue-in-cheek apology to Kader Asmal (ex-Minister of Education) at the end of this critique of the educational system, the list of lessons learnt by default in previously white secondary schools might still be recognised by learners at schools in middle-class South African suburbs (albeit that the names of pop stars will have to be substituted, and the prices of substances abused increased). Apart from these social lessons, her list includes actual subjects containing lessons no longer officially taught but nonetheless residual in the collective consciousness that white South Africans may still be guilty of passing on. One such lesson learnt in Geography is that 'Africa was completely uninhabited before civilized, godfearing Europeans docked on the shores', and another learnt in History, 'that "events in Africa have shown that it is not possible to include both White and Bantu in one political system"' (2002: 15), a quote she extracts from a standard ten history textbook produced in the 1970s, demonstrating the extent of the 'white-washing' that this particular ideological state apparatus (National Christian Education) has inculcated.

One of Thamm's favourite targets is what she refers to as 'the ghastly weight of mindless mass culture' ('It's All the Same Thing', July 2005: 14). 'Collateral Damage' (November 2004: 14) testifies to its effects on children. She redeploys the euphemism associated with war talk (used in accounting for the unintended victims of bloody onslaughts) to describe the side effects of assimilating the cultural values in mass-produced entertainment items. Firstly, she notes that it is completely acceptable for children to be presented 'with the most appallingly sexist, violent and usually Eurocentric [...] stories and nursery rhymes'. Among the 'bloodthirsty, imperialist rhymes' that include psychic 'collateral damage', is 'The Grand Old Duke of York' whose influence she mediates by means of ridicule: 'Oh, the Grand Old Duke of York, he was a stupid dork.' In addition she appropriates and redeploys another word associated with contemporary warfare, this time to describe her own uncompromising responsibility as a mother. She refers to herself as 'a Taliban Feminist Mommy (TFM)', an image made all the more subversive in carrying its own official sounding acronym, and more abrasively ridiculing in that the adjectives 'Taliban' and 'Feminist', being so obviously incompatible as dual qualifiers, *are also* in the descriptive service of 'unnaturally' describing 'Mommy'. Thus, Thamm simultaneously foregrounds the 'crude and debilitating stereotypes that skulk between the lines', and undermines the sterile euphemisms that promote mass conformity.

In a searing column entitled 'Forked Tongues' (June 2005: 14), Thamm tells the story of Terry Schiavo whose prolonged death by euthanasia caused a moral uproar in the United States. Thamm suggests the double standards of the western world's most self-congratulating free and democratic society in two ways. Firstly, by exposing what led to Schiavo's coma in the first place: she was anorexic. Thamm relates the allegation that her husband 'joked that he'd divorce her if she ever got fat again'. As Thamm scathingly observes: 'It's perfectly acceptable to make a comment like this in polite western society', thus exposing one of the norms that upholds white western middle-class femininity, a regime of bodily discipline that, as Nancy Armstrong has observed, keeps watch over itself 'in mirrors, on clocks, on scales, through medical exams' (1997: 919–920), a regime that magazines like *Fairlady* subscribe to.[103] Thamm points to the ghastly irony that the remainder of Schiavo's life consisted of being force-fed and then starved, marking the very excesses and disciplines imbricated in this originally white western middle-class disease. Secondly, the column cleverly juxtaposes two subplots that interrupt the main feature of Terri Schiavo, the first exposing the economic motivation for the laws passed legalising euthanasia, and the second effectively demonstrating the extent of the invisibility that working-class African-Americans continue to experience. At more or less the same time that George W. Bush took it upon himself to intervene in the Schiavo case, 'in the Texas Children's Hospital [...] the five-month-old son of a black working-class mother ... suffocated to death after doctors removed his breathing tube – against the wishes of his mother'. But this story did not generate public outrage and, as Thamm notes, there 'were no "armies of compassion"' keeping vigil outside the hospital. She was severely berated by two readers for her attack on 'President Bush and his band of sanctimonious, dumb and dangerous Christian zealots who put and keep him in power', in each case the responses may be read as a replication of a similar brand of sanctimoniousness that Thamm identifies with George Bush.[104]

But by far the most provocative attack on whiteness as an insular and self-preserving construct is to be found in the column entitled 'It's All the Same Thing' (July 2005: 14), in which she 'uncovers' the layers of signification in the 'burka, the headscarf, the veil, the hijab – whatever you wish to call it'. Apart from exposing the sensitivities apparent in the multiple words vying for political correctness in describing the cultural practice, Thamm rightly identifies 'several [...] key political and social issues' buried in 'its folds': 'Western Imperialism, women's liberation, human rights, religious freedom/intolerance/fundamentalism and multiculturalism'. In doing so, Thamm taps straight into the most sensitive discourses separating East from West, or western normativity from eastern otherness, in order to suggest the convenient speciousness of the dualism. It may be argued that her entry into this complex debate is too superficial to accomplish much. A counter-argument, however, would recognise the potential in her contribution for a collective challenge to masculinist prescriptions, one that attempts to engage multiple feminisms. As Mahmut Mutman has rightly observed, the veil in neo-Orientalist discourse has become a western obsession that supposedly offers 'proof of the darkness and backwardness of [Muslim] culture' (1992: 15). Thamm recognises Mutman's critique of such imperialist western obsessions in her identification of the 'commonly held view in the West that Muslim women are oppressed, and that the burka and the headscarf are outward manifestations of this'. To counter such imperialist attitudes Thamm describes what she considers to be the western equivalent, namely, cosmetic surgery, and in doing so she suggests that the prerequisites of western femininity are no less damaging than that which the 'free' west considers to be 'fundamentalist' and disempowering in the east. Mutman argues that the veil, though obviously a symbol of a kind of feudal gendered oppression, must also be understood in relation to the western 'grand narrative of progress or the language of liberation, [and that] we should read woman as the site of an ambiguity and undecidability' (1992: 19) whose representation always includes a concealed desire for the *other* woman. As Thamm suggests, both practices (plastic surgery and the veil) 'obliterate' women by reinforcing the specularity of femininity, whether one is hiding behind a facelift or a headscarf (or in a body shape designed in a death camp). Though 'fundamentalist' Islamic women and 'empowered' western women both believe that each practice respectively has nothing to do with specularity, and everything to do with self-respect, these practices are disciplinary and masquerading when seen in the light of gender as a socialised enactment of an idealisation. Thamm concludes by suggesting that there has to be a 'middle way', 'somewhere between the burka and the knife', but that it requires 'fighting off the ghastly weight of mindless mass culture' as well as the metanarratives of 'religion and tradition', a suggestion which nicely signals her own navigation of the discourses she uncovers. Somewhere between purple and green, or black and white.

A Brown Monk's Cowl and a Fool's Staff: On the Impossibilities of Duplicity
Of the more than sixty 'Unfair Comment' columns that Marianne Thamm has written since 2001, there are only three that may be said to exhibit something of the uncomfortable accessorising that a 'monk's cowl' and a 'Fool's staff' figuratively suggest, in manifesting Thamm's perhaps unconscious duplicity in falling victim herself to several normative assumptions. As I have shown, in an analysis of columns that might be considered representative of her praxis, Thamm productively uses the space afforded her to critique from within the 'mindless weight' of western normativity as it is enacted and recycled in popular mass culture. The following comparatively lengthy analysis of these problematic columns thus needs to be viewed

in relation to her sizable oeuvre that maintains a politically charged and unrelenting examination of the mores that engender and are engendered by mass indifference. In addition, these columns demonstrate something of the double bind of the court jester: it is a role that is simultaneously sanctioned and scoffed at, attended to and ignored, so that the performance requires a certain compromise, or shiftiness, that is necessarily uncomfortable and sadly inevitable. To extend the analogy introduced in the title of this subsection, the monk's moral stance might be at odds with the Fool's ethical one, and it is this distinction that is the most revealing in uncovering the impossible (or at least impeded) aspect of the writer's duplicity. This duplicity emerges in relation to the ambivalence in white women's writing where even those who claim to be astute and critical readers of white heterosexual normativity are themselves susceptible to making (moral) assumptions based on gender and racial stereotypes.

The first of these ambivalent columns is entitled 'Dead or Living in Canada'[105] (2002: 17). Here Thamm begins by launching an attack on the 'intrinsically pessimistic mien' she identifies as a white South African post-apartheid sensibility. She quotes snatches of what Dreama Moon has dubbed 'whitespeak' (1999: 188): 'The country has gone to the dogs, man. The rand is worth nothing. You can't do business with these people' (2002: 17), and identifies precisely the malaise responsible in the following hypothesis:

> Why is it that some white people feel at liberty to express racist, homophobic and sexist hate speech (the three usually occur in rapid succession) to another white person as if it were part of some greater white collective unconscious? Maybe it is. (2002: 17–18)

It is interesting to note Thamm's recognition of the interrelatedness of these responses, namely, that racism, homophobia and sexism are all part of the same mutually insulating and exclusive collective, which is why it is so difficult to disentangle gender and race (and indeed class) from the matrix of discourses responsible for promoting and sustaining human inequalities.

There is, however, the possibility that Thamm undoes some of the work in two apologetic moments that reflect something of the compromised position of the court jester. Firstly, she introduces the piece with the disclaimer that this was '[o]ne of [her] political rants that enraged readers'. She goes on to explain: 'This one was triggered by a conversation I had overheard in a bookstore. I left the place seething and bashed this out' (2002: 17). One cannot help hearing in this foreword a hint of rationalisation that is meant, at least partially, to appease the readers she may have 'enraged'. Secondly, she concludes the attack on a somewhat jarring celebratory note which congratulates young South Africans whom she suggests are 'loud and proud and don't give a toss about silly white people who huddle around the braai whingeing' (2002: 19). Though the image of white South Africans is appropriate, and though the possibility of younger generation white South Africans 'coming out' of the claustrophobic discourses recycled by their parents is beginning to surface, it may be argued that such a remark marks an untimely and simplistic resolution to South Africa's racial difficulties, thus demonstrating the impossibilities of a less conscious duplicity.

Another uncomfortable piece entitled 'Fair Play' (February 2004: 14), and reminiscent of Toni Morrison's examination of racial shaming in *The Bluest Eye*,[106] confronts one of the most damaging capitalist consumerist practices that upholds white female normativity: the production of dolls for girl children. Thamm, having recently become a parent, writes about her experience shopping for a black doll. After doing extensive market research at toyshops throughout South Africa, she notes that the major chain stores stock only 'walls and walls of [white only] dolls in pretty pink and purple packaging'. In the interchange between a sales assistant and Thamm, the faulty logic in stereotypically white South African responses is suggested: when pressed, the sales assistant admits that blacks do not buy dolls and that he is 'not going to stock black dolls to make a political point'. Thamm's rejoinder is one that underpins her awareness of the extent of an insidious sense of white right in the white South African imaginary. 'And', she enquires, 'stocking only white dolls is not making a political point?' Furthermore, Thamm points to the obvious constructedness of racial classification in her comment that she did eventually find 'a black doll ... well, a brown one'. What is interesting to note is that despite her development of a wholly convincing argument, from her reference to Barney Pityana's experience of racism, through to her quotation of persuasive statistics from the 2001 South African census (which indicate that approximately 78% of South Africa's population is black), and ending with her astute observation of the tendency (by largely white manufacturers[107]) to depict black dolls stereotypically in 'ethnic', 'authentic', 'traditional dress', curiously, she does not question the politics involved in presenting girl children with dolls to dress, nurture and cuddle. In observing only that '[w]hite dolls are caricatures of real babies' which is why 'little white girls and, sadly little black girls like them', Thamm misses an important opportunity to contest the socialisation of girls, which requires of them to imitate the attributes necessary to perform what their biology has destined. What militates against a critical reader's justifiable rebuke for this omission, however, is that Thamm very subtly in her introduction to the column suggests that her own experience of such socialisation was not successful, in hinting at her penchant for boys' toys (including 'whoopee cushions, false teeth and stink bombs'), and stuffing her doll 'in a dark cupboard'. Nonetheless, one comes to expect a certain vigilance from the columnist, especially in light of her onslaught on Barbie, written only a month or so before this one ('Barbie's Revenge' December 2003: 12). That said, Thamm's final marketing hint for would-be manufacturers who want to sell black dolls, that they should model them on the likes of Naomi Campbell (a real-life dark-skinned Barbie), may be forgiven for its pragmatism if not for its gender politics.

'Royal Male' (March 2005: 12) marks one of Thamm's most dangerous traversing of the gulf between the Wise Fool and the moralising monk. It is in the opening lines of this column that she elaborately dresses up in her court jester costume and launches a verbal attack on King Goodwill Zwelithini. Much as this attack might be warranted (the king had reneged on his responsibility to look after his extended polygamous family, allegedly), the discomfort arises in relation to the context: *Fairlady* remains, despite its attempts at social relevance and cosmopolitan 'inclusivity', a magazine marketed for and read largely by white middle-class women. There is thus little or no chance for a cultural countering of Thamm's reading of Zulu customs. The court jester is caught pandering to white middle-class sensibilities, and the reader is allowed a moment of 'civilised' self-congratulation. In this instance, one might well suggest that Thamm's own call for politically correct vigilance around racial sensitivities ('To Be or Not To Be – PC' 2002: 99–102) has perhaps been conveniently forgotten, when she stands before the Zulu king waving her Fool's staff and berating him publicly. She stands before him as 'a woman, a mother, a concerned citizen of South Africa, and lastly, as a pissed-off feminist', and though each positionality is politically 'correct' and extenuating, what she omits from the list is that she is 'white' as well, a positionality that fades into valorising neutrality.

By far the most problematic duplicity emerges in the controversially entitled 'Who's an African?' (2002: 68–70). In this piece Thamm slates a spokesperson from the ANC Youth League, Ms Nomfanelo Kota, who is purported to have criticised the 2001 Miss South Africa beauty pageant for being 'Eurocentric' and delivering a winner who was 'not African enough' (2002: 68). Thamm reads these sentiments as 'border[ing] on racial chauvinism' and as 'sound[ing] quaintly old-fashioned' (2002: 69). It is in expressing opinions such as these that liberal humanist assumptions of equality are characteristically white, and suggest that Thamm herself might be guilty of responding in the affirmative to the first of the definitively white propositions that she puts to Happy Sindane in her open letter to him: 'This letter pisses you off because it raises the issue of "race" and you think it's all nonsense that belongs in the past' (September 2003: 12).

What Thamm is patently not hearing in Ms Kota's response to the 'fairer-skinned lady', Vanessa Carreira, is the lingering effect of racial hierarchisation, which Sander Gilman has plotted in a number of intersecting discourses to have emerged during European colonial expansion (1986: 248). Though Thamm is right to suggest that the new global world order is marked by fluidity rather than fixity of identifications in noting that 'definitions of who is African, who is European, who is American and who is English are no longer clear', this is a markedly cosmopolitan phenomenon, rather than a 'universal' one, and one that runs the risk of erasing cultural difference, and at the expense of attending to the specificities that continue to divide and rule cultural practices. The ANC Youth League is justified in identifying a matrix of discourses operating in support of the globalising and homogenising influence of a white western media industry in setting the parameters of what constitutes beauty, and what constitutes a successful media event. That they were silenced (Thamm notes that only one newspaper bothered to cover the 'little verbal scuffle' [2002: 68]) may not be so much as a result of philanthropic multiculturalism, which is how she accounts for it, but might best be understood in relation to the question that Bhabha asks us to consider in understanding the complexities of our post-colonial experiences and responses:

> Do we best cope with the reality of 'being contemporary', its conflicts and crises, its losses and lacerations, by endowing history with a long memory that we then interrupt, or startle, with our own amnesia? (2002: 59)

Thamm's amnesia in this case is marked. Not only does she appear to have forgotten her earlier scathing attacks on the presumptions hidden in 'myopic' white sensibilities in her allusion to Albie Sachs's reading of white privilege – that if white South Africans 'cannot see what apartheid did to [their] fellow South Africans, [they] must be dead or living in Canada' (2002: 18) – she also appears to have completely forgotten her own fiery feminist politics. In approaching the subject of a Miss South Africa beauty pageant, curiously, Thamm does not even once allude to the demeaning parade of female flesh that the competition demands. Instead, in an editorial aside, she praises Vanessa Carreira for responding so appreciatively to

Thamm's intervention in the debate, calling Carreira 'such a well-brought up young woman' (2002: 70), and thus, perhaps unconsciously, inciting racism *and* at the expense of sexism. The role of the moralising monk in this case is clearly at odds with that of the Wise Fool, making Thamm's response just a little schizophrenic.

Conclusion

It may be argued that though *Fairlady* has 'come a long way … maybe' (April 2005: 30), Thamm's role in the magazine reflects some of the impossible duplicities that the publication itself has not managed to overcome. *The Fairlady Collection: Forty Years of Fine Writing* published in 2005 and edited by Thamm is an impressive selection which includes, among others, articles and essays by J.M. Coetzee, Nadine Gordimer and Antjie Krog. Interspersed with these literary contributions (in the magazine editions they were originally featured in) are pages dedicated to feminine regimes of body maintenance and consumer excess that effectively neutralise the social conscience that the magazine has celebrated in its 2005 anniversary editions, and this may account, at least in some way, for the licence Thamm is afforded: she may criticise the court on condition that she does not seriously undermine the queen, 'Fairlady', and all she represents.

Such a reading, however, may be tempered by considering her duplicity in the light of the productive tensions it engenders. Although one should not, as a general rule, introduce any further evidence at this stage of an argument, I wish to break with protocol, to suggest something about an emerging trend discernable in Marianne Thamm's journalistic practice that hints at a way out of the racial dualisms that Antjie Krog appears not to have successfully traversed, the ones that Krog has identified as 'freez[ing] the debate in tones of black and white and giv[ing] no guidance on how the individual can move forward' (2002: 58). Two articles penned by Thamm move towards a fluidifying polemic: 'Just Believe' (May 2005: 12) and 'Who Killed Fana Khaba?' (November 2005: 18).

In 'Just Believe' (May 2005: 12), Thamm writes her own version of the '"South Africa Alive with Possibility" campaign', and the script consists of four scenes in which representative South Africans, well known and anonymous, male and female, are given lines that contradict the stereotypes they may be likely to perpetuate, and/or the positions they would be expected to adopt. As in the original, each character is filmed paying some sort of tribute to the new South Africa, against the backdrop of proudly South African vistas. Her first cast member appears in the form of Dan Roodt, whom she uses as an example of an unreformed whiteness characterised by a eugenic obsession with the purity of the white race. Having moved on in Scene Two to indict Health Minister Manto Tshabalala-Msimang for her position in respect of the HIV/Aids debate, and Shabir Shaik in Scene Three for his fraud and corruption, her subversive advertisement culminates in an image of Thabo Mbeki staring 'straight into the camera lens' and saying:

> Today I woke up and realised that not everyone who criticises me is part of a racist, neoconservative clique determined to dictate the political agenda. I woke up and realised that people actually like me, that they're confident in my leadership and that I have made errors of judgement with regard to Zimbabwe and HIV/Aids. I woke up and realised I need not be so defensive and brittle. That I will make a significant, lasting and valued contribution to South Africa, and the rest of the continent. All I need is to believe. (May 2005: 12)

Clearly, by simultaneously allowing the president the last word and by putting her words into his mouth, Thamm is calling for an equality that succeeds the racial politics of the past, and she wants her criticisms of him to be as unequivocal as her support of him. Indeed, she wants to engage him here, not as a white middle-class woman, but as a 'concerned South African citizen'. As commendable as this egalitarian and Utopian encounter might be, it is unlikely that Thabo Mbeki will shift his responses to either the HIV/Aids debate or Zimbabwe, but it is beyond the scope of this examination to engage his oppositional stance, except to acknowledge its existence. Thamm's call, however, for connectivity beyond what Vikki Bell has labelled 'Nietzschean ressentiment' (1999: 40) is powerful, and her attempt at a balanced criticism that includes in its dramatic sweep the worst of all racialised responses, whether from an unreformed white 'neoconservative clique' with its own political agenda or from government officials acting irresponsibly or defensively, or hiding 'behind semantics', is the kind of robust debate that needs to emerge in South Africa. It can only happen productively and candidly when all traces of 'white right' which elicits black defensiveness and black solidarity have been eradicated from socio-political systems, and that is hindered by the fact that 'white money' still largely dictates the terms of those very systems, as can be seen in a publication like *Fairlady*, where the sheer excess of western mass consumerism overrides even the most progressive attempts at cosmopolitan inclusivity. Nonetheless, the court jester in the queen's court reaches a wider reading market than most other kinds of literature, and Thamm's waving her meerkat bladder at all of us indiscriminately may be one way to start the debate, though other contending voices need to join the fray.

The year 2005 drew to a close with one of Thamm's angriest contributions to the race debate, a debate which she sees as inextricably linked to the Aids debate, which at its core includes a gender and class debate. In 'Who Killed Fana Khaba?' (November 2005: 18) the complex and deeply contested politics around the HIV/Aids pandemic is brought to a polemical point of crisis that demands of the reader that she face squarely the 'moral' and 'racial' obscurants that continue to thwart a consolidated effort to stop millions of people dying. The question Thamm poses in the title of this column is provocatively accusatory, and deliberately posed to elicit more than one answer, and more than one culpability, as will be demonstrated in the following brief discussion.

Thamm's strategy is to expose the faulty logic in the formulation and application of a universal singular morality for all citizens at all times by calling up and unsettling a reliable old equation. This she manages firstly by suggesting that the 'thin air of the moral higher ground' can be breathed by more than one cultural/racial grouping, though the elevation is reached with less effort by the privileged white middle-class readership of the column, who are warned in her mimicking of media censorship disclaimers that the material before them might be considered offensive, and by exposing the insularity of white western womanhood in her introducing the life and death of a popular South African cultural figure, Fana Khaba, whom the typical reader of *Fairlady* will be unlikely to have heard of. Then, having implied the race of the people occupying that elevated reified space, she adds another figure, that of Health Minister Manto Tshabalala-Msimang, whose advocacy of safe sex and single-partner sex places her on the same elevated but unsure footing of the moral higher ground, thus suggesting that moral superiority is not prescribed by race, or at least not only by race, anymore. The columnist then deliberately invokes race, only to unsettle the terms of its binaries in the culminating equation:

> Fana was black, Adam is white.
> Fana pinned all his hopes of recovery on the minister of health's Dutch quack.
> Adam took antiretrovirals.
> Fana Khaba is dead. Adam Levin is alive.

All of which adds up to the accusation embedded in the title which is repeated in the last line. On a superficial level one might interpret the provocative equation as Thamm's attempt to suggest that it is no longer solely white privilege (which comes armed with knowledge and power) that saves Adam Levin, and that it is no longer solely colonial oppression (which carries the baggage of disempowerment and despair) that kills Fana Khaba, though clearly the residue of these historical factors is a lingering part of the equation. On another level, however, Thamm is challenging the reader to enter the debate and take cognisance of her own (moral) judgement in identifying the perpetrator of this social crime. Thus, the conservative reader might be unable to step down from the higher moral ground that she (un-)comfortably occupies, and conclude that Thamm's own sexual 'aberrance' precludes her from pronouncing on sexual promiscuity and its consequences.[108] The liberal reader might agree with Thamm's 'fair' and 'unbiased' clue to deciphering the calculation, and conclude that the Health Minister is responsible for Khaba's death on account of her reticence in prescribing antiretrovirals and in promoting an 'African Solution' to the problem. But the critical reader will battle, as Thamm does, in spite of her accusation, to 'bring [the] two worlds together' that these two figures inhabit[ed], and conclude that there is no clear-cut, black-and-white answer in a country where we 'have everything and nothing in common'. In this way Thamm precariously negotiates the narratives and counter-narratives that continue to divide and destroy us.

It is perhaps in this final column that all the elements of Marianne Thamm's role as the court jester come together in exhibiting something of the compromise *and* the productive tensions and potentialities that surface in her journalistic practice. Her 'jocoserious abnegation of big-phallus status' (Coetzee 1996: 103) as Folly is manifest in a 'transgressive aesthetic' (Dollimore 1991: 64) which is marked by a conscious duplicity, that at best and quite consistently challenges the normativity and insularity of the white middle-class heterosexual reader of *Fairlady*, as can be seen in the precariousness of the position she adopts in relation to the rivalrous AIDS debate. But, as Dale Bauer has pointed out in her reading of the Bakhtinian carnival, 'it cannot last. It is functional, a means of resisting conventions and revising them, without destroying them completely' (1997: 717). At worst then, and intermittently, Thamm's work manifests an unconscious and compromised duplicity which undoes some of her most courageous attempts to unsettle normative presumptions, as is evident in the 'unfair' position she adopts in indicting the government's official stance on HIV/Aids, which in itself is not necessarily ill conceived, but in a magazine aimed largely at maintaining white western normativity, is ill placed. What is beginning to emerge, as these last two columns demonstrate, is the potential for a balanced critical practice, in which 'concerned citizens of South Africa' might discard their ill-fitting, 'colour'-ful costumes, stop waving their fools' staffs, and, if not 'with one tongue singing', at least with one shared objective, start speaking and writing, listening and reading, less guardedly and more vigilantly.

5

The Co-ordinates of (Post-)Colonial Whiteness: A Reading of Karen Press's *Echo Location: A Guide to Sea Point for Residents and Visitors*

> *As far as I understand it, the notion of textuality should be related to the notion of the worlding of the world on a supposedly uninscribed territory. When I say this, I am thinking basically about the imperialist project which had to assume that the earth that it territorialised was in fact previously uninscribed. So then a world, on a simple level of cartography inscribed what was presumed to be uninscribed. Now this worlding actually is also a texting, textualising, a making into art, making into object to be understood.*
> **Gayatri Chakravorty Spivak (1980: 210)**

Introduction

Echo Location: A Guide to Sea Point for Residents and Visitors (1998) received some fairly indifferent reviews[109] when it first appeared, among them Kelly Berman's summation that the anthology, though lots of fun, was not important enough to be afforded serious scholarly consideration (1998: 74). In part, this chapter constitutes a response to such indifference, and an attempt to rethink the innovative achievement and continued relevance of the book. The title of the collection of poems signals the possibility of reading the work as Karen Press's re-narrativisation of Sea Point's history, a geographical/historical space, the co-ordinates of which are overtly associated with a certain kind of colonial insularity manifest in white material privilege that is residual in cosmopolitan South African suburbia. Navigational 'echo location' requires listening or hearing rather than seeing, and interpreting sound rather than visual images or words, and the text may thus be read as a search for alternative signifying practices. The reader is called upon to tune into an unfamiliar frequency, one that unsettles the normativity of the colonially mapped co-ordinates that, as Spivak has argued, are responsible for 'worlding', 'texting' and 'inscribing' the world (1980: 262).

That the subtitle aims itself at both 'residents' and 'visitors' marks the poet's unsettling of the categories 'settler' and 'tourist', which might imply her reading of both as sojourners, to a lesser or greater extent, in an alien landscape, and this may constitute a subtle reminder to residents of their status as visitors. This reading of the implications in the subtitle is borne out in the powerful sense of white displacement *and* white normativity that the poems trace. In the following analysis of selected aspects of the poetry and its presentation, I shall demonstrate what might be seen as Karen Press's examination of the damaging racial/cultural co-ordinates that continue to map power relations in post-apartheid South Africa. Her position in relation to the images she observes and records will also be plotted, and in this regard it is important to note the critical distance she maintains as the poet-observer, a position of relative safety in comparison to those adopted by Antjie Krog and Marianne Thamm.

Echo Location, a collection of poems disguised as a 'guide book', consists of a map, two epigraphs, a prologue and seven sections or 'chapters', interspersed with photographs and underscored with a baseline text. Multigeneric, the text resists comfortable and conventional categories, what Susan Stanford Friedman, following Jacques Derrida's exposé of the 'law of genre', and Celeste Schenk's noting of 'the Western will to taxonomise', conceives of as 'the tyranny of categorical boundaries, to declare what is inside, what is outside' (Friedman in Warhol 1997: 721–722). The seven chapters invoke a chronological, sequential time frame that mimics novelistic conventions. The title of 'Chapter One' is 'Wherever Land *Begins*' and 'Chapter Seven' is called 'At the *End* of the *Story*', with all the chapters in between recalling some aspect of land and (cultural) belonging, for example, 'Chapter Three' is 'A Most *Desirable Location*' (my emphases). The seven-part structure is echoed (though deliberately imperfectly) in the baseline seven-day eating plan, the implications of which I will examine in one of the penultimate sections of this chapter. These strategies collectively mark Press's awareness of the ways in which form dictates content (and vice versa), suggesting that her project is at least partly a facetious ploy to repackage poetry, a genre that has not been competitive in the publication market, and attempt to sell it in disguise.

The two words that make up the main title 'Echo Location' carry multiple intertextual echoes. It is possible that Press is invoking the mythological Echo, the Oracle of Delphi (or Sybil), whose request for eternal life without specifying the requirement of eternal youth, led to her becoming an increasingly distant 'Echo'. Sybil is also invoked in T.S. Eliot's epigraph to 'The Waste Land' (1922), and in this regard the title may be read as reflecting simultaneously the centrality and emptiness of western grand narratives. In addition, Press may well be invoking Bhabha's conception of the '*location* of culture' as a mapping of western discourses in delineating the other. Apart from these intertextual echoes, 'echo location' is a navigational strategy signalling the text as a search for geographical/historical co-ordinates, and thereby recalling the imperial promise of empty space that can be conquered and owned. The notion of land as property, though obviously not an exclusively western phenomenon, is one that, in South Africa and other colonised places, is historically linked to European imperial conquest, with the inevitable slicing up of space into walled and fenced, and (eventually) sky-scraping units, the most expensive and exclusive of which have been inhabited largely by the descendants of white settlers. 'Colonialism', says Robert Young, 'involves the introduction of a new notion of land as property, and with it inevitably the appropriation and enclosure of land' (1995: 172). In *Echo Location*, Press is aware of space, and plots the historical and present geographies of this colonially mapped co-ordinate called Sea Point as a place earmarked historically for exclusively white (expatriate) colonial landownership. The word 'echo' connotes emptiness, the hollow ring, the returning of empty sound in empty space. An echo, in fact, is characterised by the convergence of time and space. Given that Sea Point is one of the most densely populated spaces in the Cape Peninsula, one might argue that Press conceives of whiteness, the racial category most readily associated with property ownership in Sea Point, as emptiness, as a hollow haunting lack, resonating the notion of a kind of time warp. Given also that the word 'location' in a South African context has very specific connotations, I shall illustrate the ways in which Press emphasises linguistic and discursive practices as instrumental in mapping and controlling the spaces occupied by colonising forces. Press's title alerts the reader to the fact that her work seeks to reinterpret the colonial discourse of place and belonging from the point of view of one no longer sure of her settler privilege, but rather as one seeking (with all its ambivalence) a 'location' from which the white post-apartheid woman poet might speak.

Charting Whiteness: The Convergence of Opposite Forces
One of the ways in which Press charts the uncomfortable co-ordinates of post-colonial whiteness in the text is in relation to the convergence of opposite forces. A brief aside on the front cover of the anthology will reinforce my reading of the centrality of convergences in the text. The ghostly double exposure of the present absence of the (white) women traversing a borderland, where sky meets sea meets land that is occupied by scattered abstract shapes, invokes the notion of the superimposition and overt alienation that Press's poetry examines. Sea Point is charted in the text as a borderland, situated between mountain and sea, light and dark, a place of convergences. In a poem entitled 'The Fairest Cape' (1998: 50) the speaker notes: 'We are all in this place because somewhere else/sadness and money converged.' The entire narrative of *Echo Location* traces the converging of opposite forces: money and sadness; white and black; rich and poor; straight and gay; presence and absence; 'First World' and 'Third World'; east and west; past and present; the living and the dead, and, more crucially for the white western woman writer perhaps, being neither here nor there, in an echoing in-between land.

These convergences are often experienced by the colonial settler, and his or her descendants, as isolation and displacement. Zoë Wicomb's reading of Coetzee's *White Writing* as his attempt to give whiteness a 'marked meaning, the name for something incomplete, not fully adapted to its environment, something in transition' (2001: 169) provides a valuable point of reference in approaching Press's poetry, as does Valerie Babb's identification of what she calls 'the paradox of whiteness', noting that '[t]he devices employed in creating white hegemony are for the most part devices of exclusion. They articulate not necessarily who or what is white but rather who or what is not white' (1998: 42). Here Babb is implicitly invoking a border between what is and what is not white, but it is not a border that can easily be mapped. Rather, it is one that operates at the level of abstractions and linguistic constructions that make it almost impossible to discern.

In *Echo Location* Karen Press exhibits an awareness of this kind of paradox. It manifests itself in relation to the ghostly presence/absence of various figures, most notably in the 'ghosts huddled like deckchairs [...] mad with memory and boredom' (1998: 98) in 'At the End of the Story' and in 'Green Tin' (1998: 59), where the Sea Point lawns cover the 'landfill from previous centuries' (Endnotes, 1998: 100). In many of the poems in the collection she features white subjectivities that reflect the assumptions and entitlement, the exclusions and denials characteristic of white responses in post-colonial spaces, as will be demonstrated in an analysis of selected poems. But, perhaps more significantly, the poet's interrogation of whiteness is manifest in four interrelated strategies in presenting the poems, strategies that highlight the continued effects of a white western frame of reference. Briefly summarised, these are: 1) the inclusion of snippets of overheard conversation that accompany many poems; 2) 'found poems' taken sometimes verbatim from other kinds of texts and presented as poetry; 3) a baseline text which offers the kind of information the title purports to offer; and 4) the inclusion of two versions of the guidebook against which to read Press's version of this kind of publication. These epigraphs operate as an intertextual echo of the colonial narratives she plots, from the first poem in the collection to the last.

The first of these strategies is Press's inclusion in *Echo Location* of seemingly unmediated[110] snatches of conversation in italics at the bottom right-hand corners of numerous pages, as evident, for example, in 'Purple' (1998: 22), a poem that, as I shall show, must be read against the overheard 'street talk', which accompanies it. These ostensibly overheard statements are deliberately presented to highlight racialised and polarised discourses that are rendered uncomfortable, even absurd, when juxtaposed. The sense of 'immediacy' created in each case suggests Press's recognition and acknowledgement of the limits of her own representational practice.

In addition to these 'social scripts' are the accumulated 'found poems' in *Echo Location*. Press has spoken of the genesis of 'found poems' in postmodernist 'readymade' installation art such as the work of Marcel Duchamp, whose famous 'Fountain' (1917), a urinal set up in an art gallery and signed R. Mutt, represents a critique of the late capitalist world of consumerism and excess. Press's 'found poems', gleaned from newspapers, magazines and public notices, for example, and taken out of the context in which they are normally found, are included in the collection to highlight the ways in which apparently neutral statements are symptomatic of a tendency in middle-class suburbia for people to become passive recipients, malleable consumers of the grand narratives served up as truth, as is evident in the 'found poem' entitled 'Rules Binding on all Owners and Residents' (1998: 42), where the social values binding the inhabits of middle-class, predominantly white, spaces are exposed.

A related strategy is Press's inclusion of a baseline text. Traversing the entire anthology and reminiscent of pop-up sales lines in cyberspace, the baseline text initially offers a kind of scrolling marquee of conspicuous consumption. This secondary text constitutes Press's recognition of the centrality of the media industry in constructing Sea Point as a tourist destination; in effect, its commodification of the 'colourful' Cape. But the cuisine advertised in the first half of the baseline is radically undermined by the primary text which foregrounds that which is patently omitted from tourist brochures and the like. In writing a new version of the guidebook, by displacing into the secondary baseline text the kind of information expected in such a publication, Press is marking her refusal to appeal to popular tourist habits. Like Jamaica Kincaid, she is suspicious of this kind of human being, this 'you' who 'when the natives see you, the tourist, they envy you, they envy your ability to leave your own banality and boredom, they envy your ability to turn their banality and boredom into a source of pleasure for yourself' (Kincaid 1988: 19). Being rich, the tourists consume and Sea Point offers them a picturesque location in which to escape the banality of their lives. But, the poet seems to be asking, what has become of the subjectivities (the original travellers from distant lands, those historical 'tourists') that inhabit this overtly advertised tourist destination. From the beginning of time, as suggested in the first poem which features the elemental forces of rocks, sand and water (1998: 16) to 'the End of the Story' (1998: 98), or to the end of a particularly powerful colonising narrative, one that has been necessarily illegitimated, they remain stranded, washed up in the borderland between sea and granite.

The residual effects of such a colonising narrative are manifest in yet another textual strategy deployed by Press in *Echo Location*: her choice of two prose epigraphs to introduce the collection. One is a recent travelogue, and one a dated tourist brochure, and each invites a recognition of the ironic implications in the subtitle: 'A Guide to Sea Point for Residents and Visitors'. The epigraphs signal Press's rewriting of the typical travelogue and its blatantly materialist offshoot, the tourist brochure, as well as point towards the dubious genealogy of 'guide books' as seemingly innocent and supposedly factual or non-fictional texts. Sander Gilman has examined the complicity of travel writing in a web of nineteenth-century European discourses (including medical science and graphic art) in advancing the metanarrative of white superiority (1986: 231). Press's invocation of the genre and its offshoots, and her deliberate misuse of them, suggests that her project is, at least partially, to expose the discourses concealed in such literature. 'One of the key distinguishing characteristics of colonialist discourse' (1995: 52), notes Elleke Boehmer in her discussion of 'travel metaphors', is the '*transferability*' (my emphasis) of a certain set of ideas about conquered terrains that engender the dialectic of self and other, and that the ubiquitous guidebook has come to replace the travelogue, reinforces the transferability of a discourse of superiority associated with the privilege of touring, observing, judging and 'worlding'.

The first epigraph, taken from James Hamilton-Paterson's *Seven Tenths: The Sea and Its Thresholds* (1993), may be read as a traveller's poetic prose description of the magnitude and awesome loneliness of the sea: 'Out here we are on the edge of something: of drowning, fear, and loneliness'. These may be read as precisely the co-ordinates of (post-)colonial whiteness that Press identifies as pivotal in her exposure of the displaced and alien condition of whiteness in *Echo Location*. As 'carbon based-beings', the epigraph reads, we are 'nothing but the point at which three axes plotting this three dimensional borderland intersect' and we are therefore 'stranger than we imagine'. The second epigraph constitutes a 'real', historical visitors' guide to Sea Point, as published (anonymously) in 1908, and signals the huge historical divide between the early twentieth-century guide and the one that Karen Press produces in the last decade of the same century. The sweep of history and the discourses responsible for washing us up at this particular historical juncture are underpinned by the matter-of-fact tone of the earlier 1908 brochure, concerned as it is primarily with the weather in Sea Point ('It prides itself on having a very much better climate than other suburbs of Cape Town' and on its 'comparative immunity from the south-east gales'), and consequently the comfort of potential residents and visitors who might be interested in obtaining a publication entitled *Tramps In and About the Peninsula*. The juxtaposition of these epigraphs mark wholly opposing responses to travel, the second overriding the first in its colonising sense of entitlement, evident in the preoccupation with trivialities and physical comfort. Or, read differently, the first overriding the second in its refusal to grant supremacy to these 'carbon-based', 'borderland' 'beings' whose co-ordinates of survival are, in effect, slowly being erased.

After the two epigraphs and the prologue poem, and signalling Press's attempt to plot or chart her way through the officially sanctioned historical narrative towards an alternative one, is the first poem, entitled 'Wherever Land Begins' (1998: 16), one that offers a lyrical genesis of the world. Press animates the shoreline as a meeting place uncontaminated by human history. The water droplets are personified as 'children with a secret', which may be read as an attempt to write against the taming of the landscape (and the concomitant anthropomorphising colonial trope of the land as lover's body), in figuring it within the tentative grasp of child-like wonder, and in doing so to signal the violence that a narrativised history launches in relation to imperial conquest and colonial settlement, what Spivak has suggested is a textual 'worlding' of the world (1980: 42). The poem invokes a timeless, frozen, elemental meeting somewhere 'out here on the edge: of drowning, fear and understanding' (Epigraph No. 1), and is elusive and suggestive rather than official and historically verifiable.

The poet's challenge to the official historical narrative of white settlerhood commences after 'Wherever Land Begins'. The poem '19th Century Gratitude' (1998: 20) plots, sequentially and consequentially, the procession of linear historical time and the arrival of a colonial and domesticating presence in the Cape. The poem may best be described as a catalogue of ingratitude and entitlement, with ominous tragic echoes into the future. The first stanza sets the tone of the kind of ingratitude that will be bequeathed to future generations: 'Sea captains come to anchor here,/unloading the fattened dreams of dark barbarity,/shaking the crumbs of insignificance from their beards.' The poem is marked by similar images of synaesthesia, and the mingling of sense perceptions effectively erases (by confusion) the sense of entitlement and privilege entertained by the sea captain and his descendants. The culminating image of 'the women swapping recipes for wreaths' incorporates the life sustaining ('recipes' usually connoting the preparation of food) and the death dealing ('wreaths' associated with mourning) as complementary co-ordinates of the same gesture. Images such as these (in the poem as a whole) serve as constant reminders that the assumptions responsible for empire and colonial expansion might still be residual in the norms and gestures (the 'recipes' and 'wreaths') that white western subjectivities have inherited.

Presumptions and Anxieties: White South Africa Disintegrating
The residual elements of a colonising prerogative become evident in a number of poems that introduce more recent subjectivities inhabiting Sea Point, and in many instances Karen Press appears to be setting herself up as the speaking subject, recording aspects of her own complicity in inadvertently promoting such discourses. Many of these accounts of life in Sea Point may be read as satire, which in turn suggests something about Press's positionality in relation to the scenes she observes, experiences and records. The deployment of satire marks her own uncomfortable and ambivalent position of partial complicity in the discourses she uncovers. In Press's sixties poem called 'Purple' (1998: 22), which represents the settler descendants inhabiting Sea Point in the mid-twentieth century, the speaker might well be the poet,[111] looking back on her formative years and the influences that she would have been likely to have experienced. It is a poem that bears witness

to the penchant in the insular white bourgeois world of the Cape during the height of apartheid to hanker after, borrow and assimilate European/American values and norms, in this case the trappings of the psychedelic sixties' sexual revolution, which seem so ludicrously misplaced in Africa – purple, the colour of passion, wilts when the young women return from their travels abroad. And it is the African climate that proves to be unfavourable in supporting such an excess of fashion accessories. In this poem Press is clearly playing on the notion of the 'Colourful Cape', especially in relation to the snippet of overheard conversation spoken in Cape 'coloured-ese':

> *Jou ma se poes*
> *Walk the dog. Walk*
> *the bloody dog.*
> *Jou piss poes! Piss*
> *poes! Jou – jou –*
> *Ek sal jou fokken naai! Ja, jy! Jy!*
> *Moenie weg loop nie!*
> *Jou naai!*[112]

The placement of these two texts on the same page serves to underpin what Press sees as the 'absurd juxtapositions' of metropolitan South African life, where 'some people are starving and some people have three houses and five cars' (1993: 27), in that the white women in the poem clearly have all the material possessions they desire and the coloured woman walking the dog has only her menial labour and the derision it provokes. In addition, the juxtaposed texts mark the poet's interest in examining 'the interface between people's psychological collaboration in identity and the fact that identities are constructed by social means' (27), especially in relation to the underlying attitudes expressed in each text. It is the voice of a coloured man we hear in the overheard conversation, one who has internalised and reproduces the race hatred learned from the white master, and it is the voice of the younger cousin in 'Purple' who has internalised and who reproduces white middle-class mores in wishing to emulate the older women's sense of style and displayed sexuality ('Purple was as good as sex in 1968/for my grown-up Sea Point cousins/from good homes'). Furthermore, the exploited coloured housemaid, who walks the madam's dog, makes possible the leisured classes' travels abroad with their 'Lavender tights' and 'Mulberry boots' and their 'Sugarplum lips' (22). The white western sexual revolution of the sixties and seventies has clearly not liberated this 'third world woman' who, in a snatch of street talk, is reduced to serviceability ('Walk the bloody dog'), violent objectification ('Ek sal jou fokken naai') and spent fuckability ('Jou piss poes'). But it is the opposing dialects represented, and the spatial co-ordinates they occupy on the page, that reinforce the enormity of the gulf between white privilege and coloured despair and they emphasise the absurdity of the juxtapositions Press has identified as characteristic of South African metropolitan realities.

'In Those Days' (1998: 23) evinces a similar set of responses to those espoused by the 'purple'-clad cousins Press represents in the previous poem, and may also represent something of the confessional aspect of Press's project; her avowal of her own insular white middle-class background. In a sense, the companion poems share the implications of the snippet of overheard conversation, placed strategically between them. The title of this poem signals a nostalgic recollection of mid-twentieth-century white South African urban insularity, and the poet's self-conscious use of the plural pronoun 'we' throughout the poem forces the reader to confront the complicities that made possible at least one generation's 'exempt[ion] from politics'. Press's repetition of the isolated and capitalised abstraction 'Politics' in the next line reinforces the solipsistic remoteness of a lifestyle associated with 'summer/ice creams/Sunday walks on the beachfront before lunch'. Equally revealing of the attitudes bequeathed to the descendants of colonial settlers is the matter-of-fact tone the representative speaker adopts, which is at odds with the observations recorded. We are told, for example, that battles were fought 'over dustbins, maid's rooms, prostitutes' and that 'our corruption stretched no further/than the servant's quarters', as if these preoccupations are completely natural and normal. But, much like Press's 'found poems' do (discussed further on in this chapter), these seemingly trivial observations of daily life emerge as powerful understatements, especially when read in the context of the accompanying snippet of street talk. It is the coloured woman, once again, whose denigration is at the silent centre of the domestic disputes and intrigues that dominate middle-class white suburbia. Her labour allows the leisure of the middle class, but it is a dialectic increasingly experienced as paradoxical (especially in relation to the images being so at odds with the matter-of-fact tone in which they are recorded), even absurd, as is suggested in the final image of the poem in which 'our children and their architects [...] sunbathe all day as if they want to look good/in the news footage from the war front'. This image reinforces the reproductivity of white normalcy in its invocation of the notion of social engineering.

'The First Thirty-Seven Years' (1998: 25) may also suggest something of the poet's own experience of settlerhood, that is, of being a descendant of the 'Sea Captains' of '19th Century Gratitude' (1998: 20) with their 'fattened dreams of dark barbarity'. The speaker's youthful experience of the politics of the nuclear family is marked by a sense of 'unhomeliness', with her father 'dropping the anchor/year by year', her mother buying 'carpets', but it is the repetition of the phrase 'just camping out' that epitomises the family's experience, and the impossibility of 'dropping anchor' is suggested in the futility of the father's actions. He is figured, in the present continuous, as 'lowering the rope' – the action is never completed, and finally, he leaves 'no rope' for his daughter to hang on to. The rope may be read as a metaphor for a 'lifeline', one that is offered from one generation to another, promising stability, anchorage and belonging in middle-class white suburbia.

Two companion poems about growing up confirm the sense of loss and lies endemic to settler experience into the twentieth century. The first of these is 'Rehearsal' (1998: 64), and the first-person persona recording the experience once again suggests a memory likely to be the poet's, marking her recognition of the social conditioning of which she is a product. This poem is juxtaposed with a poem about a boy called Gerald, and together they demonstrate gender prerequisites at the same time as exposing the trauma and presumption upon which normativity is built, as will be shown in the following analysis.

The very title 'Rehearsal' signals the performative nature of normative social practices which children must learn, and the poem illustrates a complex and ambivalent response to an incident involving a dance lesson, which is the arrival in a wheelchair of a dying girl, and a snatch of overheard speech in the bottom right-hand corner of the page. What becomes evident is that the speaker is rehearsing not only the moves of an amateur ballet performance, along with the social graces that such training inculcates, but more significantly, though less obviously, she is rehearsing the manoeuvres necessary in surviving the burden of guilt. This is evident in the children's response to the girl wheeled in to the town hall by her mother: 'She was dying, and we danced without looking at her/but her eyes followed us everywhere' (1998: 64). And if the young girl fiercely but unsuccessfully ignores the sick child in the wheelchair, the older narrating self cannot ignore the implications of what the young experiencing self may not have understood: the conversation outside in which a child shouts, 'Take me to the *beach*!' (heard from within the narrated experience the poem recalls) and the domestic servant's response (recorded from outside of that experience and transcribed in italics in the bottom corner):

Uthe umntwana angahlala ngamexesha
Esikolo, qha angangeni ebesini.[113] (1998: 64)

Once again, the immediacy of the 'unmediated' speech is intrusive in its insistence on being heard, and disallows any easy manoeuvrability on the part of the reader out of acknowledging the ubiquity of black labour upon which white leisure is premised. The black nanny in charge of the white child is interpreting the culturally remote and indecipherable proscriptions of rich white landowners as she interprets the madam's command and negotiates the child's demand. The reader is involved in a similar task (of interpreting and negotiating the politics involved), while the child in the poem tries to avoid the 'dark pools' of the dying child's eyes in which all the envy and unfairness that the poem throws out accumulates.

On the opposite page a version of official history or myth-making plays itself out. Entitled 'The Iliad (Cont.)' (1998: 65), the poem explores what boys might be doing while girls are attending ballet rehearsals. Gerald is plotting the demise of a rat which is intent on his sandwich during break at playschool. In the spirit of epic conquest, rehearsed and replayed as the parenthesis in the title suggests, and as 'Achilles had Paris./Dingaan had Pretorius' before him, little Gerald becomes the (unsung) hero and victim of a skirmish (in the process of chopping off the rat's tail, he is bitten and poisoned) that is deliberately unheroic, except in Press's facetious appropriation of the western epic which she undermines by suggesting that:

> History will show
> one less property developer,
> one more small corpse with tooth marks on its chubby palm, [...]

That Gerald is envisaged as growing up to be a 'property developer' must be read against the snippet of overheard speech sandwiched between the juxtaposed poems, and, in that context, perhaps, the equation drawn from the history of male aggression ushered in with 'The Iliad' is complete:

> Achilles had Paris.
> Dingaan had Pretorius.
> Gerald will have the rat.
> The rat will have Gerald.

Whereas 'Rehearsal' is a personal account leading at least to the speaker's half-acknowledged sense of the discipline brought to bear on her young self, 'The Iliad (Cont.)' is an objective, third-person account, rendered without emotion. Press's satirical criticism of the echoes of white masculine mythologies of conquest and scientific certainty is evident in Gerald's unnecessary death, as well as in the pseudo-scientific equation quoted above, but perhaps more forcefully in the final image of the rat's tail chopped off by Gerald, which will be 'preserved in a forensic laboratory/until the space is needed'. If that tail issued 'no warnings', the 'tale' in the overheard speech in IsiXhosa does, even if only in its portentous indecipherability to the average white reader.

In 'View' (1998: 95), like 'In Those Days' (23), Press employs the first-person plural pronoun to acknowledge her complicity in the discourses she examines, in this case the real-estate value of a sea view from Sea Point residences. The white inhabitants of Sea Point are envisaged collectively as borderland beings anxiously 'scanning this blue country/we are on the edge of, watching/for signs that we may go home'. It is only the birds diving for fish visible from balconies[114] and windows that have experienced the continent that is the backdrop of this expensive, exclusive 'view': they have 'flown in from Mombasa [...]. Dakar [.../...] from distant outposts at Omboué, Mtwara, Laâyounne', while those with the view that is paid for remain alien observers and are 'sucked in/by some buried current, our uninhabitable past/pulling us back'. In this, the third last poem in the collection, one hears the hollow empty ring of 'echo location', and recognises the uncomfortable un-belonging evident in the inability of settler descendants to move out of an 'uninhabitable past', which is also a mythic past, recycled and anxiously repeated as an investment in white normativity.

In addition to the 'personal' poems, which suggest something of the experience of the writer herself, are the poems in which Press imaginatively enters the subjectivity of typical residents of Sea Point, the people who occupy the same geographical 'location' as the poet does and whose conversations 'echo' in the streets below. One of the most significant of these, apart from 'The Iliad (Cont.)' (1998: 65) discussed above, is 'Single Passage' (1998: 24). Recalling the arrival of the 'sea captains' in the nineteenth century, the poem appears to follow their first- and second-generation descendants, 'old men' who 'had not expected to be abandoned'. Their sense of abandonment is reinforced in Press's description of what their lives have been reduced to:

They had the choice of playing cards
with each other; arguing about politics
or folding silently inside a nurse's shadow.

These activities collectively suggest most notably a profound lack of agency: playing cards with each other implies not only that they may not have anyone else with whom to play but the unproductive passing of time; arguing politics would inevitably throw out the (only) two white responses to apartheid (*verligte* and *verkrampte*),[115] neither of which proves to be effectual against the massive injustice that apartheid generated, and 'folding silently inside a nurse's shadow' is the ultimate image of emasculation.

But it is the final stanza that provides the most powerful image of agentless displacement. These ageing men of Empire are described as follows:

> Just ships some gene was using
> to get from Vilnius to Perth. You could see
> the thought flickering in their eyes:
> bloody long detour.

The sea captains of yore, navigating the circumference of the new world, metamorphose into the vessels that they had previously steered. In addition, the impulse responsible for such imperial navigation is figured in relation to a biological/territorial imperative which has the effect in the context of the poem of ridiculing the 'naturalising' of white western right. This is borne out in the trajectory of the journey from 'Vilnius to Perth', a journey from the 'centre'[116] of Europe to the 'last colonial outpost'.[117] These are the co-ordinates of (post-)colonial whiteness, which in the thoughts flickering in the old men's eyes seem to mean nothing more than 'a bloody long detour'.

Identity and the Other: 'Alida is not my name'

Apart from the 'unmediated' snatches of street talk, there are several poems in the collection that reflect (on) the lives of black and coloured inhabitants of Sea Point. In these poems Press consciously navigates the difficulty, impossibility even, of entering the subjectivities of those 'down there', visible from the elevated Sea Point balconies. They are immersed in the world of exploitable black labour and predominantly involved in domestic employment, the nameless 'maids or caretakers' (1998: 36) of 'Reconciliation', for example, requisite in sustaining white leisure. They 'stand to one side, arms folded,/no idea which way the wind is blowing for them'. In this concentrated description, there are powerful implications in the body language and the surmised response, both of which indicate that they anticipate being accused of the crime being investigated. The intrigue[118] however is short lived, and in no time the status quo is resumed: the white inhabitants redecorate and 'exchange names of contractors, bricklayers', etc. – the list is deliberately extended to suggest the preoccupations they can afford, while the 'maids and caretakers return to their old,/unexcavated warrens'. The last line of the poem, 'It never stops', demonstrates the impossibility of 'reconciliation', except as a superficial masking over by the 'bricklayers, plasterers, painters' that the incident (and the poem) summons.

The nameless 'maids and caretakers' of 'Reconciliation' appear in two additional poems in the collection. 'The Caretaker' (1998: 49), a poem juxtaposed with a 'found poem' called 'The RDP Comes to Sea Point' (48) (discussed in the following subsection), in seven spare lines offers a 'job description' of the ubiquitous caretaker of the apartment blocks that dominate Sea Point's landscape. The caretaker's anonymity is reinforced in several ways: firstly, he will be wearing 'blue overalls', the uniform of menial labour; next, he 'has a name like John or Klaas', conveniently generic, familiar and easy to remember or forget, so as to discourage individuality. In addition, he is recognisable only by what he does, which the ensuing catalogue demonstrates: 'He collects [...]/He sweeps [...]/He waters [...]' And finally, we are told, 'You will know him when you see him', which has the effect of diminishing him to not much more than a visual signifier of the social strata and status quo in Sea Point. A similar strategy is employed in 'Glimpses of Women in Overalls' (1998: 52). In this case the poem offers an oblique response to the ramifications of the most sought-after kind of domestic employment available to the nameless black and coloured 'maid' in the italicised subheadings that 'define' her: the *'live in'* variety who is never *'off duty'*, who is expediently labelled *'one of the family'*, and who is *'yet somehow apart'* (italics in original). Press catches a glimpse of her life in the servant's quarters where she drinks from a tin cup while dreaming of drinking from china, and anticipates the 'door bursting open' with interrogatory accusations. As 'one of the family' she is ironically hardly there, just a 'shadow/moving quietly along the world's outline', which suggests powerfully that the world, at least the one she inhabits, is white. Her dehumanisation is reinforced in the image of her as a 'bridge on heavy legs'. But the tragedy of her anonymous but indispensable existence is captured in the image of her arms, one of which ceaselessly supports 'untold numbers of children and their parents,/maltese poodles, hot water cylinders, supermarkets, lavatories', and the other figured as 'jointed like a cracked wing,/reaching into the mist'. In this image, her serviceability is incompletely but potentially counterbalanced with her yearning for freedom, which threatens to destabilise the 'world', the outline of which she has been forced 'quietly' to inhabit. One senses in the trajectory of the poem a gathering of momentum in the 'natural' order of things: the final image of the pigeons with the 'soft-throated rumbling of their incomprehensible songs/barely audible' echo the earlier image of her arm 'jointed like a cracked wing' and embodies her yearning.

Apart from the nameless workers, there is one figure who repeatedly emerges, Alida, though she remains so elusive that she slips just beyond any attempt to define or categorise her. What the reader can deduce is that Alida is a young attractive possibly coloured woman, a prostitute, who has experienced mixed fortunes, which have at times provided her with comfort and security and at times lead to her homeless wandering. These aspects of the persona emerge piecemeal from subtle and cumulative hints embedded in the numerous poems that feature fragmented aspects of her life story ('100% Silk' 1998: 30, 'Rotten Fish': 31, 'Probability': 32, 'Klip in die Bos': 33, 'Truth': 35, 'Her Watery Legs Led Him Deeper': 72, 'Alida at Home': 93). Her nameless anonymity is ironically invested in her name, Alida, which is not her name, as the opening line of '100% Silk' (1998: 30) records. The name, originating from Greek, means the 'beautifully dressed, small winged one' according to various websites that provide definitions of first names,[119] and the brand name ('Alida Creations') of the '100% Silk' dress she finds discarded on the beach. Alida thus inherits and inhabits not only another woman's dress but the name attached to the label, demonstrating Press's negotiation of the power of naming in constructing identity. She 'becomes' Alida and attempts to reinvent herself in opposition to the damaging race and gender shaming she has been exposed to. The humiliations she has suffered are numerous: she has had her teeth broken, her body abused, and is dirty (1998: 30); she has been told she smells 'like rotten fish' (1998: 31), and she has been embroiled in murder and bribery (1998: 31, 35). Much of the shaming she experiences is recorded in '100% Silk', which offers a first-person account of Alida's traumatised past, one that involves repeated physical abuse. The narrative ends, however, with her identification of herself as 'a piece of rubbish. 100%' an image that reinforces her humiliation and despair. But it is Alida's elusive unrepresentability that is possibly the most striking aspect of her characterisation. Despite this life of destitution and violence, she emerges in one of the last poems in the collection entitled 'Alida at Home' (1998: 93), having escaped her humiliations, if only in the poet's imaginative effort to provide her with a happy ending. The quaint rhymes, and unreal, fairy-tale-like images in the poem reinforce the unlikelihood that Alida's existence could ever culminate in her drinking 'darjeeling tea' and being 'happy, quite free'. It is thus plausible to read her story, which is told only in fragments, as Press's conscious negotiation of the impossibility of knowing Alida, and her recognition that she can only rescue the character imaginatively. Such a reading is borne out not only in the fragmentation and incompletion that characterises Alida's story but in the focalising perspective from which it is delivered. The first poem, '100% Silk', is offered as a first-person account but from there on she emerges as a figure in third-person versions ('Rotten Fish', 'Klip in die Bos' and 'Her Watery Legs Led Him Deeper', for example). In one instance before her arrival 'home' (1998: 93), she is figured in pseudo-headlines from a newspaper and as a fictional insert in the gossip column. In the 'poem' entitled 'Truth' (1998: 35) the headlines run: 'ALIDA EATS BREAKFAST EVERY DAY' and 'Alida opens a building society account'. These, and the insert hinting at shady dealings, emphasise the difficulty of representing her, except through layers of mediation. Ultimately, Alida remains a kind of haunting present absence and a reminder of the unrepresentability of other.

Found Poems: Raiding the Archives
In addition to the scraps of conversation recorded as adjuncts to several poems in the collection are the ones from pre-existing texts which have simply been transcribed from their original context into the gallery-like aesthetic space of a poetry collection. These texts carry the traces of western epistemological imperialism in the sense that in the original publications they appeared in they would be likely to be received as merely factual. In each case, the discourses informing the original texts are thrown into sharp relief in the new space they occupy. 'CONTACT ZONE' (1998: 17), for example, rendered in capitals, is either a direct or partial transcription, intended to mimic, in reproducing an official factual discourse, the language of the informative plaque found at historical sites, and aimed at the edification of consumer-travellers. The supposed neutrality of such formal and factual discourse is undermined in two ways. Firstly, there is the obvious implication of the settler/native encounter in the very rocks under scrutiny, which are read as 'an impressive contact zone of dark slate with pale intrusive granite'. Secondly, Press is foregrounding the notion that the rise of natural sciences was not an innocent enterprise – the last line refers to Charles Darwin's visit to the site in 1836. This invites us to recall the echo of his particular legacy in contributing to race theories which, at least partially, informed some of the justifications for imperialism and colonial expansion.

'Recreation' (1998: 18) provides another transcription of an existing text, with a similar effect achieved. Using direct quotations from museum archives, Press records and simultaneously destabilises the official history of the origins of Sea Point, or, perhaps more poignantly, the origins of the species inhabiting Sea Point. The abiding effect is the invocation of the past, complete with the attitudes and norms associated with a particular historical moment, and simultaneously a reminder that present-day visitors and settlers are themselves the products and perpetrators of exclusionary and privileged white practices, that they are interlopers with a considerable sense of their self-importance. This is borne out by Press's reminder in the poem that Sea Point was originally designated as a colonial 'country club' aimed at promoting cultural insularity in bringing a little piece of the 'Old World' to the 'dark' places, as she records the official deliberations that led to its settlement:

> The locality they favoured was –
> In the language of their document –
> *Achter de zoo genaamde Waterplaats, aan de voet des Leeuwenberges*

In this appropriated historical fragment, Press challenges textual and generic boundaries and exposes the motivation for the development of Sea Point: the alleviation of boredom for isolated colonials. Press meticulously transcribes the language of colonial officialdom, pointing to the capacity of language to carry and echo the sense of entitlement associated with settlerhood. Clauses such as 'knowing that it cannot prejudice the interests of others' and 'inasmuch as slaves and miscreants are wont to befoul the place by watering cattle there' (1998: 18) bespeak this sense of entitlement of the leisured classes, and the poem as a whole signals the reverberation of such attitudes into the future. The last line of the poem, suggesting that the petition was successful and that the 'country club was in full swing' (19), coupled with the unfolding narrative in the collection which the poem introduces, suggests the continued effect of such preoccupations, so that it becomes apparent that Press is drawing attention to the sense of settler entitlement upon which South African history is built. If these are the origins of Sea Point, she seems to be suggesting, a country club for bored colonials, then she will have to look elsewhere, find alternative co-ordinates to navigate other possible identifications.

In 'Recorded History' (1998: 26) Press provides an incomplete and 'found' collection of newspaper headlines and captions accompanying descriptions of photographs in square brackets. These deliberately hacked snippets are extracted from the catalogue of the South African Library, and recorded imperfectly to highlight the preoccupations of the reading public and the media industry that both panders to and creates its sensibilities. Item number 18, for example, hails the arrival of the 'New Seekers in Cape Town' and item number 19 records the creation of a new 'Doggies' Loo', followed by an incomplete bracketed description of the accompanying photograph: a 'small enclosure on the Sea Point Beach Front'. Interspersed with these references to entertainment and leisure activities are items that contain only the bracketed description of a photograph, such as items 103 and 107, which are juxtaposed to highlight the stereotypes in conventional and normative western practices:

103 [Woman in bikini posing on double decker open
107 [Man in white coat apparently conducting scientific experim [*sic*]

Apart from the gender stereotypes that emerge in the above extract, the overall effect achieved in the listing of hacked phrases and incomplete images in this found poem is multifaceted: Firstly, the strategy reinforces the textuality of our shared experience of 'reality', by drawing attention to the mediated, media-driven record of our collective history. Secondly, the sudden omissions, at times mid-word, signal the other more significant gaps and silences in the recorded and partial footage. The world depicted is exclusively white and the preoccupations recorded are insular and privileged, as is evident in the repetitions of wholly trivial activities, which include the defecation habits of dogs (items 19 and 45), the routines of bathers (items 27, 30, 103, and 131) and leisure walkers (items 35 and 97) and the notification of celebrity visits (items 18 and 41), amongst others. The catalogue conceivably materialises out of Press's search for historical documentation relevant in tracking Sea Point's history, and items 2 through to 148 might then be considered representative of the archival material she discovered. With the exception of item 83, proclaiming the miscellaneous and generalising heading 'African Facts', it is a record that excludes and omits any reference to the political struggle that must have been raging concurrently. Thirdly, the catalogue reinforces the notion that our experience of the world, in addition to being received textually, through words, is also, as a result of global media practices, reliant on visualisation. Indeed, such practices have been instrumental in constructing the difference between 'fact' and 'fiction', in their elevation of photographic documentation as proof of the verisimilitude of the account. That the pictorial proof is in fact missing from Press's appropriated 'recorded history' (represented as it is in signs rather than images), further reinforces society's reliance on pictures to tell the truth, and may be read as Press's critique of the media in recording history and constructing reality. And finally, the snippet of overheard conversation directly beneath the 'poem' appears to have been included to reflect the attitudes that such narratives engender:

What naches?
You give your kids everything,
And then they turn around and do this to you.
A schoch she's living with. Here in Fresnaye.

A world as divorced from, but as afraid of, South African realities as the one depicted in the 'found poem' appears to be, might necessarily produce sentiments as prejudiced and resentful as the speaker of this overheard pronouncement implies. Despite the culturally specific colloquial clues,[120] the speaker is white, and thus unquestionably right, at least in relation to the discourse he espouses, which, as Press's 'Recorded History' demonstrates, emerges from a position of privileged insularity created and maintained at least partially by the media industry, but one which is threatened, as the extract suggests. Indeed, the snippet of conversation suggests the potential for a fluidifying of racial identity, even as the speaker vehemently and xenophobically rages against such a possibility, thus threatening to destabilise the conviction and its accompanying sense of superiority.

One of the most challenging 'found poems', called 'Rules Binding on all Owners and Residents' (1998: 42), demonstrates the difficulty of finding alternative co-ordinates, and the persistence of an inherited value system. The poem is reminiscent of Foucault's notion of social discipline and punishment, according to which we are conditioned into becoming good citizens. Panoptikon-like, the huge apartment blocks in Sea Point carry the insignia of conventionality. Each flat will almost certainly contain, usually as part of the lease agreement, the rules for social living, which attempt to police the boundaries of this 'most desirable location' (1998: 40). The rules, transcribed without intervention (and exposing Press to charges of real-estate copyright infringement!), provide a veritable catalogue of middle-class suburban mores. Here is the summarised version:

1. Overcrowding is strictly forbidden …
2. All refuse should be securely wrapped …
3. Washing must not be visible above the balcony parapet.
4. … windows should be covered with suitable curtaining …
5. Noise must be kept to a minimum …
6. The keeping of animals (including birds and reptiles) is strictly forbidden …
7. … taps are [to be] FULLY turned off …
8. The owner shall not place or do anything … aesthetically displeasing or undesirable …
9. [No] … gambling, running a brothel, [etc.] …
10. No unit may be used as a storeroom …

My interpretative list would appear as follows: remember the sanctity of the nuclear family, and subscribe to capitalist consumerism; do not display your dirty washing, keep up with the Jones's, and other related idiomatic 'universal truths'; maintain control and decorum, and promote proprietorship, uniformity and moral hygiene; uphold the boundaries between nature and culture, and the division between the public and the private spheres. Yet, the fact that these rules have to be drawn up (and in some cases displayed) suggests that society has not been successful at keeping 'undesirable' elements out of this 'location', and recalls Eric Lott's charge that the condition of whiteness (or at least the residue of middle-class western hegemony) 'requires continual effort to sustain' (1999: 241). In *Mythologies* (1972), Roland Barthes examines the ordinary ways in which bourgeois values are encoded in even the most seemingly trivial everyday texts and Press's interpolation of an actual list of rules for the tenants of Sea Point flats into an aesthetic space allows us to 'examine the normally hidden set of rules, codes and conventions through which meanings particular to specific social groups (i.e. those in power) are rendered universal and "given" for the whole of society' (Barthes in Hebdige 1993: 363).

In 'A Most Desirable Location' (1998: 40), the title itself mimicking the discourse of estate agencies, Press anticipates the regime reflected in 'Rules Binding on All Owners and Residents' (1998: 42) by recording the original documentation promoting and prescribing residency in Sea Point. A snippet of 1839 archival auctioneers' advertising highlights some of the reasons for 'the avidity with which ground is sought for' in Sea Point, the first being that:

> None of the lower class of the population
> either coloured or white
> reside within the limits of the Municipality
> except those in service and residing
> with the several proprietors.

The replication here of colonial officialdom's language of propriety and entitlement notwithstanding, it is precisely the dependency on the services of the 'lower class' that is responsible for the infiltration into this 'most desirable location' of the coloured maid and her entourage who trouble the following generations of settlers, as witnessed in the poem 'In Those Days' (1998: 23). This in turn accounts for the explicitness and ponderousness of the rules to which all future owners and residents must adhere (1998: 42). In addition to the early auctioneers' advertisement of a locality where there are no lower-class people, is their promise of one in which, since '*There are no Canteens*', 'crimes of drunkenness and theft are of more rare/occurrence than in any other district of the colony'. What these stuffy and self-righteous proclamations fail to predict is the extent of the leisured classes' will to consume, and Press's ironic invocation of these archival documents emerges in the residents' and visitors' contemporary experience of Sea Point, which as the baseline text demonstrates, as will be examined in the following subsection, is filled to capacity with 'canteens' selling 'wines spirituous' and 'malt liquors', and anything else that money can buy.

Press's endnote on 'The RDP comes to Sea Point' (1998: 48) states:

> The RDP, or Reconstruction and Development Programme, was a government programme of social welfare initiatives that existed briefly after the election of South Africa's first democratic government in 1994. (1998: 100)

The 'found poem' itself is a selection of extracts from local newspapers that comment on aspects of the initiative, mostly obliquely. For example, the first extract, entitled 'Dreams Do Come True', instead of featuring a redemptive story of social welfare for previously marginalised groups, as would be anticipated, contains a description of 'prime real estate' once inhabited by the coloured community, and now potentially the 'dream home' of some rich white man with 'architectural vision' and money enough to covet and own the view. In lieu of real reconstruction and development in the area, residents are apparently more concerned about default reconstructions necessary to keep Sea Point fully developed, perfectly appointed and safe, as the insert entitled 'New Abuse for Drain Covers' suggests, drain covers having become a popular instrument to aid car and house theft. Even further removed from the RDP is the third extract from local papers, this one hailing a 'New Gay Club for Sea Point'. Though it may suggest at first glance, at least an attempt to redress past imbalances, though in relation to gender rather than race and class, in its pseudo-acceptance of a homosexual community, it does so only to reinforce Sea Point as a place earmarked for exclusively upmarket tastes, accustomed to 'jacuzzis and steam baths', with the proviso that '[e]ntrance is by membership only'. The fourth extract appears to have been selected by Press to suggest the presumption that informs privileged white responses to their gathering sense of 'unhomeliness', and, along with the previous newspaper quotations, reinterprets the RDP as an empty gesture in the face of continued white power. Apparently written from the perspective of an irate taxpayer, the piece offers the city council some advice on how to manage the vagrancy problem in Sea Point, which entails moving the homeless out of the city, and 'appoint[ing] people with the right know-how to assist them to become self-sufficient'. But this 'commonsense wisdom' is radically undercut by the extract from the Smalls column that follows, one which advertises employment opportunities in Sea Point, the likes of which in many ways account for the vagrancy commented on in the previous insert, that is, casual domestic labour, in one instance offering employment in exchange for accommodation only. The quotation ascribed to Nelson Mandela ('RDP ONLY FOR THOSE WHO PAY'), and taken out of context, can only be read as hugely ironic in the light of these white responses during a time in which 'reconstruction and development' was being touted, and reinforces the tenacity of the sense of entitlement associated with white South African middle-class sensibilities.

Baseline Text: Advertising Excess
The baseline text, offering another apparently trivial text to examine, mimics a quintessential tourist brochure/guidebook discourse with its allure of exotic destinations neatly packaged for easy digestion. Hailing Sea Point as the 'gastronome's paradise' (1998: 16) and playing on the illusion of choice, a concomitant of capitalist commodification, the text moves from the most to the least desirable cuisine titbits, incorporating the mediocrity and ubiquity of fast-food chains in its trajectory, and ending with the waste found lying on the sidewalks and in garbage bins. Not even the seagulls want these morsels imbibed by the homeless, unemployed, largely coloured population. In moving from descriptions of mouth-watering upmarket cuisine to destitute garbage pile scraps, the text increasingly undermines the edible, 'consumerable' product it purports to advertise, from white privilege to black need.

Following the seven-part structure of the book, the baseline text offers a seven-day eating plan to the tourist/visitor and clearly Press is invoking biblical genesis here – God's creation of the world in six days, and His resting on the seventh – in order to suggest something about the interrelatedness of the mythical linear patterns governing western value systems, a point which will be reinforced in the following discussion. Mimicking the discourse of media advertising with references to 'Special Offers', the baseline text consciously foregrounds the commodification of difference, in relation to food. Each day in the seven-day eating plan marks an eating experience that decreases in value and satisfaction. The text begins with overtly cosmopolitan exotic tastes, purposefully eroticised[121] in sensually rich vocabulary in which the reader is invited to 'taste' 'the cuisine from every country, from British roast beef to Thai coconut and lemon-grass curry'. Day 1 recommends a 'quintessentially Sea Point' (1998: 26–27) eating experience, which in the context of the rest of the text must be read as quintessentially white, that is, expensive and exclusive. Day 2, consisting of 'Family Fare' (35), suggests a return to a wholesome bourgeois family value-for-money mode of consumerism in its recommendation that the visitor supports fast-food multinationals, citing a 'Wimpy Breakfast', a 'Spur' lunch and a 'St Elmo's' dinner. Day 3 announces itself as 'Detox Day' (45) and marks the consumerist 'desiring machine's' necessarily ambivalent relationship to food. In addition, it serves as a well-timed reminder that it is only the financially secure who can afford the binge-and-starve programme characteristic of eating disorders. Day 4 invites the visitor to try 'Traditional Treasures' (51), which is ironically a series of European establishments, offering traditional European menus, for the discerning cosmopolitan traveller, or at least for those with pretensions to being discerning and cosmopolitan. Day 5 is a 'Rediscovering Roots' day, which, besides the breakfast suggestion to ask any 'domestic worker to share her breakfast with you' (59), is a continuation (though a slightly seedier one) of the commodification of difference and the advertising of excess. Day 6 offers 'Special street treats [that] are plentiful and cheap' (68–72), which is just the next step away from the culminating images offered on Day 7 when God took his well-deserved rest: 'Bergie Basics' (84) is on the menu for this Sabbath. 'Be adventurous', the tourist is told, 'discover how local street survivors make it through the day', and thus, what ostensibly sets out to supply valuable information to prospective tourists, gathers ironic momentum and launches a scathing attack on the sensibilities of the passive white consumer of middle-class comfort and respectability. In pseudo-marketing and packaging sheer poverty, Press belies the easy assimilation of difference, and exposes the depth of the entrenchment of hierarchical practices policing the borders of social propriety.

The baseline text may be read in relation to an intricate web of race, class and gender discourses. It signals the assimilation and internalisation of cultural values and demonstrates, quite graphically, the continued effects of a race and class hierarchy in a seven-day diet plan – which in itself signals a western, specifically gendered, obsession with dieting and weight-loss, one related to the impossible ideal of a female form dictated to in patriarchal narratives of desire. What is interesting to note in this regard, as Robert Young has pointed out, is the conflation in the etymology of the word 'commerce', which 'includes the exchange of both merchandise and of bodies in sexual intercourse', since 'respectability, marriage, economic and sexual exchange were intimately bound up, coupled with each other from the first' (1995: 181–182). A western, middle-class, and largely gendered, obsession with food (the domestic responsibility for the purchasing and preparing of it and the dieting regime it produces) is an immediate association of a seven-day eating plan. It is the echo of these discourses that the baseline consciously navigates.

The baseline does not keep pace with the chapter divisions governing the poetry and may thus be read as deliberately destabilising the ordered chronology of linear time. However, each new day scrolled out in the seven-day eating plan coincides with a poem that may be read as an oblique response to the values embedded in the baseline. For example, Day 6 coincides with a poem entitled 'Twinkle Twinkle Little Star' (1998: 68), and constitutes a rethinking of the ontological certainties inscribed in the Christian account of the world's genesis (God's creation of the world in six days) and its subsequent history; and, by implication, in other central mythical and narrative accounts mapping western temporal and spatial co-ordinates. The nursery rhyme, for example, evoking a childish innocence, does not offer answers to the question posed in the line 'How I wonder what you are'. Instead, Press asks us to imagine other possible answers to that question, ones not dictated to by scientific (or religious) certainty. In an interview with Jane Rosenthal, Press has suggested that the poem was partly inspired by a newspaper story concerning a young girl's hang-gliding adventure (1998: 20). In this country, even now, one would not be off the mark to surmise that the hang-gliding girl was in all probability white, or at the very least, privileged enough to pursue *Getaway*-type high adventure sports. That the poet may have imagined a young white girl as the representative human presence in the poem, pushing 'you', the reader, over the edge of your frame of reference, may be read as Press's negotiation (whether conscious or not) of an inevitably recycled set of associations that seem to govern our responses:

> ... a little girl is running behind you
> pushing you as you float off the edge
> into the thermals that will carry you
> along the axes of your time-space continuum

It is the little girl who, as she 'keeps pushing the space/that you are flying in', is charged with the responsibility of 'carrying you along on another set of axes/outside your system of co-ordinates'. Though at first this image may suggest a new direction, since the girl is pushing you *out* of a particular continuum, the last lines of the poem return us to viciously cyclical replication:

[as] ... you move
further and further away ... she gets closer
to the edge where the thermals will fetch her
when whoever is running behind her
pushes

The little girl hang-gliding may have momentarily escaped some of the social constraints responsible for producing acceptable feminine behaviour, but she will almost certainly grow up to be one of any number of bigger white girls who might be heard to be partaking in the snippet of overheard conversation that appears on the opposite page:

Did you see his eyes?
I swear if he asks me out I'll just die. Is it true
he's the one in the Coke ad? My folks will kill me
but I don't care. I hear he takes girls
to Llandudno and they do it behind the rocks,
with wine and everything.
Do you think I should dye my hair black? (1998: 69)

These are the co-ordinates that are so damagingly limited, being, as they are, those of objectified, vulnerable and stupefied femininity, as well as of a consumerist, media-generated and depleted value system; in effect, a white suburban insularity that continues to exclude and exude a presupposed sense of its own normative neutrality.

End Poems

Throughout *Echo Location*, Press has adopted varying perspectives. Many of the first-person accounts, I have suggested, may be regarded as the writer's experiences, and demonstrate her recognition of herself as a product of the discourses she challenges. The few imaginative first-person accounts of other people's experiences contextualise and challenge the poet's own experiences and perspective, and here one recalls Press's imaginative entry into the subjectivity of Alida in '100% Silk' (1998: 30). Interspersed with these third-person narratives are the scraps of overheard, 'unmediated' conversation which add immediacy in creating a sense of the densely populated, layered and multiple realities to be found in Sea Point. Furthermore, there are narratives with no identifiable focaliser (i.e. the 'found poems'), which suggest an agentless and transparent perspective carrying social prescriptions and universal truths. There is even, as in the case of 'Twinkle Twinkle Little Star'

(1998: 68) and the entire baseline text, the second-person invocation of the reader which demands that she/he confronts her/his own positionality in relation to the discourses uncovered.

These fluctuations in focalising perspectives invite an examination of the final culminating perspectives recorded in the collection. The poems collected in the last chapter, which is entitled 'At the End of the Story', offer an increasingly elusive focalising perspective. 'Alida at Home' (1998: 93), for example, as has already been suggested, presents an almost disembodied present absence of one of the principle focalisers in the collection, to the extent that she merges with her surroundings, with her 'mountain top walls', and becomes not much more than a ghostly reflection: 'her chandeliers/light mirrored glass'. In 'View' (1998: 95), the autobiographical 'I' is replaced with the plural pronoun 'we' and incorporates all the residents of Sea Point who have paid an enormous price for their sea view, a price which the last lines identify not as monetary but psychological, in relation to 'our uninhabitable past pulling us back'. The first-person perspective appears to re-emerge in the final two poems, but the 'I' is no longer autobiographical, nor even singular, in that it seems to incorporate all of the perspectives that have been included thus far, as the following analysis of each will show.

'Seaworthy' (1998: 96), the penultimate poem, offers an alternative to the 'uninhabitable past' that much of the collection has demonstrated is residual in the present. The title recalls, at least implicitly, the earlier voyages of discovery that brought settlers to the southern tip of Africa, but the poet offers a vision of a different kind of journey and it is conceived of as a journey through time rather than space ('we are sailing into the deep century'). The 'I' persona may be read as a disembodied potentiality (with its 'childhood shoulders') that may emerge from the 'uninhabitable past', one that comes to terms with the trauma that the past has instilled, acknowledging the 'cuts and bruises', the 'weeping pavements', and the 'acid kisses' associated with the multiple realities of the inhabitants of Sea Point. It is an 'I' that offers the possibility of healing and protection as an alternative to arrogance and assumption. The strong present continuous verbs reinforce the protective, regenerative potentiality: 'I am rising [...]/I am coming out/to gird you [...]/I am casting my nets/over your glass sails with their arrogant wings [...]', and the false dreams of 'diamonds stashed in your wicked crow's nest'. It is a poem that laments the deep divisions of the past, with its 'northwest memory' and 'southeast curses' and offers a lifeline of a different kind to the anchoring ropes of occupation. In the transferred epithet the new amalgamated 'I' holds out a 'hand-knotted song, [as] your sounding line', and together with the plural incorporated in 'we are sailing into the deep century rising under us/not sinking', all of the elements of 'echo location' culminate in an alternative time/space continuum.

The last poem in the anthology, 'At the End of the Story' (1998: 98), to some extent counters the redemptive potential of 'Seaworthy' in the sense that the ghosts of the past return to haunt the speaker, who emerges in her capacity as poet-representative to suggest that there is no end to the story:

> I found them there, huddled like rotting deckchairs,
> counting their grievances off on transparent fingers.
> Passing around pictures of their grandchildren –
> the members of parliament and TV stars.
> Oblivious of time.

With their 'transparent fingers', their resentment, their nostalgia and their stereotypical preoccupations, these figures may be read as the echoing emptiness of whiteness as a ghostly present absence, and that Press is anticipating the end of their story or history. But the story does not end there: caught between 'memory and boredom', these apparitions continue to haunt the present, and '[o]bviously things aren't over yet'. The last line of the poem invokes the presence of 'Oupa Boeli' whom Press identifies in the endnotes (1998: 100) as a mythological 'disciplinary force' to keep children in line in nineteenth-century Sea Point, described as a 'malevolent old man, who would do nasty things to bad children'. Here the Law of the (white) Father is apparently fading, but still felt, and the story resists closure. The psychological baggage of an 'uninhabitable past' is carried into the 'deep century', and the echoes of the regime responsible for promoting social law and order, though fading, may still be located in the interstices ('in the invisible room, behind unseen walls') of the narratives inherited.

Conclusion

Of all its reviewers it is only Jeremy Cronin who offers a serious engagement with Karen Press's innovative achievement in *Echo Location*. For Cronin, the poems that are the most convincing are those 'that strike a personal note', though he would 'have preferred a little more integrative work from the poet herself, a little less of the merely found' (1998: 20). What I have attempted to demonstrate in this analysis is that the poems are never 'merely' found, and that the personal is always political. Dan Wylie's review, rather than offering a serious engagement with the poetry, is peppered with such phrases as 'feistily charming', 'winsome fun' and 'humane delicacy' (1998: 33), and one cannot help but hear a note of patronising dismissal in such observations, especially in his final recommendation to buy the book and 'drink it down', like a cold beer or a glass of cheap white wine. Similarly, Kelly Berman suggests that '[a]nyone who reads it with earnest analysis in mind will be duped' (1998: 74). The final question to be asked then is whether Press's contribution to post-apartheid literature is indeed worthy of scholarly consideration.

In an attempt to answer this question and to counter these reviewers' responses both to the collection of poems and this 'earnest' analysis, I turn to Biddy Martin and Chandra Mohanty, whose 'Feminist Politics: What's Home Got to Do With It!' seeks to answer a related question: that is, the adequacy and relevance of white western feminism in relation to the post-colonial concerns and experience of non-western women. The essay offers a favourable examination of a white woman writer's explicit negotiation of 'the relationship between home, identity and community that calls into question the notion of a coherent, historically continuous, stable identity ... by politicis[ing] the geography, demography, and architecture of communities' called 'home' (1997: 296). Press's poetry is marked by a profoundly political awareness of the relationships (outlined above) in her exploration of 'home'. If navigational echo location, as has been suggested, requires listening rather than seeing, and interpreting 'sound' rather than words, the text demonstrates the unconscious, unspoken ways in which white normativity continues to echo into the future.

Richard Dyer has pointed out that 'white power secures its dominance by seeming not to be anything in particular [and] also because when whiteness *qua* whiteness does come into focus, it is often revealed as emptiness, absence, denial or even a kind of death'. He goes on to suggest that contemporary post-colonial and postmodern centring of minority group issues has to some extent led to the reinforcement of the norm which 'carries on as if it is the natural, inevitable, ordinary way of being human' (1999: 457). In *Echo Location*, Press examines these seemingly 'ordinary' ways of being human, both historically and in the present, and shows them to be marked by a very real sense of echoing emptiness.

'Whiteness, the condition once assumed by diverse European settler communities, is no longer one to be cherished. Indeed, it is no longer a nice word', says Zoë Wicomb (2001: 169). White women writers such as Karen Press, who are themselves the products of this legacy, are actively negotiating their whiteness (and their womanhood) in relation to (post-)colonial realities and this particular collection of poems calls into question many of the assumptions that underpin the reifying myths that map a particularly narrow and limiting set of cultural co-ordinates.

6

Narratives of Madamhood in Suburban South Africa in Short Stories by Nadine Gordimer and by Marlene van Niekerk

> *I regard fiction [...] both as the document and as the agency of cultural history. I believe it helped to formulate the ordered space we now recognise as the household, made it totally functional, and used it as the context for representing normal behaviour. In so doing fiction contested and finally suppressed alternative bases for human relationships.*
> **Nancy Armstrong (1987: 26)**

Introduction

White South African suburbia in 2008 is much the same kind of space as it used to be during the height of apartheid. Though there are blacks moving into previously white residential areas, the ethos of these areas remains largely unaffected. Walls are still high, security gates and alarm systems are still compulsory, and black domestic employees present the same problems they always did: they are a necessity in maintaining excessively big homes and gardens, but 'they cannot be trusted', as whitespeak in South Africa would have it. The owners of these establishments are primarily middle class, mostly white, and anxiously protective of the goods accumulated inside. Security is the abiding preoccupation in white suburbia. Neighbourhood watches are popular and the general consensus is that the residents are sitting ducks, victims of rampant crime, unprotected by an overburdened police force and unassisted by the new black government that is accused consistently of not addressing the problem of urban crime adequately. The domestic spaces of white suburbia are overseen largely by white 'Madams',[122] whose representations are the focus of this chapter. Nadine Gordimer and Marlene van Niekerk have both written about the Madamhood phenomenon in short stories that depict the unhomeliness and discomfort of white women occupying these comfortable and privileged spaces.

The stories appear in David Medalie's 1998 collection, entitled *Encounters: An Anthology of South African Short Stories*, and in Michael Chapman's revised collection of South African short stories published in 2004, *The New Century of South African Short Stories*. That both anthologies were compiled in post-apartheid South Africa is partly the justification for including in this chapter stories not necessarily written since 1994. The other part of the rationale is that all are angry indictments of white suburban insularity that has its roots in apartheid but has not disappeared in the new South Africa. Whereas Gordimer's stories 'Enemies' (1956), 'Comrades' (1991) and 'Once Upon A Time' (1991) depict white suburban anxieties for suburban Madams before the demise of apartheid, Van Niekerk's story 'Labour' (2004) examines a similar set of anxieties in post-apartheid South Africa. The stories thus lend themselves to analytical juxtaposition in which the symptoms that each of the writers interrogates is examined, and one which foregrounds the residual effects of Madamhood, traced back to the 1950s and forward into the twenty-first century, thus demonstrating the power of past narratives in symptomatically informing contemporary racial dynamics. None of the stories may be said to be representative of the extraordinary oeuvre of these two important South African writers and it may be argued that their full-length works offer much more scope in studying whiteness and womanhood in South African women's writing. The inclusion of these stories in particular, however, apart from facilitating the multigeneric character of this study, is meant to reflect something of the ways in which two prominent writers have scrupulously interrogated whiteness in an ostensibly less important genre perhaps more effectively than writers such as Antjie Krog who have written weighty tomes on the subject.

Michael Chapman has suggested a possible rebirth of shorter fiction in a country marked by the painful negotiation of transition in his rationale for the inclusion of the multiple and previously marginal perspectives emerging in post-apartheid South African storytelling:

> Such a variegated landscape, or cityscape, is not suited to the novel. The variety is better captured in an anthology of individual stories: stories that grasp the

future possibilities of what the past has made available to us; stories that help us think backwards (how did I arrive where I am?) while understanding ways forward (what shall I, or we, do next?). (2004: xx)

The short stories under scrutiny in this chapter reflect something of the stranglehold the past still exerts on us, and embody Chapman's bracketed questions in confronting the violence of exclusion that inheres in maintaining white privilege and insularity. That both Medalie and Chapman chose to include *these* short stories amongst the dozens that Gordimer has written to represent one of South Africa's most famous writers in their overtly post-apartheid collections of South African short fiction suggests their recognition of the power and continued relevance of each story. In addition, as Ileana Dimitriu has noted (2000: 147–148), relatively little critical attention has been expended on Gordimer's short fiction, with the exception of Dominic Head's study published in 1994 and her own more recent contribution. This seems a curious omission, given the centrality of Gordimer as one of South Africa's most anthologised short-story writers, but perhaps, as Dimitriu suggests, this phenomenon may be attributed to a general perception amongst Gordimer scholars that her short stories are more 'universal' and do not engage seriously with the sociopolitical crises that her novels examine (147–148), though this, as I will argue, is a fundamental misperception of the short story generally, and of Gordimer's deployment of the genre specifically.

Nadine Gordimer's Short Fiction
Nadine Gordimer's fiction has typically offered a severely critical reading of white women's complicity and/or ineffectuality in facing South African racialised realities. One need look no further than her characterisation of Maureen in *July's People* (1980) for confirmation of this tendency, but her depiction of the ethical impossibilities confronting middle-aged, middle-class white women in the case studies of Mrs Clara Hansen in 'Enemies', Mrs Hattie Telford in 'Comrades', and the anonymous Wife in 'Once Upon A Time', bears witness to her enduring remonstration with insulated, lonely, selfish white womanhood. The portraits in miniature of Clara Hansen and Hattie Telford are largely modernist 'slice of life'[123] stories rendered in minute and detailed gestures, the significance of which reverberate and resonate so that the reader recognises the peculiarly South African predicament that marks these women's experiences of 'race'. A 'fundamental property' of the short story is its capacity to render 'ambiguity', according to Dominic Head (1994: 162), and

Gordimer's short stories have consistently offered 'problematic ambiguities between self and other', notes Barbara Eckstein (1985: 343). These ambiguities between self and other are crucially political in the three women characters featured in the stories, as the following analysis will demonstrate.

In 'Once Upon a Time', Gordimer uncharacteristically abandons her (anti-) realist mode of representation in favour of the fairy-tale format, which she deploys in much the same way as Alexander Pope employed the epic format (in *The Rape of the Lock*) to satirical effect: that is, in foregrounding simultaneously the ways in which form and genre dictate 'reality', and 'reality' dictates form and genre, and in doing so, to expose the artificiality of both.[124] The white suburban bourgeois nuclear family is the central 'reality' in all three stories, regardless of the ages or marital status of the white Madams depicted: they are all products of a profound sense of 'unhomeliness', which, no matter how comfortable and spacious the house is that each occupies, makes it impossible for any of them to live 'happily ever after'. Grant Farred notes that the 'real hegemony, white property, remains in place' (1999: 65) and that South Africa is 'a country rapidly becoming inhospitable to, if not uninhabitable by, its white occupants. The unhomeliness derives [...] from post-apartheid South Africa's inability to provide physical and mental sanctuary for a community accustomed to such protection by virtue of its race' (1999: 73). Though Farred is describing contemporary South Africa, apartheid South Africa was no less 'unhomely', only less uncomfortably so.

'Enemies'

Mrs Clare Hansen of 'Enemies' is an elderly aristocratic widow who embarks on a train trip from Cape Town to Johannesburg, leaving her 'faithful' and long-serving Malay chauffeur and manservant, Alfred, to look after her worldly possessions in her six-week absence. The story's ambiguous title draws the reader's attention initially to the curiously intimate and simultaneously antagonistic dialectic that characterises the relationship between Mrs Hansen and Alfred, whom she suspects of devious mismanagement of her orders, but who is nonetheless clearly devoted to the old woman, ensuring that she remembers her spectacles and sleeping pills while equally prepared to take advantage of her unsupervised amenities in her absence (1998: 53). Though most of the story is rendered from the point of view of Mrs Hansen, Gordimer's employment of free indirect speech allows her momentarily to enter Alfred's consciousness to confirm his employer's suspicion that his intentions are not above reproach:

Did she know; with that face that looked as if it knew everything, could she know, too, about the two friends in the house in the Malay quarter? (1998: 53)

This isolated entry into Alfred's thoughts may at first appear to be an authorial inconsistency, but it has the effect of reinforcing the lack of control that Mrs Hansen dreads exhibiting. If indeed Alfred is planning to fetch his friends in Mrs Hansen's car as soon as the train departs, then clearly she is not in control of her servant, and consequently not as in control of her life of white privilege as she would like to be. We hear in the opening paragraph of the story that she had once been 'a baroness and a beauty' who had 'survived dramatic suffering' and that her demeanour reflects her past, making her unapproachable in her dignity, her 'face withdrawn as a castle' (1998: 52). It is not long, however, before it becomes apparent that her public persona of rigidly guarded superiority is at odds with her private persona, whom she refers to in the third person as 'old fool' (1998: 55) – her ageing, vulnerable self.

Whereas Alfred may pose some kind of vague threat in her perception of him as a potential enemy, it is Mrs Hansen's encounter on the train with an elderly woman that provides another possible enemy in the form of Nemesis. This other woman remains anonymous and Mrs Hansen despises her on account ostensibly of her weight ('Fat overflowed not only from her jowl to her neck, but from her ankles to her shoes' [54]), and her *petit bourgeois* vulgarity. It becomes apparent, however, that it is neither the bourgeois mannerisms nor the buxom shape of the fellow traveller that Mrs Hansen really despises, but the lonely, marginal existence that she experiences in her own life, reflected in the other old woman with whom she reluctantly has dinner on the overnight train trip, and who dies in her sleep that same night. What Clara Hansen fears is that she is even more of a lonely, isolated and insignificant 'old fool' than the bumbling, bloated old woman in the next compartment. Gordimer's confrontation here is with the politics of gender, class and race as she exposes the exclusions and denials in the service of white upper middle-class womanhood. These exclusions and denials become apparent in the closing moments of the story. Mrs Hansen's final gesture, in anticipation that the woman's death might have been reported in the local newspapers, is to send Alfred a telegram: 'IT WAS NOT ME. CLARA HANSEN.' (1998: 62), which despite being expedited with calculated glee, constitutes a failed attempt at validating her own existence – she may have safeguarded her possessions against Alfred's covetous advances, but her eventual demise might well be more anonymous and unnewsworthy than the old woman's in the adjoining compartment is likely to have been. And her attempt at validating her existence is ironically cast in the negative: 'It was *not* me.' Both women on the train have been abandoned by the world because they are women who have grown old. They are in fact known solely by what they are not. They are not young, they are not accompanied, and they no longer have husbands or families to look after, and neither of them even has a name (Mrs Clara Hansen has her husband's name, and her travelling companion is anonymous). Having outlived their market value of pro(re-)creation, they have been relegated to endure each other's unremarkable and painfully self-obsessed company, and though the anonymous old woman makes the best of what is left over, munching away at high-cholesterol ox-tail stew along with everything else on the menu (and dying possibly 'of greed', as her travelling companion would have it), her regaling Mrs Hansen with the dead-boring details of her clichéd existence (1998: 58–59) allows Mrs Hanson only momentarily to believe that she is superior. Indeed, so self-absorbed are these two elderly women, but particularly the protagonist, that their real enemies are themselves (1998: 55) rather than the dark Other at the borders of their consciences, or perhaps more accurately, *because* of the dark Other at the borders of their consciences, though the narrative only hints at their presence. Africa does not exist for Clara or her alter ego, except in the vague and ambiguous threat posed by Alfred, whose dark figure we last saw lurking at the edge of the old woman's vision as the train departed from Cape Town Station. While the train moves through the African night, Mrs Hansen pictures only darkness, grass and telephone poles. Nothing else. In her insulated little world, she might never have left Europe, and the letters in her handbag notwithstanding, she might as well not have.

The 1950s would most certainly have produced women such as these in South Africa. Mrs Hansen's loneliness and anxiousness coupled with her vigilant sense of social decorum makes her a pathetic victim of patriarchal oppression on one hand, and a perpetrator of sexist, classist and racist prejudices on the other. Her travelling companion's obsession with food and her daughters' lives suggests that despite her lack of the measured control that Mrs Hansen exhibits, her life is equally as empty and as insular. What remains disturbing, though, is that the kind of white South African womanhood this story depicts remains wholly recognisable more than half a century later. Rather than sending Alfred a telegram, a contemporary Clara Hansen might send him an SMS, but technological advancement aside, the racial anxieties of Madamhood, and the social dictates of white class-conscious womanhood continue to rule much of suburban South Africa.

'Comrades'

If Mrs Hansen fails to identify the real enemy in Gordimer's 1950s story, it is left to Mrs Hattie Telford of her 1991 story 'Comrades' to understand the real implications of comradeship in a climate antipathetic to anything but animosity. In contrast to the initial identification of Mrs Hansen as ageing baroness and beauty, in this story the female protagonist is identified in the opening paragraph as an educated, leftist, liberal activist, a 1990s (stereo-)type no less plausible than the 1950s Mrs Hansen. The reader encounters Mrs Hattie Telford as she is emerging from a university conference on People's Education at which black and white activists have been sharing in the comradeship of mutual resistance to apartheid. The efficacy and ethical value of her participation at such an event, however, is undone before it is even narrated, in the opening lines of the story:

> As Mrs Hattie Telford pressed the electronic gadget that deactivates the alarm device in her car a group of youngsters came up behind her. Black. But no need to be afraid; this was not a city street. This was a non-racial enclave of learning, a place where tended flowerbeds and trees bearing botanical identification plates civilised the wild reminder of campus guards and dogs. (1998: 148)

Despite the liberal humanist political affiliation of Hattie Telford, it is her gut response here that Gordimer is foregrounding. In white South Africa, now as then, a group of black youths materialising next to a parked car occupied by a white person typically means instantaneous and unbridled fear, hence the author's signalling of this in the singular 'sentence', 'Black', which has the effect of demonstrating the conditioning that promotes such a knee-jerk response. Gordimer appears to be equally critical of the insularity of academic institutions that host such conferences in her recognition of the paradox signalled in the botanical order on one hand and the campus guards and their dogs on the other, all of which is filtered through the focalising perspective of Mrs Hattie Telford, recipient of the privilege and paranoia that white academia, white guilt and white anxieties have respectively bestowed on her. The group, it turns out, is a delegation from the ANC Youth Movement with whom she was sharing comradeship only moments earlier in the hall. For this misjudgement she will have to make amends in order to ease the burden of guilt.

If her ambivalence is pronounced in this initial encounter, it is as evident in her next response, which is elicited when one of the youngsters asks whether she is going in to town, because they need a lift. Instead of saying that she is going in the opposite direction as she intends to, she finds herself 'entering the spirit' of the conference she has just attended with its 'stamping and singing Freedom songs' (1998: 149) and complying with the request. It is now that she has committed herself to acting on her liberal, leftist sentiments that her position becomes more and more uncomfortable. After some small talk the group indicates that they are hungry, a simple fact that clearly cannot be ignored by someone who claims, as she does, to be humanist. After this announcement there is silence in the car, and the reader is exposed to the thoughts that someone like Mrs Hattie Telford might be thinking:

> These large gatherings both excited and left her over-exposed, open and vulnerable to the rub and twitch of the mass shuffling across rows of seats and loping up aisles, babies' fudge-brown soft legs waving as their napkins are changed on mothers' laps, little girls with plaited loops on their heads listening like old crones, heavy women swaying to chants, men with fierce, unreadably black faces breaking into harmony tender and deep as they sing to God for his protection of Umkhonto weSizwe, as people on both sides have always, everywhere, claimed divine protection for their soldiers, their wars. (1998: 149)

It is no surprise that the white liberal woman feels conflicted but mostly vulnerable in such situations: neither her insular and self-preserving white suburban lifestyle, nor her educated liberal humanism has prepared her for this mass of oppressed humanity, and her alienation is manifest in the very images she uses to describe the event. She does not see or hear people. What she hears is the 'rub and twitch of mass shuffling' and what she sees is dislocated body parts, 'fudge-brown soft legs waving', 'plaited loops' of hair, and anonymous 'heavy women swaying', men 'with fierce, unreadably black faces'.

The settler, as Fanon has shown, does not *see* the native,[125] or as Arundhati Roy more recently has argued, the white person does not see the person of colour.[126] Despite educated and liberal proclamations to the contrary, it is the dehumanised image of the inalienable other that Mrs Hattie Telford sees. And though the generalisation about all armies calling on God to be on their side is moot, it does rather diminish the one this white woman is ostensibly supporting. Having identified the cause of her anxiety, Mrs Hattie Telford admits to herself that '[at] the end of a day like this she wanted a drink, she wanted the depraved luxury of solitude and quiet in which she would be restored (enriched, oh yes! by the day) to the familiar limits of her own being' (1998: 149–150). Essentially what she wants is to appease her superfluous white guilt without having to sacrifice an iota of her comfortable white privilege, a desire she only half acknowledges in her choice of the phrase 'depraved luxury' but belies in the over-qualifying parenthetical aside, the sentiments of which, were she to have articulated them, could only have been met with derision by her black comrades with whom she shared the day's proceedings. The word 'hungry', however, returns her to the immediate crisis of appeasing her white guilt and she is required to suppress her desire for 'iced whiskey and feet up' in order to accommodate the less luxurious needs of the hungry youths in the car. Her hesitation in replying to the implied request when they tell her that they are hungry constitutes the third in a series of gestures that signal Mrs Hattie Telford's difficulty in converting liberal sentiments into genuine action.

Having invited them back to her house for something to eat before she takes them into town, our protagonist finds that there are a few unforeseen domestic realities to negotiate which make her position seem increasingly compromised. Her home signifies sheer opulence to the young boys, and once the Madam has safely kept the big dog in check, and silently and self-consciously justified her decision to lead them in through the back door, her next dilemma emerges when the lunch is ready to be served: 'she suddenly did not want them to see that the maid waited on her. She herself carried the heavy tray into the dining-room.' If her gestures thus far have been marked by ambivalences, this one is nothing short of an outright lie. It is a lie which ends the first section of the story, and hangs in the air, as it were, during the course of the meal. Her life of excess is made manifest in relation to the youths' deprivation: at one point she realises that the meal may not be adequate and offers them fruit from the big copper bowl which is described as a laden 'edible still life' (1998: 151), the abundance of fruit it contains thus placed on the dining-room table for visual delight rather than basic sustenance.

In addition, her attempt at polite conversation exposes her ignorance of the very realities she is supposedly committed, as an activist, to change. She asks one of them whether he goes to school and realises almost immediately that the question emanates from a space of comfortable bourgeois safety: these boys are 'not going to be saying they've been selected for the 1st Eleven at cricket or that they're off on a student tour of Europe in the school holidays' (1998: 152). To break the next uncomfortable silence, she asks them if they like her wooden carving of a lion, and in an attempt at some kind of identification with them, remarks that the artist responsible is a Zimbabwean called Dube. It is at this point, in the final moments of the story, that her 'foolishness' becomes apparent to her:

Dumile, in his gaze – distant, lingering, speechless this time – reveals what has overwhelmed them. In this room, the space, the expensive antique chandelier, the consciously simple choice of reed blinds, the carved lion: all are on the same level of impact, phenomena undifferentiated, indecipherable. Only the food that fed their hunger was real. (1998: 152)

This may certainly be read as an 'equivocal epiphany' similar in effect to those that mark the short fiction of modernists such as Virginia Woolf and Katherine Mansfield.[127] Mrs Hattie Telford's sense of momentary displacement is powerful, as she observes her taste, her values, her subjectivity and individuality, indeed her white western womanhood, through the eyes of those who have been forcibly displaced to make room for her, and that constitutes her epiphany. The equivocation resides in the fact that she will continue to occupy that space of comfort, albeit a little less comfortably.

'Once Upon a Time'

In order to examine the 'unhomeliness' and 'dis-ease' of white suburbia more vigorously, Gordimer adopts, in 'Once Upon A Time', the 'universal', 'recognisable' and wholly fabricated and fantastical 'happily-ever-after' fairy-tale mode of storytelling. Though all cultural groups generate their own folk tales, which are passed on traditionally from one generation to the next, the fairy-tale format upon which Gordimer is drawing is a white western European phenomenon, and its 'universality' reinforces the effects of western hegemony. Gordimer claims in the framing narrative to have been inspired by a request to contribute a story to a children's anthology, and to have rejected it on account of the fact that she does not 'write children's stories' and does not believe she 'ought' to be obliged to write anything on command (2004: 236). Of course, the story she produces as a result of this incident is hardly an appropriate bedtime story for children, though no less gruesome and violent than the average fairy-tale, only just a tad too close to home for comfort. I interpret her choice of the fairy-tale as hinging on several possible considerations which I shall address consecutively in the following discussion of the story.

'Once Upon A Time' is Gordimer's radical rewriting of conventional fairy-tales, those seemingly innocent children's stories that are morally didactic in purpose, presenting children with 'universal' truths that teach them to accept their allotted role and space in the world. Much work has already been done by feminist writers and scholars in rewriting and rethinking the fairy-tale[128] in order to examine the gender politics embedded in the stories as they have passed through the ages and travelled to different places. These stories, which emerge out of European traditions and were appropriated from orality and censored by the Brothers Grimm, amongst others, became vehicles for passing on the gender prescriptions needed to sustain the heterosexual status quo. Gordimer's tale subverts the standard fairy-tale in several ways: firstly, it does not feature the prerequisite passive female heroine in need of rescuing – an unnamed little boy is the (anti-)hero of the story; secondly, it begins at the end of the standard tale when the married couple are already living the 'happily-ever-after' bit; thirdly, the tale offers no 'happily-ever-after' resolution at the end, and finally, having subverted all of the above expectations, the tale exposes the dangerous reproductivity of the moral lessons inherent in fairy-tales, and the racial and gender norms espoused in them, and thus the potential for subversion that emerges is one of the major considerations in Gordimer's deployment of the genre.

The fairy-tale format, like the Van der Merwe joke, is so instantly recognisable that it offers the writer plenty of scope for satirical appropriation. The stories have universal appeal, in the sense that having emanated from Europe and travelled beyond the western world in the suitcases and psyches of European settlers across the globe, Sleeping Beauty and Snow White are better known characters in the world at large than, for example, Tokoloshe or Tsotsi have been. Primarily, then, it is the 'universality' principle that Gordimer is exploiting. The story begins '[in] a house, in a suburb, in a city, [where] there were a man and his wife who loved each other very much and were living happily ever after' (2004: 237). Thus, Gordimer's tale begins at the end of the traditional tale and in doing so challenges linear and teleological narrative as well as questions the honesty of such unlikely narrative closures in foreclosing on the more probable, untold outcome for the compulsory bourgeois nuclear family, which is the most essential unit in maintaining the current economy of being. In addition, the repetition of the indefinite article 'a' suggests that the house in question could be any house in any suburb of a city anywhere, and that the couple are Everycouple, representative of Man and Wife living representative compulsory heterosexual lives in the service of compulsory procreation and conspicuous consumption. Indeed, if one were to encounter this story in some other anthology *sans* the framing narrative with its reference to Chopi and Tsanga migrant miners and gold mining, and in the unlikelihood that one had never heard of Nadine Gordimer, one might be left guessing about the geographical setting of the story, at least initially, so universally western is the set of criteria by which this couple live their lives: they have the prerequisite cat and licensed dog, a car and a caravan, a swimming pool and medical aid, a housemaid and a gardener and a subscription to the local Neighbourhood Watch. But what becomes increasingly apparent is not so much the universality of the white couple's material circumstances but the universality of the violence upon which it is built, and the ways in which the violence is simply more overt, being officially sanctioned in apartheid South Africa. Being more overt, it is also simply more absurd, fantastical even. Thus, the fairy-tale mode, satirically deployed, sets up white South Africa as an allegorical kingdom, replete with castles and thorny briars protecting its perimeters, and like the sign informing would-be intruders: 'YOU HAVE BEEN WARNED' (2004: 237–238), the reader of this subversive fairy-tale is warned that such a lifestyle comes at a price.

That price is revealed in a related explanation for Gordimer's use of the fairy-tale: there is always a moral lesson to be learned. The villains and the wicked witches get punished, the heroines get rescued, the rich princes get to marry the most beautiful damsels, and social order is restored. In Gordimer's story none of these ingredients is mixed in correctly: the villains and wicked witch go unpunished, the Man and his Wife are clearly not living happily ever after and the illusion of social order is all but destroyed. But the most significant variant is that the little prince, rather than obtaining his just reward, gets severely punished. The villains in this tale are 'the people of another colour' who live outside of white suburbia, who are so bad that 'police and soldiers and tear gas and guns' (2004: 237) are needed to keep them away. They are allowed into suburbia only in the capacity of 'reliable housemaids and gardeners', but when they return to their quarters they experience 'buses [being] burned, cars stoned, and children shot by the police'. So to protect themselves from these dangerous enemies Everycouple build themselves an impenetrable fortress in the likeness of the average white South African suburban home. The wicked witch of the tale is (inevitably in white suburban nuclear family life) the Mother-in-Law whose interfering, overbearing presence is suggested rather than felt, in being labelled 'Wicked Witch' and making Everycouple beholden to her in sponsoring their fear-induced alterations to their suburban abode (2004: 239). The Man and his Wife are living the opposite of the fairy-tale promise: their existence is dictated to by an increasing fear of the dark villains inhabiting the quarters beyond suburbia, and despite every home comfort their responses are only ever ill at ease. When Husband and Wife and Little Boy take a walk in the leafy suburb they no longer stop to 'admire this show of roses or that perfect lawn'. Having become so obsessed with security, all they notice is the 'aesthetics of prison architecture' (2004: 239) dominating the neighbourhood. But it is the son of Everycouple who is ironically both the little prince *and* the victim in the story. For Christmas he is given a book of fairy-tales and one day, after having heard the tale of the prince 'who braves the terrible thicket of thorns to enter the palace and kiss his Sleeping Beauty' (2004: 240), he decides to re-enact the scene. The tale of Prince Charming teaches him the qualities that white masculinity requires of him: he learns that boys are brave and active, and that girls are passive and in need of rescuing, and that white boys will in all likelihood grow up to be brave and handsome princes, own castles, and rescue pale and ailing maidens in distress. By this time, having put up warning signs, installed alarms, extended the height of the walls, the married couple have taken the ultimate step in protecting their property in the form of 'DRAGON'S TEETH', consisting of a 'continuous coil of stiff and shining metal serrated into jagged blades' which has been placed along the length of the property's six-foot walls, creating the perfect thicket of thorns for the young prince to test his courage against. Needless to say, the social order is maintained only at extreme expense.

But there is one final reason for Gordimer's deployment of the fairy-tale: above all it is an oral tale, passed on from generation to generation, subject to revision and reinterpretation, depending on the teller and the audience. This story ends with the 'bleeding mass' of the little boy's body being 'hacked out of the security coil with saws, wire-cutters, choppers' and carried into the house by 'the man, his wife, the hysterical trusted housemaid and the weeping gardener' (2004: 240). Whether he is dead or alive we do not know, but the standard closure to a story that begins 'Once Upon A Time' is violently undercut. However, if this tale, like others in the genre, carries the potential for oral transmission from one generation to another, then it carries the potential also to be revised. At the end of *Beloved* (1987), Toni Morrison's narrator repeats three times: 'It was not a story to pass on' (1997. 274–275). The repetition constitutes an almost spiritual incantation to ward off the trauma and humiliation inflicted on future generations of African-Americans as a result of slavery. In a sense, Gordimer might be saying the same thing to white South Africans: that this is not a tale to pass on. So we leave the typical South African suburban nuclear family there, carrying the body of a mutilated child, and as the couple and their dark doubles disappear into the house, it strikes the reader that it is perhaps the very configuration of this nuclear assembly itself that has to be transformed to prevent the story from being endlessly and tragically reproduced.

As long as Man and his Wife, and all of the politics that controls the formal marital relationship, remain the custodians of children's realities and dreams, as long as the couple remains trapped behind big walls and barbed wire, and as long as they are religiously accompanied by a pair of subservient and docile slaves, the story will, inevitably, be passed on.

Margaret Atwood's 'Four Basic Victim Positions' (1996: 37–39) may be invoked as useful co-ordinates in analysing the white women in Gordimer's short fiction. The widows and wives in all three stories appear to be trapped in denial, yet all three are victims of the fairy-tales (or grand narratives) that delimit their lives as women. Simultaneously, as white South African middle-class women, all three are perpetrators of the class and race narratives imbricated in those self-same social fictions. Gordimer's use of free indirect speech in the first two modernist stories, and her patent exploitation of omniscience in the third story make it interesting to plot *her* responses to the women characters she depicts. Clearly she is scathingly critical of the generic Wife in 'Once Upon A Time', but she is not as unambiguously disapproving of Mrs Clara Hansen and Mrs Hattie Telford. The care with which she attends to the most trivial gestures and minutiae that adorn the lonely, empty lives of these ageing women suggests her ambivalence, in sympathising with their predicament as women, but at the same time challenging the assumptions that their whiteness engenders. Gordimer's contributions to a precarious sense of *be-longing* facing white South Africans in the three stories re-anthologised in post-apartheid short-story collections are arguably as valuable and relevant today as barometers of white western preoccupations as they were when originally published, and they make the writer a creative non-perpetrator in white South African women's writing of the racist discourses that inhere in suburban myths. The women she depicts in each story reflect aspects of white western Madamhood that continue to make white South African suburbia the uncomfortable and 'unhomely' space it has always been, where once upon a time their enemies are mistaken for comrades, their comrades for enemies, and happily ever after remains the little white lie that continues to sustain their miserable *un*-belonging.

'Labour' or 'Small Finger Exercise on the Notion of Hybridity'
Marlene van Niekerk's short story 'Labour' demonstrates that the legacy of white Madamhood that Gordimer has so accurately observed lives on in the new South Africa. The story was originally published in 2001 in an anthology entitled *Briewe deur die lug*, edited by Etienne van Heerden.[129] Translated by Michiel Heyns, the

English version appeared in Michael Chapman's anthology, *A New Century of South African Short Stories*, published in 2004. The story was originally entitled 'Klein vingeroefening rondom die nosie van hibriditeit'[130] and appears in a subsection of the anthology dealing with issues of hybridity. Unlike Antjie Krog, who publishes in both English and Afrikaans, and whose prose is largely categorised as non-fiction, Van Niekerk is a writer known primarily for her Afrikaans fiction (though she also publishes literary criticism). Both writers, however, are equally preoccupied with a current crisis of whiteness in post-apartheid South Africa. The inclusion of Van Niekerk hinges on one important consideration: as both Melissa Steyn's and Zoë Wicomb's scholarship suggests, the historical divide between English- and Afrikaans-speaking white South Africans, at the risk of over-simplifying, may best be understood in relation to the ostensible innocent and benevolent liberalism of the former, and the supposed conservative culpability of the latter group. As Steyn has rightly observed, there is a marked cultural chauvinism of Englishness in South Africa, and though, as Wicomb has suggested, in the light of Antjie Krog's examination in *Country of My Skull* of the ways in which 'Afrikaner' like 'whiteness' is 'no longer a nice word', 'the struggle [to rehabilitate the cultural category 'Afrikaner' in contemporary Afrikaans literature] implicates the other binary opposition, relations with Englishness. And whilst English in fact assumes national language status, that space of cultural and linguistic capital is necessarily one where whiteness will continue to reside in silence and anonymity' (2001: 180). Given the English claim to liberalism, it is 'poetic justice' that the white Afrikaner woman writer, rather than her English counterparts, provides this final and most indicting examination of the politics of suburban domestic whiteness in post-apartheid South Africa.

As Bhabha has pointed out in 'The White Stuff':

> [s]ince 'whiteness' naturalises the claim to social power and epistemological privilege, displacing its position cannot be achieved by raising the 'gaze of the other' or by provoking the 'return' of the repressed or the oppressed. The *subversive* move is to reveal within the very integuments of 'whiteness' the agonistic elements that make it the unsettled, disturbed form of authority it is – the incommensurable 'differences' that it must surmount; the histories of trauma and terror that it must perpetrate and from which it must protect itself, the amnesia it imposes on itself; the violence it inflicts in the process of becoming a transparent and transcendent force of authority. (1998: 21)

Van Niekerk's 'Labour' is a subversive story that reveals 'the very integuments of "whiteness"', and confronts the 'violence it inflicts' in becoming 'a transparent and transcendent force of authority'. Serving as noun, verb and adjective, the word 'labour' carries multiple meanings, not the least of which are its associations with capitalism and reproduction, and in South Africa, 'black labour, white guilt' to quote a notorious brand satire T-shirt slogan.[131] Indeed, 'labour' serves as a euphemism in this story for a particularly South African suburban labour practice: the shameless exploitation in white suburbia of black labour, with men, often called 'boys', working in the garden and women, often called 'girls', working in the house. Suburbia in South Africa remains as insular as ever a decade into democracy, though not as secure as it was during apartheid when laws protected whites from '*die swart gevaar*'.[132] Van Niekerk is powerfully aware of the connotations the word 'labour' will conjure in its solo capacity as title, signalling what Dreama Moon (1999: 188) has called 'euphemistic whitespeak' as ludicrous in its effort to sustain its 'unsettled, disturbed [though powerful] form of authority' (Bhabha 1998: 21).

The story is set in Stellenbosch, a place steeped in Cape Dutch history and symbolising the strength and wealth of Afrikanerdom, boasting multiple successful and lucrative wine estates and, of course, the University of Stellenbosch, home of the white Afrikaner intellectual. Much like Sophiatown or District Six have come to symbolise the violence and trauma of forced removals during the apartheid regime, Stellenbosch, in this story, may be read as symbolising a comfortable white suburban gentility, the kind that K. Davy suggests is 'a bedrock concept of imperialism [...] that encompasses a plethora of values, morals, and mores that determine [...] the tenets of respectability in general' (1995: 198). The dramatis personae needed to stage what Ruth Frankenberg has conceived of as the drama of imperial history appear in Van Niekerk's story: 'White Woman, White Man, Man of Color, Woman of Color' (1997: 11), though the primary characters are, to use Frankenberg's terms, White Woman and Man of Color. It is the complementarities that Frankenberg is interested in examining, finding, as she does, that White Woman has to be 'frail, vulnerable, delicate, sexually pure but at times led "astray"' in order for Man of Color to be 'sexually rapacious, sometimes seductive, usually predatory, especially toward White Woman' (1997: 11–12). What she also notes is the unstable position of White Woman as the imperial drama plays itself out: her 'ambiguous and ambivalent status' means:

she is, on the one hand, accorded privileges and status by this race/gender positioning, and, on the other hand, confined by it. In any case she is advantaged only conditionally on her acceptance of the terms of the contract. This includes especially her sexual practices, for the trope-ical family is strictly heterosexual and monoracial in its coupling (with the exception that White Man may have unofficial liaisons with Woman of Color, with or without her consent). (1997: 12)

It is precisely this position of ambivalence confronting White Woman, descendant of the earlier 'trope-ical' family, that Van Niekerk is examining in 'Labour'. One of the first and most significant manifestations of this ambivalence is in relation to a noticeable shift as the narrative unfolds between first- and third-person perspectives. Indeed, the narrator, who calls herself 'Marlene', and is clearly the barely disguised figure of 'Marlene van Niekerk' the writer, admits at one point that her 'tongue is forked' (2004: 306), an image of doubleness, of duplicity, discussed later in this section.

The story begins conventionally enough with the narrator adopting an informal first-person present continuous stance: 'My sister who knows about gardening is standing with her hands on her hips surveying the wilderness surrounding my new house, "nifty little piece of property", according to my father' (2004: 301). Here, in the opening sentence/paragraph, the reader is presented, not only with the entrance of one half of the 'simple quartet' involved in acting out Frankenberg's drama (1997: 11) – members of the white nuclear family – but in such a way as to suggest a particular point of view. This perspective, however, shifts within the first ten paragraphs at the precise moment that the narrator's mother warns her daughter about security, reminding her that she is 'a woman alone', the most vulnerable, and, at the same time, most dangerous member of the cast, in threatening the stability of the heterosexual, patriarchal contract that is in the service of maintaining the status quo. The narrator now refers to herself in the third person, thus signalling her awareness of the role assigned to her, and which, like it or not, she is now required to play: 'Woman alone', she records, 'rummages in her not yet unpacked crates' (2004: 301). The very phrase 'Woman alone' is accusatory, and carries with it an eminently recognisable set of connotations in gender politics, not the least of which is that White Woman is incapable of protecting herself, thus in need of the protection White Man is created to provide, in addition to which is the implication that she has clearly failed in her duty as Woman because she is Alone. The deployment of the proper noun order here suggests that she is aware of being objectified as an unclaimed possession.

A similar switch in perspective occurs in the narrator's encounter with Piet, the coloured gardener she has employed. She asks him what he *would like* (thus endowing him with agency) for lunch and in so doing steps dangerously out of the role required of her as 'Madam'. This unexpected gesture prompts Piet to foreground the discrepancy between gesture and expectation by a) requesting salad rather than meat for lunch and b) referring to her as 'Madam' in the same breath (2004: 303). The word 'Madam' launches the shift from first to third person once again, requiring of her, whether consciously or not, to encounter the unavoidable contingency that there is no place for any kind of relationship available to them beyond the one historically and (still) unofficially sanctioned by a persistent Hegelian master/servant dialectic. Indeed, on the first day that the narrator and Piet spend in their respective capacities as Madam and Labourer, they discover that '[t]hey enjoy each other' (2004: 304), which already sends out warning sounds to them and to the reader, all of whom are aware that such a response is not officially scripted in the stage directions of the drama outlined above in which 'sexually vulnerable White Woman' must be protected at all costs from 'sexually rapacious Man of Color' (Frankenberg 1997: 11). The property agent who has in a sense 'leased' out Piet's labour, tells Marlene that she is 'setting a dangerous precedent' in overpaying Piet and providing a full-blown Greek salad for his daily lunch. The final switch in the story from first to third person hinges on the notion of the 'setter of precedents [who] is left with her head in her hands', despairing at her inability to step out of the discourses that define her. It is precisely during instances in which the narrator feels compromised and/or complicit that she resorts to the third person, as if watching herself from a distance inevitably acting out a part she genuinely does not want to play. 'She decides to leave them both just there without any explanations', speaking of herself in the third person, caught as she is between sympathy and guilt, between 'labourer and estate agent' (2004: 305), in a gulf of space not yet bridged in post-apartheid South Africa.

This ambivalence is repeated in her encounter with the white overseer of a team of domestic cleaners, such an outfit being a fairly new development in the Madam and Eve politics of white South African domesticity. Here, though, she is relieved of the immediate guilt of having to play the role of Madam, since that role is already accounted for in the persona of Mrs Uys, the supervisor of 'Northwest Breeze' (2004: 305), the domestic cleaning team consisting of four coloured 'maids' 'leased' to clean houses in white suburbia. The narrator's precarious position in this moment is marked, not by the shift in perspective which has the effect of caricaturing the role expected of her, but by an awareness of the danger, and indeed the violence, of words in shaping responses. Van Niekerk, in this story, as well as in *Triomf* (1996), is aware of the capacity of language to perform the work of ideology and, in particular, the capacity of idiomatic language to contain those common sense truths endemic to social propriety. In relating the precautions taken ahead of the cleaning service's first visit (such as locking her handbag in the study), the narrator recalls one of her mother's Calvinist truisms: 'What the eye does not see […] the heart cannot desire'. Her response, ironically, is: '[y]ou can't even trust the idioms' (2004: 306). The irony lies in the fact that she has been grappling with the effect of idioms right from the start of her experience with domestic labour, at times resisting them, at times falling prey to them.

An idiom is always a quotation, spoken from an agentless perspective, in Foucault's terms, representing the 'tyranny of the transparent', a comforting, reassuring and neatly packaged Truth upon which 'we' (with all of the universalising implications of the plural pronoun) may morally depend in order to do the right thing. The narrator is right to point out that they can no longer be trusted – the ones that shored up apartheid have certainly turned out to be lies, but, Van Niekerk's story seems to suggest, are still in common usage in the suburbs of South Africa. An early exponent in the story of Dreama Moon's 'whitespeak' is the narrator's sister, whose invocation of the generic 'They' delineates the other half of the caste of colonial characters conjured by Van Niekerk to enact our collective racial heritage. 'They', we are told, cannot be trusted because 'on Saturday they're drunk, and during the week you can't leave them here on their own, they'll rob you blind' (2004: 301). Only after these undisputed 'truths' have been spoken are we enlightened as to who 'they' are, Van Niekerk knowing full well that the description in itself will suffice in stereotypically establishing the racial identity, for a South African readership, as being, not white, not black, but very specifically Cape coloured.

Though the discourse of the narrator's siblings may provide the initial benchmark for (stereo-)typical middle-class whiteness, replete as it is with the crass racial observations they so glibly spout, Van Niekerk demonstrates that even the liberal intellectual, 'Marlene' (Van Niekerk) herself is not above or exempt from these normative and righteous proclamations indicative of suburban insularity and self-preservation. At first, safely occupying the moral higher ground, the narrator is able to rationalise her position as white landowner and employer of coloured labour, in her confession that 'at least she doesn't own a firearm' to use against those who would 'rob her blind', and in the decision to adopt a laissez-faire working relationship with said labourer in which '[s]he'll be cautious and correct. Firm and friendly, with distance [...] Give good food and regular refreshments, a bonus for commendable work' (2004: 302). However, she soon finds herself on precariously shifting ground in finalising the terms of the contract with her hired help. Her unsure footing is humorously depicted in Van Niekerk's rendering of the scene: 'The negotiations are in full swing, that we both know. I push the Volkswagen harder to stay ahead' (2004: 303), clearly a move which does not help the narrator's cause, because now the negotiations inadvertently include the car she is driving, which Piet appears to covet. From this moment on both Madam and labourer test but fail to surpass the limits of the social contract they have entered and the roles each is consequently required to play, and if Marlene's Greek salads are gestures in 'quotation marks' (meant to symbolise her liberal humanity in matters of race relations), she becomes uncomfortably aware that Piet's gestures, like the rose cuttings he brings her from his garden, are also metaphorically in inverted commas – 'triple, quadruple ones' (2004: 305), more heavily emphasised in that he is responding to, rather than initiating, the duplicitous act and thus less culpable than she is. That they are both stymied by a kind of rigid rhetoric signalled in sets of inverted commas suggests an inability to communicate beyond the terms that continue to bind their social contract, from which, it seems, there is no escape. Clearly, this first foray into 'Madamhood' for the narrator offers little scope for what Vikki Bell has termed 'connectivity' beyond Nietzschean 'ressentiment' (1999: 40) between white woman and black man. Each remains trapped in a dialectic that empty gestures, couched in inverted commas, only superficially conceal. Piet thus disappears from the story, requiring the narrator to look elsewhere for manual labour.

To this end she is forced to phone Beauty du Toit, who is 'cheap [and] has her own truck' (2004: 309). In asking Beauty's labourers if they would be interested in picking up some casual garden work, the narrator once again becomes aware of just how forked her tongue is, confessing to the reader:

> You can no longer say even the most ordinary things with a clear conscience in this country. It's almost as if you can only quote. I had a garden in Africa. I wanted a garden in Africa. We used to have a garden in Africa. Roses, foxgloves, snowdrops, blue forget-me-nots. Richman poorman beggarman thief. (2004: 309)

In this culminating insight, the narrator marks a set of volatile chain reactions that European imperialism set in motion. The 'You' she refers to might easily be replaced with the universalising pronoun 'One' and is clearly aimed at incorporating exclusively white sensibilities. This is reinforced in the repeated intertextual echoes from the famous opening line of Karen Blixen's colonial memoir *Out of Africa*: 'I had a farm in Africa', which is reduced to 'I had [...]. I wanted [...]. We used to have a *garden* in Africa' (my emphasis). The repetition in variation of the sentiments expressed in colonial literature serves to suggest Van Niekerk's awareness of white South Africans' sense of ambivalence: on one hand, the past tense signals a sense of displacement and alienation, and, on the other hand, the string of first-person singular and plural pronouns signals a perpetual sense of entitlement – though perhaps less imperious in scope in that the farm is now a suburban garden. The chain-reaction effect is given further momentum in the cataloguing of exotic flowers, the names of which, reminiscent of English country gardens, may be construed as Van Niekerk's reminder of the presumption of Eurocentric attitudes, especially as they manifest themselves in the colonising predilection for transforming (sub-)urban spaces into little replicas of Europe, à la Stellenbosch – a little piece of Mediterranean Provence. Furthermore, another kind of chain, this time 'of being', is signalled in the ditty: 'Richman poorman beggarman thief', the last three links in the chain being corollaries of the first. In a sense the entire story may be read as enactment of the chain reactions spewed forth in this little outburst. That the ditty is associated with the nursery rhymes used in children's games to include and exclude is also significant. Though not as racially offensive as the discredited 'Eeny Meeny Miny Mo', which has fallen into disuse for obvious reasons, 'Richman poorman beggarman thief' marks a strictly plotted continuum from most to least desirable, and is totally exclusionary in its trajectory.

It is in the presence of Mrs Uys and her team of Northwest Breeze cleaners that Marlene experiences the most violent reaction to the chain (of being) outlined above. In many ways Mrs Uys symbolises what Nancy Armstrong observes as the power wielded by white western middle-class women in the domestic sphere, in reinforcing and perpetuating class [and race] hierarchies (1997: 919). The very names of both the character and the company she manages are indicative of the force she represents as a white woman in South Africa. Van Niekerk may well be playing on the association of the word 'Uys' with the English word 'us' as opposed to 'them', and the Afrikaans word 'ys' which means 'ice' that is cold and white; while the 'Northwest Breeze' (apart from its obvious opposition to the predominant, dust-swirling southeasterly wind that blows through the Cape Peninsula) may be read as having ushered in what Melissa Steyn has suggested are historically the very integuments of whiteness, that is, in assuming the mantle of providing 'order, government, leadership [… of taking] charge [and] assign[ing] roles' (1999: 270). Mrs Uys's assumption of a shared white experience between herself and Marlene is the catalyst that sets in motion a series of reactions requiring the narrator to confront her own complicity in maintaining the 'yskoud' (ice cold) world of white suburbia. On several occasions Mrs Uys winks at, or glances at the narrator conspiratorially, followed by some painfully racist comment. The first of these gestures takes place when one of the workers complains of a headache (2004: 306), and Mrs Uys gives them all a painkiller, as if they were sweets being dispensed to a bunch of toddlers who would throw a tantrum if they suspected favouritism. Marlene's response is to pretend not to hear, though it is an act that she cannot sustain for long. Directly after this, Mrs Uys eagerly awaits Marlene's response to Gladys's query upon seeing the warning sign: 'This Property is Protected by Snakes.' Here, the narrator knows that she is going to lie, and that the lie will be witnessed by the smug Mrs Uys, whose first conspiratorial wink is now justifiably followed by a second. But it is the third that causes the most interesting response. It occurs on completion of the task, when Marlene hands over a cheque to the winking Mrs Uys and watches as the workers' gaze 'follow[s] the cheque's progress into her handbag' (2004: 308). The 'sincere', 'meaningful', 'matter-of-factness' of Mrs Uys's ruthless and socially sanctioned exploitation of the utterly destitute inhabitants of a squatter camp, and her assumption that the narrator approves of 'the work provider's' self-righteous 'rescuing' of these people, prompts Marlene to enact an imagined rebellion on their behalf:

> Suddenly a brilliantly bloodthirsty fantasy blossoms in my mind. A quick grip, strong hands throttling and wrenching, blood against the windscreen of the Cortina, handbag eviscerated, Rainbow Warriors gone with the wind scouring the shacks, no word breathed about it. I think of Pirate Jenny in Nina Simone's version. (2004 308)

The violence of the images goes some way to neutralising the effect of the uncomfortably confidential winks bestowed on Marlene by Mrs Uys. In this moment, however compromised she may have felt previously, the narrator's allegiance is now firmly with the black women, celebrated and liberated in the image of Rainbow Warriors[133] (a cynical version of Archbishop Desmond Tutu's vision of a post-

Narratives of Madamhood in Suburban South Africa ▪ 181

apartheid South African 'Rainbow Nation', and a clever subversion of consumerist branding and its co-option of 'exotic' cultures to sell products – the vacuum cleaners are 'Rainbow Warriors'), and of Pirate Jenny[134] who will rise up from her knees, from scrubbing other people's floors, and destroy the oppressor. This imaginative enactment of their revenge and their liberation momentarily vindicates the narrator, as Van Niekerk is well aware, in counteracting the complicity she feels earlier, but in a sense, what she must, and ultimately (in the final moments of the story) does acknowledge, is that this fantasy will inevitably remain as empty a gesture as her salad in inverted commas if she simply continues to support the structures (and people) responsible for perpetuating such inequalities. A partial acknowledgment of her culpability may be suggested in the suddenness of the switch in narrative focus. 'Winter comes' is the next statement, and it finds the narrator once again in need of manual labour. This time, however, she is determined to maintain some degree of anonymity in her dealings with service providers, having been made far too conscious of the uncomfortable ambiguities of her own responses to the conspiratorial gestures made by Mrs Uys.

In her brief conversation with the team of workers overseen by Mrs Uys, Marlene becomes aware of the difficulties communicating across the deep chasm that constitutes the race/class divide in South Africa. If she has struggled to find common ground with Piet, the gardener, and with Mrs Uys, service provider, she struggles even more poignantly with the four black women who are cleaning her house. On arrival, Dolla 'fixes her stare on the ground with a fuck-you expression on her face' (2004: 305), and the conversation that follows revolves largely around the warning sign: 'This Property is Protected by Snakes', the tone of which is set by the expression on Gladys's face when she asks the narrator where the snakes are, an expression that says, 'Right on, ignore her, the old cunt' (2004: 306). This is a familiar expression to many white South African women who have had households to clean. It demonstrates the dynamic that transpires when 'Madam', in this instance, and in Gayatri Spivak's terms, the First World scholar meets 'Eve', the Third World Woman regardless of the women's social standing. At the same time as Marlene may be said to be 'speaking for' Gladys, she may also be listening to her in ways that Mrs Uys cannot, or more accurately, will not; and in listening, she hears anger and hatred that the seemingly neutral question asked ('So where are the snakes?') does not articulate. However, the narrator appears unable to traverse the impasse which Spivak identifies as the western academic's being caught between granting an 'expressive [western] subjectivity and total unrepresentability' (1987: 209), an impasse that Van Niekerk is well aware of as a white scholar, and who thus simply demonstrates the problem satirically, without offering any all too easy solutions. The interaction becomes even more fraught as the hour wears on and Van Niekerk's rendering of it is ludicrously stereotypical (the women spit and cackle and grab at each others' crotches' (2004: 305, 307, 308). Their 'unreadable' responses mark the writer's awareness of the impossibility of any genuine dialogue between these women and herself. At one point, having been asked what the snakes eat, the narrator decides to 'improvise with a straight face and an ironic tone' in the hope that she 'can find favour with them'. 'I shall make my lies visible', she declares. 'Then I will be safe' (2004: 307). Clearly, the only person, besides perhaps Mrs Uys, that Marlene has made her lies visible to is herself, and found favour with no one. The women these lies (in a set of quotation marks) are addressed to, are not interested in her, or her inverted commas, only in their own mimicking of white paranoia as it manifests itself in a pair of four-foot snakes called Michael and Raphael. And, clearly too, she will not be safe as long as white South Africans can only ever speak in inverted commas. Her story about the snakes becomes taller and taller and when Dolla, in effect, cuts her off with the rejoinder, 'Yow, what's the miss saying', the narrator responds: 'The miss is saying everything [...] fucking everything.' Or nothing, at least nothing new, read from a perspective other than her own. And herein lies the central paradox: much as Marlene would like to unshackle the chains that govern their responses to one another, she is locked into the hierarchical position she occupies, and so are these women, whose humiliation seems 'powerful' (2004: 308) to the narrator, in the face of her deception, her manipulation, her control, and ultimately her ongoing reliance on cheap black labour.

Van Niekerk, though, is not exclusively preoccupied in this story with black domestic labour, but also with the ways in which white existence is premised on, but ought to move beyond, exploitative, cyclical, economically dictated race dynamics. The narrative features a vignette in which Van Niekerk exhibits something of what Zoë Wicomb has argued may be conceived of as a re-narrativisation of Afrikanerdom as alterity in Afrikaans writing, evident particularly positively, Wicomb suggests, in Van Niekerk's subversions of 'the dominant meaning of Afrikaner, the Calvinist self from which debased, landless "poor whites" have been excluded' (2001: 173). Both Beauty and Gerrie serve as foils to the stern Stellenbosch image of the Calvinist Afrikaner, to varying degrees. Beauty mouths the familiar idioms that contain their fair share of racial slurs and self-righteousness, though she is represented by Van Niekerk slightly more sympathetically than the condescending, ingratiating Mrs

Uys is. Marlene describes her as: 'Friendly. Gullible. Unsuspecting.' (2004: 310), and, in a sense, though Beauty complains bitterly about the coloured labour she employs, Marlene tentatively approves of her tenacious independence (as a woman) hurtling along on their way to the dump, slapping the outside of the truck 'with the flat of her hand'.

The initial approval, however, is short-lived, as the next in a series of impossible paradoxes emerges: the narrator turns to look at 'Them', the workers in the back of the truck whom Beauty refers to as a 'class of people' one ought to be afraid of, and sees only a dehumanised 'bundle of rags amongst the branches [...] Only the rough hands and the dull gleam of eye betray[ing] the presence of bodies'. At this precise moment, Beauty draws Marlene's attention to noises emerging from the dog pound, and bemoans the fate of the dogs that bark for a fortnight and 'if they still haven't found homes then, they get put down, too terrible, I tell you' (2004: 310). One cannot but hear echoes of the final moments of J.M. Coetzee's *Disgrace* (1999), and of David Lurie's eventual occupation – taking care of dogs in the pound that have been earmarked for euthanasia. In a sense, the men in the back of the truck *are* just 'bundles of rags' if the white woman driving the truck hears, above all else, the sounds of doomed dogs barking, keeping her awake at night, but the existence of her labourers matters only to the extent that they are useful (or useless) and in the possible threat they pose for White Woman Alone. Both Coetzee and Van Niekerk appear to be pointing to the limits of the continued presence of white people in Africa (or at least those white people who cannot give up the narratives of the past). The cruelty of the juxtaposition (those bundles of rags in the back of the truck, and the 'dear little things, terribly neglected' that Beauty brings home from the pound) expresses a profound incommensurability, and introduces a macabre version of the folk tale 'Beauty and the Beast', one that emerges from the same source that most South African urban myths[135] do: a debilitating fear of the other.

The dump represents the excess of western consumer capitalism in Van Niekerk's painstaking recording of the items to be found there, and in her recognition of the 'sweet rich smell of first world compost' (2004: 311). It is at the dump that the narrator encounters what appears to be an isolated instance of genuinely 'white labour'. She meets Gerrie and his son, characters whose presence in the story both suggest and resist alternative white responses. Though the first symbolic connotation regarding these men is that they represent 'white trash' in their association with the place in which they are encountered, Van Niekerk immediately engenders the reader's sympathy, for both father's and son's entrepreneurial effort in making extra money to support their mutual dream of the son becoming a professional wrestler. But it is 'an up-side down world' (2004: 311), as Marlene rightly notes, and the downside of this commendable joint effort is manifest in their reliance on the racial status quo to bolster their implausible dream of Olympic heroism. Hellish as Gerrie's existence may be, as the image of an 'upside-down Hephaistos', 'gatherer in the a throw-away zone' suggests, the 'poorman' needs the 'beggarman' to sustain his dream, so he sets the 'black men and women[136] in ragged clothes' to 'chipping away at the bricks' for 'half-shares', and he keeps enough to help his son (2004: 310–311). The tragedy for this 'upside-down Hephaistos' is in the unlikelihood, impossibility even, of the Olympic dream ever materialising, he being, as a poor white man in post-apartheid South Africa, lame and flung out of Olympus. Similarly, his son, hard-working and ambitious as he may be, relies on money he earns as a bouncer at coloured clubs 'where things get rough' and where he 'bounces on command' and, it seems, indiscriminately. They make a sorry pair, the lame celestial artist booted out of Olympus, and his Greek god of a son beating up drunk coloured people to make extra money so that he can 'wrestle his way to the top',[137] an unfortunate pair, relegated to the trash heap of white western history.

The last of the narrator's encounters with black labour is the most powerful in its acknowledgement of the absurdities of social living in South Africa, where white suburbia remains as insular and simultaneously as threatened as always. Jan and Simon from the shelter come to finish off the work that Piet started. If there is the slightest possibility for connectivity beyond Nietzschean 'ressentiment' it occurs when Marlene and Jan realise that they have a shared linguistic (and therefore, however remote, social) heritage. When Marlene goes to fetch them, she recognises a particular idiomatic usage associated with her hometown, Caledon, when Jan comments on 'the madam driv[ing] half-and-half[138] fast with the little beetle' (2004: 312). Whatever possibility this moment may have offered them to move beyond the allocated roles of Madam and Labourer is buried under the weight of history and its relations of power and authority. Jan's response to the narrator's observation is 'all affectation, he mimics the tone in which his betters make insincere small talk. The power of mimes, [she thinks]' (2004: 313). Earlier, she noted the 'power of the humiliated' in relation to the team of domestic cleaners. Here, too, in noting the 'power of mimes', she confronts her own powerlessness, ironically, in countering what white privilege has bestowed on her. And, indeed, her ineffectual and superfluous white guilt is no match for the power residing in the justice demanded to compensate the humiliated, and the hostility that produces mimicry. Bhabha's work on mimicry and ambivalence is significant in this regard. He describes mimicry as 'at once a resemblance and menace' (1984: 127), and, as Robert Young reads Bhabha, 'the coloniser sees a grotesquely displaced image of himself' (2004: 188), an image the narrator finds hard to contradict, even harder to confront.

So much for Jan, who is in any case more interested in Marlene's 'dubious' personal relationships than in her merely academic linguistic/geographic affiliation with him. It is Simon who wrenches the narrator out of her comfortable white suburban space, even if only figuratively. He arrives at her door unexpectedly, telling her that he has not eaten for three days. She hears him but smells only the alcohol on his breath. The words she then utters are the ones that define her despite her very real effort to seek alternative identifications. If he hasn't eaten for three days, she wants to know, where does he find the money for alcohol? Instantaneously, she is aware that she has '[p]ronounced the greatest cliché in the Boland' (2004: 317). Simon takes the cue and acts out in front of her the role that she, in articulating the accusation, demands of him – that of grovelling servitude, and in doing so, he 'advances with the leverage of centuries'. It is a leverage that insists on being addressed, and one which Van Niekerk does address in the final moments of the story. Marlene makes amends, gives Simon money and some food and takes him back to the shelter. This final journey elicits three last laughs at three different levels. On the way she reminds Simon to fasten his safety belt. This engenders in the narrator the first of the three last laughs, but it is a hollow, empty 'laugh' that runs down like 'a clockwork gadget' (2004: 318). It is a laugh not of delight but of despair, of automation, a laugh that contains the recognition of centuries of leverage, epitomised in the absurdity of 'a handshake between somebody with an empty stomach and somebody who gets off on snow-covered peaks' (2004: 317). It is a laugh in response to the madness of the pseudo protection of safety belts in the face of the death-dealing blows of racial injustice that are endemic in contemporary South Africa, and epidemic in their persistence and in their proportions. Simon's humour, however, ends the story: it is he who is allowed the last laugh, as it were, when he tells Marlene that had Jan been there he would have said: 'Now what is now so half-and-half funny, madam?' (2004: 318). Though 'Marlene' has not been able to manoeuvre her way out of Madamhood, Van Niekerk has at least exposed the predicament. And she has proposed that an ambiguous, even compromised 'half-and-half' laugh is perhaps one of the few effective antidotes for the poisons that white mythologies have engendered.

But the *last* last laugh belongs to Marlene van Niekerk in her authorial control of the central reverberating image in the story: the snake with its forked tongue.

To speak with a forked tongue is inflicted rather than chosen. It is to be painfully divided against yourself. Her pair of phallic and fictional snakes invoked in the fake signage may be a novel way of warning of intruders,[139] but they may also be a way of articulating an alternative identification: Hélène Cixous calls us to 'look at the Medusa straight on' and discover that 'she's not deadly. She is beautiful and she is laughing' (1997: 355). Though the main element of the serpent symbolism is its association with the biblical account of the temptation in the Garden of Eden, there are multiple other connotations. Van Niekerk may deliberately be invoking the image to unsettle its power as a central trope in western mythology. Along with the Cross, it constitutes one of the most influential symbols upon which the values and mores of western civilisation are premised. Van Niekerk would certainly be aware of the interchangeability in the myth of the snake and Eve, both being mutually responsible for bringing evil into the world. But she would also be aware of its phallic associations, and of the Medusa figure (with hair of snakes) lurking just behind the psychosexual and the biblical mythologies. In a sleight of hand move, Van Niekerk appropriates the image, with all its layers of meaning, in the service of protecting not only her property but herself. From the very beginning of the story, the narrator is made to feel socially suspect. Like Eve, the fallen woman, she is damned, having eaten of forbidden fruit,[140] – being as she is Woman Alone, that is, Woman Without Man, or more explicitly Woman With Another Woman. She has had to fend off inquisitive probes from both Mrs Uys and Beauty (2004: 305, 309) regarding her marital status, as well as from Jan, who does not buy the lie that 'Mrs Robinson' (2004: 313) is her sister. The forked tongue of the snake suggests not only the duplicity she exhibits in her white responses to the labourers she employs but another no less laden doubleness, in feeling it necessary to hide her lesbian identity (along with her wallet and cellphone) in the closet. Her lover has taken a photograph of Marlene 'with a chameleon on her shoulder',[141] another duplicitous reptile, with 'eyes in the back of its head' and the capacity to change colour according to its surroundings. Marlene's identification with the snake is powerful, and underpinned, tongue-in-cheek, when she notes that her lover 'tends to think we are in paradise'. If they are in paradise, it is a fool's paradise, well hidden from probing eyes for lesbian lovers, and a Paradise Lost for white South Africans.

The original title of the short story, translated as a 'Small Finger Exercise on the Notion of Hybridity', in addition to the series of epigraphs omitted from the English version, offer useful material for a concluding remark. The duplicities exposed in this analysis, most notably in the image of the snake with its 'forked tongue' may be read in relation to Mikhail Bakhtin's definition of a 'hybrid construction'[142] which is quoted in the first epigraph, as well as in relation to Bhabha's exploration of ambivalence as a trope suggesting 'the simultaneous complicity and resistance that exists in the fluctuating relation between the coloniser and the colonised subject' (in Burrows 2004: 13). The conflicting discourses rendered in the story through Van Niekerk's satirical exposure of her own complicities, as well as the implicit subversive alternate identification uncovered, unsettle the conventional authority of white suburban domesticity.

Conclusion

The four short stories that have been the focus of this chapter are finely crafted vignettes of white suburban life in South Africa. Michael Chapman may indeed be accurate in his assessment of the potential of the short story to convey the multiple responses to a country in transition (2004: *xx*), particularly because coffee-table anthologies such as Chapman's include stories against which the ones I have chosen may be read, surrounded as they are with stories by black, coloured and Indian South Africans. David Medalie would concur, in his suggestion that a short-story collection provides the possibility of exploring the 'encounters across […] categorical divisions [that] have constituted and continue to constitute the rough fabric of many South African experiences' (1998: *xii*). Perhaps the time has passed for full-length works focussing on white 'unbelonging' such as Antjie Krog's *A Change of Tongue* (or J.M. Coetzee's *Disgrace*), so that in a less idealistic spirit of multiculturalism than official narratives of rainbow nationhood have managed, our stories can converge and confront one another more directly, more readily.

Though the temporal and spatial settings of each is vastly different, ranging from 1950s Cape Town through to the struggle years of the earlier 1990s in Johannesburg, and culminating in a post-apartheid, early twenty-first century which takes us back to the Cape, I have explicitly chosen each to illustrate some of the abiding preoccupations confronting white western Madamhood in South African society. Apartheid South Africa may indeed have been officially dissolved, and the 1950s image of womanhood may have been eradicated, but the residue of the attitudes, practices and values of those temporalities, as depicted in all three of Nadine Gordimer's short stories, continue to 'colour' life in white suburbia. This might well be, at least partially, the reason for their inclusion in post-apartheid South African short-story anthologies, and constitutes the main justification for their presence in this book. Apartheid's demise has done little to change materially the circumstances of white middle-class realities, which are marked by a continued need for cheap black labour, a sense of insecurity and unhomeliness, entitlement and fear, now as then. Gordimer's contribution to South African literature has been prolific and invaluable, and the decision to include three fairly minor, fairly dated short stories might in some way reflect the truism that essentially she is a giant of apartheid writing, and that her centrality in English South African literature is a twentieth-century rather than twenty-first-century phenomenon. Nonetheless, she remains one of South Africa's most outspoken woman writers, and one who has examined whiteness in many of its sepulchral guises.

Perhaps Gordimer's successor in post-apartheid South Africa will be Marlene van Niekerk. Certainly, *Triomf* (1996), 'Labour' and her novel, *Agaat* (2005), translated into English in 2006, suggest that she is telling the world about white South African preoccupations as fearlessly as Gordimer did in the twentieth century, and there would be some kind of poetic justice in an Afrikaans writer becoming the twenty-first century's most widely read white South African woman writer, given the English claim to liberalism and universality. Van Niekerk's 'Labour' is the text that demonstrates most effectively a writer grappling with her own complicity in contributing to discourses that maintain white suburban (in)securities.

7

Conclusion

Mind you don't step in it.
Now look what you've done.
Karen Press (1998: 70)

I have demonstrated that white women's writing is marked by an ambivalence that emerges in relation to residual and continued white normativity that is at odds with transformation and reconciliation. This ambivalence has been traced through a range of texts, and in each case it has manifest itself in different ways. The body of work that has become known as whiteness studies has contributed in examining and making whiteness visible as an identification, and as a cultural construct. This proliferating field of cross-disciplinary studies has assisted in articulating the persistence of racial hierarchisation despite post-colonial and, in the case of South Africa, post-apartheid decentring of white western subjectivity, and manifestations of this phenomenon have been examined in the literary representations of racial identifications in white women's writing.

One of the primary aims of this project was an attempt to plot a continuum of writers from those who are least through to those who are most aware of their positionality in relation to whiteness as both a lived experience and an empty signifier. This proved more difficult than anticipated, with the exception of the writers of mass-produced fiction discussed in Chapter Two. It may appear glaringly obvious to have notched up this kind of writing as the least self-conscious, given that the very genre and its perceived popularity demand a standard set of ingredients in order to sell to an established and viable market. It was not as obvious to position Antjie Krog's *A Change of Tongue* ahead of Marianne Thamm's work, nor Thamm's literary journalism ahead of Karen Press's narrative poetry, nor for that matter, to position Press's work ahead of Nadine Gordimer's seminal studies of white womanhood and/or Marlene van Niekerk's relatively minor short story. If there is any progressively more engaged continuum to plot with regard to these writers, it is not readily discernable, may well be open to contestation, and emerges out of complex interconnecting considerations in relation to the genre, the profile of the writer, the cultural and linguistic affiliation of the writer, and the accessibility of the material, in terms of both circulation and popularity.

As has already been suggested with reference to the major criticisms from reviewers of Antjie Krog's *A Change of Tongue*, and in relation to Nadine Gordimer's satirical deployment of the fairy-tale, genre often dictates content and vice versa. The genre that sells is mass-produced fiction and its content is dictated to by white middle-class sensibilities, and, in turn, these dictate what gets published and promoted. It is not surprising then that the fiction most readily published by a largely white-owned publishing industry targets an established bourgeois market and panders to (and promotes) the sensibilities of that readership. That Pamela Jooste and Susan Mann are readily published internationally and locally by some of the most influential names in the industry reinforces this phenomenon. Conversely, it is not surprising that Karen Press's *Echo Location* is out of print, and in danger of being entirely forgotten. Antjie Krog, on the other hand, established a profile largely as a result of her journalism which was translated into a full-length account of the Truth and Reconciliation Commission, and her reputation as far as an English readership is concerned is not resultant on her primary role as Afrikaans poet. Marianne Thamm may not be as much of a household name as either Pamela Jooste or Antjie Krog, in the sense that she is not taken as seriously, but she very probably enjoys a wider readership than either of them. And were it not for Michael Chapman's conscious selection, in his latest collection of South African short stories, of material reflecting representative writing, and not exclusively English writing, Marlene van Niekerk's 'Labour' would not have been available except in Afrikaans. These comparisons emerge out of the politics of publishing, which influences the circulation and accessibility of literature and sets the parameters of generic viability. It is perhaps inevitable then that the least popular genres, namely, poetry and short fiction, offer the most scope for a concentrated engagement with the politics of representation.

A summarising rationale is thus called for, one that takes cognisance of these interrelated aspects of the writers' relative achievements in negotiating the politics of identity in post-apartheid South Africa. Arguably, it is genre that emerges as the single most important factor in examining the complex elements that inform the sequence in which each text has been positioned in this study, though language/cultural affiliations may be as significant.

Pamela Jooste's *People Like Ourselves*, though clearly a flawed novel, is also a bestselling one and the reviews it received on publication suggest that the white middle-class market of women readers at which it is aimed identified powerfully with the new South African suburban realities facing white women that the novel explores. The question posed in the introduction of Chapter Two was whether such an identification would reinforce or challenge the average reader in negotiating her own complicities in promoting whiteness as normative. My reading of Jooste's representation of white and black subjectivities demonstrates that despite the writer's bleak comments on a growing sense of white displacement (particularly in relation to Caroline's empty mansion and Julia's increasing estrangement), the sanctity of the white western heterosexual status quo is not significantly challenged, given the revealing vignettes of deviance against which white normativity is situated. I have also suggested that one might view the very literal charge of plagiarism analogously as a symptom of derivative narrative plot manipulation which becomes a vehicle for rehashed grand narratives that reinforce white hegemony.

In the case of *One Tongue Singing* by Susan Mann, I have demonstrated that the writer's representation upholds the sanctity and sovereignty of the European self. Indeed, the decorum and civility of European whiteness is offset by the parochialism of South African whiteness, particularly Afrikanerdom. In this regard Mann reifies western civilisation even as she attempts to celebrate the new multicultural possibilities invested in a post-apartheid younger generation of South Africans. The danger of such investments is that vindication precedes any effective (re-)negotiation of complicity and culpability, which in turn relieves white English-speaking South Africans, in particular, of having 'their' racial identity examined or made slippery.

A Change of Tongue might be considered the fulcrum text around which all the others are precariously balanced. Krog's increasing centrality in South African English literature suggests that she is emerging as a spokesperson for a white South African crisis of identity. In a sense she has blurred the boundaries, not only between fact and fiction and other tenuous binaries but has unsettled the historically firm division between Afrikaans- and English-speaking South Africans, and in doing so, she encourages solidarity among white South Africans premised on a new-found sense of displacement. Writing in the mode of the testimony or the confessional, Krog succeeds in foregrounding as exemplary her own battle with transformation, and her own desire to belong as a white African in South Africa. As such her struggle will inevitably resonate loudly amongst white South African readers, who arguably need to hold on to the hope that such an identification is possible. That she courageously invites the reader to share her 'voyages of personal discovery' in order to demonstrate the difficulty of transformation at the level of 'deep structure' is not in dispute. What is open to contestation, however, as my analysis of the text has illustrated, is whether her call for a 'change of tongue', or of being, has been effectively negotiated.

The most regularly repeated criticism of the book is in relation to structure, and although it might be argued that some of the critics are simply responding negatively to Krog's alienating postmodernist strategies, it may also be argued that the structure reflects the content, which is shot through with an unresolved ambivalence. It is an ambivalence that manifests itself most saliently in relation to the focalising perspective which shifts uncomfortably between the first and the third person, and in the scatological preoccupation at the centre of Krog's work, which is difficult not to read as an obsession with the colours and textures of South African race relations. In a sense these aspects of the book assist in 'freez[ing] the debate in tones of black and white' (2002: 58) even as the writer attempts to do the opposite. This reading of Krog's project in *A Change of Tongue* returns one to the primary proposition cited at the outset of this book, namely, to demonstrate that contemporary women's writing from South Africa is markedly ambivalent (even at times duplicitous), and that it *undoes*, at worst, inadvertently and crassly; at times, consciously and carefully; at best, self-consciously and courageously, the very project of 'reconciling' races and celebrating multiculturalism that emerging literature often champions. Krog's work consciously and carefully deconstructs the project of an idealistic post-apartheid reconciliation, thus deliberately problematising notions of multiculturalism, and exhibits moments of a courageous negotiation of the white writer's own complicity in maintaining white normativity, but it also exhibits moments of refusal, of dis-ease, of a reticence in negotiating the continued effects of the universal sanctity of whiteness. The ambivalence that emerges may be read as the residual effects of white normativity that is at odds with personal and political attempts to move beyond race and find other ways of being.

It is the placing of Krog and Thamm on the continuum envisaged that unsettles the notion of a conventionally scientific investigation informing such an attempt to 'measure' the relative effects and efforts of each writer's negotiation of whiteness. Both have provided courageous challenges to the politics of identity as it relates to white western hegemony and the fact that it flourishes in a late capitalist global world economy, and both are unafraid to use themselves as subjects, and to make public their personal experiences, in order to scrutinise the ways in which racism and sexism operate in daily ordinary interactions. To claim that either has 'done a better job' would be to return to a new critical Leavisite tradition of literary hierarchisation. And the same may be said for the writers who have been placed ahead of both. Marianne Thamm's columns in *Fairlady* exhibit a similar ambivalence to the one identified in Krog's work. However, it may be argued that Thamm's 'transgressive aesthetic', coupled with her wider readership, allows her a conscious duplicity that unsettles the 'Conversations with Women' that *Fairlady* promotes, or that TRC confessions can conceivably accomplish.

In her role as officially sanctioned court jester, Thamm is given licence to criticise from *within* the world of white western normativity. The price exacted is self-censorship at times, and at other times the censure of a readership that is at liberty to take heed of or ignore Thamm's wise foolishness. But it is precisely the precariousness of such a positionality and the potential for transgression that it engenders that may be read as a conscious duplicity, and a way beyond 'freezing the debates in shades of black and white'. Though it may be argued that Thamm's ambivalence reflects the duality of *Fairlady*, in the sense that the magazine's proclaimed social conscience is often at odds with the white western feminine values that emerge in its advertising practice and in its standard set of ingredients, that is to say, food, fashion and celebrity glitz, it has been suggested that an alternative reading of Thamm's work is plausible. Like Moria in Erasmus's play, Marianne Thamm is the '*propagatrix*' and her playful, comical teasing may be read as an attempt to write against the transcendental signifier of the Phallus, and produce instead 'a *thing* of sport, of free play, of carefree dissemination rather than patrilinearity' (in Coetzee 1996: 96), and in doing so she negotiates a thing or two that dares not speak its name.

Whereas Thamm writes against the general tenets of journalistic praxis from within a popular women's magazine, Karen Press deliberately and ironically invokes another brand of ubiquitous reading matter, this time the travelogue or tourist brochure, in order to expose and oppose the values and mores governing such publications. *Echo Location* may be read as a guidebook not only of Sea Point but of multiple points of reference that map a particular world-view in spaces occupied largely by white settler-descendants of global western imperialism.

One of Press's most effective strategies is her use of multigeneric and fragmented perspectives which succeed in demonstrating the extent to which our knowledge of the world comes to us through textual production and reproduction. Amongst these is the poet's inclusion of the 'found poem', a concept which Jeremy Cronin's epithet, 'merely', (1998: 20) reduces and dismisses. These 'found poems' are never 'merely' found. They are records that, as a result of their displacement, become amplifications of the hidden assumptions, the white noise, or the most normative and unconscious attitudes that allow a white western frame of reference to be optic, washing out the detail and investing a universality principle that is hard to discern, even harder to counter.

Press remains at a safe distance, though. She is the poet-observer who watches and listens, presumably from one of the balconies of the apartments described in 'View' (1998: 95). Though there are several poems in the collection that suggest Press's own experience, the ultimate response from the reader is towards the poetry rather than the poet. Whereas Krog and Thamm are the subjects, in many ways, of their explorations of identity and difference, Press remains elusive as a persona. The critical distance, however, makes her an astute observer and recalls Nadine Gordimer's similar (dis-)stance in relation to her subject matter.

Gordimer's vignettes of white western Madamhood, though written during apartheid, not only provide a useful background to the reading of Marlene van Niekerk's 'Labour' but in themselves are records of suburban South African women whose unhomeliness is experienced in relation to gender, race and class. Gordimer's female characters are victims, rather than 'creative non-victims' who appear unable to move beyond 'wounded attachment' to their worldly possessions. The modernist 'slice of life' portraits of Mrs Clara Hanson and Mrs Hattie Telford suggest an angst that is not universal but gendered and raced, and their middle-class insularity is shown to be a suffocating mantle that ensures that they do not have to confront their enemies, nor engage their comrades, except superficially. However, Gordimer's bloody fairy-tale suggests that ultimately there is a price to pay for maintaining such insularity.

As a counterpoint to the pulp fictional explorations of identity and belonging in post-apartheid South Africa with which this study began is Marlene van Niekerk's 'Labour'. Whereas *People Like Ourselves* and *One Tongue Singing* are confessional and reconciliatory in each writer's attempt to discover and celebrate a new multicultural South African experience, 'Labour' resists any easy solution to the racial tensions that white suburban madamhood entrenches. Van Niekerk's layered irony registers her awareness of the difficulty in moving beyond black and white by illustrating that cheap black labour sustains white suburban privilege in 2001, much like it did in 1991 when Gordimer wrote her violent South African fairy-tale. Like Antjie Krog does in *A Change of Tongue*, Van Niekerk sets herself up as a character in order to study her own complicity in perpetuating the discourses responsible for racial hierarchisation, but unlike Antjie Krog, Van Niekerk sustains the distance between author and character and the switches between first- and third-person perspectives are ironic and comic rather than awkward or troubled. Just as Thamm's most courageous work emerges out of a 'transgressive aesthetic', it may be argued that Van Niekerk's deployment of the forked-tongued snake suggests an alternative identification beyond the compulsory heterosexual nuclear family, the basic unit upon which white western suburbia is built. Both Van Niekerk and Press inhabit upper middle-class and privileged areas of the Cape Peninsula and observe the minutiae of white suburban normativity which is at odds with transformation, and both investigate the power of language in sustaining a white western frame of reference in illustrating the difficulties of speaking except in inverted commas, whether in relation to the 'rules binding on all residents' or having a 'farm or garden in Africa', or, in Gordimer's reading of suburbia, a 'castle' surrounded by wire briars.

It is in Marlene van Niekerk's 'Labour' that all the elements comprising white women writing white converge and become apparent. It is a powerful short story, translated and anthologised for wider distribution. That the culminating insight into whiteness comes from an Afrikaner perspective is perhaps not surprising, given that it is Englishness, as both Valerie Babb and Robert Young have suggested, that has often been considered the preferred form of whiteness in a neocolonial global world. Van Niekerk's 'small finger exercise on the notion of hybridity' confronts white displacement as an inevitable concomitant of white normativity in a world in which normativity of any kind is exposed as a queer fiction.

Many of the theorists and critics who have contributed to the study of whiteness have called for an examination of the subject rather than the object of the gaze, or, put differently, to study whiteness from within and demonstrate the ways in which such an identification continues to operate as a tyranny of the transparent. This book is an answer to that call in its endeavour to render whiteness visible in the representations of identity in literature written by white South African women.

8

Addendum:
Poems from Antjie Krog's
Kleur Kom Nooit Alleen Nie

Ná grond-invasions in Zimbabwe
There is one type of fear more devastating in its impact than any other: the systematic fear that arises when a state begins to collapse. Ethnic hatred is the result of the terror that arises when legitimate authority disintegrates.
Michael Ignatieff: *Blood and Belonging – Croatia & Serbia*

1. Sal ek altyd wit wees
   maak nie saak waarvoor ek staan
   by wie ek skaar wat ek doen
   wie my ondersteun nie?

   sal 'n swart man op 'n dag in my gesig gil
   Voetsek! Fokôf! en my huis oorvat
   en my President bly stil en sy Kabinet
   en die oorblywende wit comrades?

   sal 'n ek op 'n dag forseer word om te besef
   swart en wit het niks gemeen nie
   nie waardes nie nie medemenslikheid nie
   selfs en veral nie geslag nie

   Is kleur die allesbepalende factor ek kan hoe
   Liefhê hoe hoort wit-wit-wit-wit klop my hart?

2. wat doen ek dan? wie is ek dan
   met my voëlvryverklaarde vel?

leer ek die brutale onderskeidinge aan
tussen 'plaas hê 'n huis hê 'n shack hê

is ek slegs aanvaarbaar sonder besittings
of is besitting van die wit vel dié uiteindelik
ergste oortreding hoe sal ek diegene verafsku
wat my forseer om halsoorkop te vlug terug na die wit

vel, my skaar by ander wittes omdat hulle wit is
wit as die enigste herkoms, uitkoms en deurslag
te herken my lewe, my hele lewe se uitkyk verniet
moet ek my bloed uitdeel en my hart en my niere

want wie dink mense herken in mekaar medemenslikheid
is blykbaar 'n dwaas en verdien nie die lewe van 'n African nie

From *Kleur koom nooit alleen nie* by Antjie Krog (Kwela 2001). Reproduced by kind permission of nb Publishers.

After Land Invasions in Zimbabwe

There is one type of fear more devastating in its impact than any other: the systematic fear that arises when a state begins to collapse. Ethnic hatred is the result of the terror that arises when legitimate authority disintegrates.
Michael Ignatieff: *Blood and Belonging – Croatia & Serbia*

1. Will I always be white
   no matter what I represent
   with whom I identify what I do
   or who supports me?

   and should a black man one day yell into my face
   Voetsek! Fuck off! and take over my house
   and my President and his Cabinet and the
   last remaining comrades keep quiet?

   will I be forced someday to realise
   that black and white have nothing in common
   not values, not even fellow feeling
   and particularly not gender

       is colour the all-determining factor no matter
       how deeply I love or how intensely I belong
       white-white-white-white beats my heart?

2. what do I do then? who am I then
   with my outlawed skin?
   I learn the more brutal distinctions
   between owning a farm, owning a house, owning a shack

   am I only acceptable without owning anything
   or is ownership of this white skin the only
   serious transgression how shall I loathe those
   who force me to flee helter-skelter back to this white

   skin, to unite myself with other whites because they are white
   to recognise white as the only heritage, the only outcome, and the only
       decisive factor
   that my life, my whole life's perspective is in vain
   must I divide and dispense with my blood and my heart and my kidneys

   because the one who sees in another a fellow human being
   is apparently a fool who does not deserve the life of an African

Translated by Helize van Vuuren and Mary West

ai tog!
ek is moeg
vir dié wat so hewig tuiskom teen die Afrikanerbors
die ou prostrate met die gekroonde tande and die bifocals
die male vanity wat die laaste woord spreek
oor die voorwaardes van hulle hoort

ek is moeg
vir hul onbetaamlike haas om te brandmerk, in te stoet en op te pis
almal sit helaas met 'n spul stinkende identiteite in die skoot
(en 'n taal gestroop van die grammatika van menslikheid en berou)

mens sê maar gereeld
mens is niemand se Afrikaner nie
mens praat niemand se taal nie
mens is nie 'n moer iemand se meriete nie
mens is drolwit en pisswart
mens skyt graag op die manne
wat werk by die nuwe barcounter van identities

mens hoort by haar wat daagliks woordeloos
nuwe wolle by die mat vleg

From *Kleur koom nooit alleen nie* by Antjie Krog (Kwela 2001). Reproduced by kind permission of nb Publishers.

ag shame!
I am tired
of those who come home so vehemently to the bosom of Afrikanerdom
the old prostrate with the crowned teeth and the bifocals
the male vanity that always has the last word
on the prerequisites of belonging to them

I am tired
of their indecent haste to brand, to herd in and piss up
alas, everyone sits with a heap of stinking identities on their laps
(and a language stripped of the grammar of humanity and of remorse)
one says over and over
one is no-one's Afrikaner
one speaks no-one's language
one is not a moer anyone's merits
one is turdwhite and pissblack
one likes shitting regularly on the men
who work at the new barcounter of identities

one belongs to her who daily and wordlessly
weaves new wool into the rug

Translated by Helize van Vuuren and Mary West

9

Bibliography

Abel, Elizabeth, Barbara Christian & Helene Moglen (eds). 1997. *Female Subjects in Black and White: Race Psychoanalysis and Feminism*. Berkeley: University of California Press.

Althusser, Louis. 2001 [1969]. 'Ideology and Ideological State Apparatuses' (Notes Towards an Investigation). In: Leitch et al. (eds). *The Norton Anthology of Theory and Criticism*. New York and London: W.W. Norton & Company. 1476–1483.

Anderson, Benedict. 1992. *Imagined Communities: Reflections on the Origin and Spread of Nationalism*. London: Verso.

Armstrong, Nancy. 1987. *Desire and Domestic Fiction: A Political History of the Novel*. New York and Oxford: Oxford University Press.

——— . 1997. 'Some Call It Fiction: On the Politics of Domesticity.' In: Warhol, Robyn & Diane Price Herndl (eds). *Feminisms: An Anthology of Literary Theory and Criticism*. New York: Routledge. 913–930.

Ashcroft, Bill, Gareth Griffiths & Helen Tiffin. 1998. *Key Concepts in Post-Colonial Studies*. London and New York: Routledge.

Atwood, Margaret. 1996 [1972]. *Survival: A Thematic Guide to Canadian Literature*. Toronto: McClelland and Stewart Inc.

——— . 1998. *Eating Fire: Selected Poetry 1965–1995*. London: Virago.

Awerbuck, Diane. 2004. *Gardening at Night*. London: Vintage.

Babb, Valerie. 1998. *Whiteness Visible: The Meaning of Whiteness in American Literature and Culture*. New York: New York University Press.

Back, Les. 2002. 'Guess Who's Coming to Dinner? The Political Morality of Investigating Whiteness in the Gray Zone.' In: Ware, Vron & Les Back. *Out of Whiteness: Color, Politics and Culture*. Chicago and London: University of Chicago Press. 33–59.

Bakhtin, Mikhail. 1997. 'Dale Bauer's Gender in Bakhtin's Carnival.' In: Warhol, Robyn & Diane Price Herndl (eds). *Feminisms: An Anthology of Literary Theory and Criticism*. New York: Routledge. 708–720.

——— . 2001. 'Epigraph on Hybrid Constructions. From Marlene van Niekerk's "Klein Vingeroefening rondom die Nosie van Hibriditeit"'. In: Van Heerden, Etienne (ed.). *Briewe deur die Lug*. Cape Town: Tafelberg. 147.

Barnett, Adrian. 2002. 'Fair Enough.' *New Scientist*. 12 October: 34–37.

Barthes, Roland. 1972. *Mythologies*. London: Cape.

——. 1984. *Camera Lucida*. London: Fontana Paperbacks.

Bauer, Charlotte. 2005. 'Plagiarism Isn't Ambiguous; It's Just Theft, Plain and Simple.' *Sunday Times*. 6 February 2005. www.sundaytimes.co.za. Accessed 16 May 2005.

Bauer, Dale. 1997. 'Gender in Bakhtin's Carnival.' In: Warhol, Robyn & Diane Price Herndl (eds). *Feminisms: An Anthology of Literary Theory and Criticism*. New York: Routledge. 708–720.

Behr, Mike. 2005. 'A Man's View.' In: *Fairlady*. Cape Town: Media24. April: 106–108.

Bell, Vikki. 1999. *Feminist Imagination*. London: Sage.

Berman, Kelly. 1998. 'Review of *Echo Location*.' *New Coin*. 35(2): 74–77.

Bhabha, Homi K. 1984. 'Of Mimicry and Man: The Ambivalence of Colonial Discourse.' *October*. 28: 26–37.

——. 1992. 'The World and Home'. *Social Text*. 10: 141–153.

——. 1995. *The Location of Culture*. London: Routledge.

——. 1998. 'The White Stuff'. *Art Forum*. May: 21–24.

——. 2002. 'Culture's In-Between'. In Hall, Stuart & Paul du Gay (eds). *Questions of Cultural Identity*. London: Sage. 53–60.

Biko, Steve. 1987 [1979]. *I Write What I Like*. Oxford: Heinemann.

Blixen, Karen. 1970 [1938]. *Out of Africa*. New York: Random House.

Bloch, Graeme. 2003. 'Review of *A Change of Tongue*.' Transcript of *The Bookshelf* at: www.safm.co.za/transcripts. Accessed 3 February 2004.

Boehmer, Elleke. 1995. *Colonial and Postcolonial Literature*. Oxford: Oxford University Press.

Bonnet, Alistair. 1997. 'Constructions of Whiteness in European and American Racism.' In: Werbner, Pnina & Tariq Modood (eds). *Debating Cultural Hybridity: Multi-Cultural Identities and the Politics of Racism*. London: Zed Books. 172–193.

Booth, Michelle. 2004. 'Interview.' In: Smith, Gail. Getting Beyond the Guilt Trip. *This Day*. 16 January: 9.

Brink, André. 2004. 'Superb Novel about Life's Unpredictablilty.' *Sunday Independent*. 8 February: 18.

Brown, Lesley. 1993. *The New Shorter Oxford English Dictionary (New SOED)*. CD Rom.

Burrows, Victoria. 2004. *Whiteness and Trauma: The Mother-Daughter Knot in the Fiction of Jean Rhys, Jamaica Kincaid and Toni Morrison*. Hampshire: Palgrave MacMillan.

Butler, Judith. 1993. *Bodies That Matter: On the Discursive Limits of 'Sex'*. New York and London: Routledge.

Chance, Jean & William McKeen (eds). 2001. *Literary Journalism: A Reader*. California: Wadsworth/Thomson Learning.

Chapman, Michael (ed.). 2004. *The New Century of South African Short Stories*. Johannesburg: Ad Donker.

Chow, Rey. 1996. 'Where Have All the Natives Gone?' In: Padmini Mongia (ed.). *Contemporary Postcolonial Theory: A Reader*. London: Arnold. 122–146.

Cixous, Helene. 1997. 'The Laugh of the Medusa.' In: Warhol, Robyn & Diane Price Herndl (eds). *Feminisms: An Anthology of Literary Theory and Criticism*. New York: Routledge. 347–362.

Coetzee, J.M. 1987 [1980]. *Waiting for the Barbarians*. Harmondsworth: Penguin.

——. 1988. *White Writing: On the Culture of Letters in South Africa*. New Haven: Yale University Press.

——. 1996. *Giving Offense: Essays on Censorship*. Chicago and London: University of Chicago Press.

——. 1999. *Disgrace*. London: Penguin.

——. 2001. *Stranger Shores: Essays (1986–1999)*. London: Secker and Warburg.

Conrad, Joseph. 1988 [1899]. *Heart of Darkness*. New York and London: WW Norton and Company. (A Critical Edition, edited by Robert Kimbrough.)

Crocker, Jennifer. 2003. 'Jooste Has Earned Her Place among SA's Best Novelists.' *The Cape Times*. 20 June: 9.

Cronin, Jeremy. 1998. 'Poet Demystifies Her Art with a "Howzit Clive?".' *The Sunday Independent*. 8 November: 20.

Davy, K. 1995. 'Outing Whiteness: A Feminist/Lesbian Project.' *Theatre Journal*. 47. 189–205.

De Beer, Diane. 2003a. 'Author Dissects a Slice of SA Life.' *Pretoria News*. 9 June: 21.

——. 2003b. 'Antjie Bares Her Soul in Latest Book.' *Pretoria News*. 27 October: 3.

De Lauretis, Teresa (ed.). 1988. *Feminist Studies/Critical Studies*. Houndmills: MacMillan.

Dentith, Simon. 2000. *Parody*. The New Critical Idiom Series. London and New York: Routledge.

Derry, Debbie. 2003. 'Easily Recognisable SA Characters.' *Eastern Province Herald*. 23 April: 8.

De Vries, Fred. 2004a. 'Singular White Females.' *This Day*. 30 May: 9.

——. 2004b. 'Mann Roer Clichés Flink om Roman te Skryf.' *Rapport*. 25 April: 28.

Dhairyam, Sagri. 1994. 'Racing the Lesbian, Dodging White Critics.' In: Laura Doan (ed.). *The Lesbian Postmodern*. New York: Columbia University Press. 25–46.

Dimitriu, Ileana Şora. 2000. *Art of Conscience: Re-reading Nadine Gordimer*. România: Hestia.

Doane, Mary Ann. 1997. 'Femme Fatales.' In: Abel, Elizabeth, Barbara Christian & Helene Moglen (eds). *Female Subjects in Black and White: Race Psychoanalysis and Feminism*. Berkeley: University of California Press.

Dollimore, Jonathan. 1991. *Sexual Dissidence: Augustine to Wilde, Freud to Foucault*. Oxford and New York: Oxford University Press.

Downing, John & Charles Husband. 2005. *Representing 'Race': Racisms, Ethnicities and Media*. London: Sage.

Driver, Dorothy. 1992. 'Women and Nature: Women as Objects of Exchange. Towards a Feminist Analysis of South African Literature.' In: Chapman, Michael, et al. (eds). *Perspectives on South African Literature*. Johannesburg: Ad Donker. 454–474.

Du Bois, W.E.B. 1986. *Du Bois Writings*. New York: Library of America.

During, Simon (ed.). 1999. *The Cultural Studies Reader*. London: Routledge.

Dyer, Richard. 1999. 'White.' In: Jessica Evans & Stuart Hall (eds). *Visual Culture: The Reader*. London: Sage. 457–467.

Eckert, Penelope & Sally McConnell-Ginet. 2003. *Language and Gender*. Cambridge: Cambridge University Press.

Eckstein, Barbara. 1985. 'Pleasure and Joy: Political Activism in Nadine Gordimer's Short Stories.' *World Literature Today*. 59(3): 65–74.

Elam. Diane. 1994. *Feminism and Deconstruction: Ms. En Abyme*. London and New York: Routledge.

Eliot, T.S. 1980 [1922]. 'The Waste Land.' In: *Collected Poems: 1909–1962*. London: Faber & Faber. 61–86.

Ellison, Ralph. 2001 [1952]. *Invisible Man*. London: Penguin.

Erasmus, Desiderius. 1941 [1509]. *The Praise of Folly*. (Trans. Hoyt H. Hudson). Princetown: Princetown University Press.

Fairbairn, Tessa. 2003. 'Disquieting Mix of Fact and Fiction.' *Cape Argus*. 18 July: 10.

Fanon, Franz. 1967 [1952]. *Black Skin, White Masks*. New York: Grove Press.

———. 1967 [1963]. *The Wretched of the Earth*. London: Penguin.

Farred, Grant. 1999. 'Bulletproof Settlers: The Politics of Offensive in the New South Africa.' In: Hill, Mike (ed.). 1997. *Whiteness: A Critical Reader*. New York: New York University Press. 65–73.

Ferguson, Russell, Martha Gever, Trinh T. Minh-ha & Cornel West. 1990. *Out There: Marginalization and Contemporary Cultures*. New York: The New Museum of Contemporary Art.

Foucault, Michel. 1977. *Discipline and Punish: The Birth of the Prison*. Trans. Alan Sheridan. London: Allen Lane.

Frankenberg, Ruth. 1993. *The Social Construction of Whiteness: While Women, Race Matters*. Minneapolis: University of Minnesota Press.

Frankenberg, Ruth (ed.). 1997. *Displacing Whiteness: Essays in Social and Cultural Criticism*. Durham: Duke University Press.

Friedman, Susan Stanford. 1997. 'When a "Long" Poem Is a "Big" Poem: Self-Authorizing Strategies in Women's Twentieth Century "Long Poems".' In: Warhol, Robyn & Diane Price Herndl (eds). *Feminisms: An Anthology of Literary Theory and Criticism*. New York: Routledge. 721–738.

Gallagher, Charles A. 1995. 'White Reconstruction in the University.' *Socialist Review*, 94(April): 165–187.

Gilman, Sander L. 1986. 'Black Bodies, White Bodies: Toward an Iconography of Female

Sexuality in Late Nineteenth Century Art, Medicine, and Literature.' In: Gates, Henry Louis, Jr (ed.). *'Race', Writing and Difference*. Chicago: University of Chicago Press. 223–261.

Gledhill, Christine. 2002. 'Genre and Gender: The Case of the Soap Opera.' In: Hall, Stuart (ed.). *Representation: Cultural Representation and Signifying Practices*. London: Sage. 337–389.

Gordimer, Nadine. 1981. *July's People*. London: Jonathan Cape.

——. 1990. *My Son's Story*. London: Jonathan Cape.

——. 1998. 'Enemies' and 'Comrades'. In: Medalie, David (ed.). *Encounters: An Anthology of South African Short Stories*. Johannesburg: University of Witwatersrand Press. 52–63 and 148–152.

——. 2004. 'Once Upon a Time'. In: Chapman, Michael (ed.). *The New Century of South African Short Stories*. Johannesburg: Ad Donker. 236–240.

Gqola, Pumla Dineo. 2004. '"… as of this burden disguised as honour did not weigh heavily on her heart": Black Women, Struggle Iconography and Nation in South African Literature.' *Alternation*. 11(1): 44–70.

Hall, Stuart & Paul du Gay (eds). 2002. *Questions of Cultural Identity*. London: Sage.

Harding, Sandra. 1995. 'Subjectivity, Experience, and Knowledge: An Epistemology from/for Rainbow Coalition Politics.' In: Roof, Judith & Robyn Wiegman (eds). *Who Can Speak? Authority and Critical Identity*. Urbana and Chicago: University of Illinois Press. 139–143.

Head, Dominic. 1992. *The Modernist Short Story: A Study in Theory and Practice*. New York: University of Cambridge Press.

——. 1994. *Nadine Gordimer*. Cambridge Studies in African and Caribbean Literature. Cambridge: Cambridge University Press.

Hebdige, Dick. 1999. 'From Culture to Hegemony.' In: During, Simon (ed.). *The Cultural Studies Reader*. London: Routledge. 357–367.

Heyns, Michiel. 2005. 'Hissy Fit.' *Mail & Guardian*. 11–17 February: 29.

Hill, Mike. 1997. 'Introduction: Vipers in Shangri-la: Whiteness, Writing and Other Ordinary Terrors.' In: Hill, Mike (ed.). *Whiteness: A Critical Reader*. New York: New York University Press. 1–20.

Hollands, Barbara. 2003. 'Gently Nuanced Character Study.' *Saturday Dispatch*. 10 May: 4.

hooks, bell. 1994. *Outlaw Culture: Resisting Representations*. New York: Routledge.

Horrell, Georgina. 2004. 'A Whiter Shade of Pale: White Femininity as Guilty Masquerade in "New" (White) South African Women's Writing.' *Journal of Southern African Studies*. 30(4): 765–776.

Ignatiev, Noel. 2005. 'Whiteness and Class Struggle.' *Historical Materialism*. 11(4): 227–235.

Ingram, David. 2005. 'Towards a Cleaner White(ness): New Racial Identities.' *The Philosophical Forum*. 36(3) Fall: 243–277.

Jacobson, Celean. 2005. 'Top Novelist Admits Copying Academic's Work.' *The Sunday Times*. 30 January. www.sundaytimes.co.za. Accessed 16 May 2005.

Jooste, Pamela. 2004. *People Like Ourselves*. London: Black Swan.

Journalist (Unknown). 2003. 'Ons Beeldebestormer – Nou Wilde, maar Snaakse.' *Insig*. December: 69.

Kelen, Christopher. 2005. 'Hymns For and From Australia.' In: López, Alfred J. (ed.). *Postcolonial Whiteness: A Critical Reader on Race and Empire*. New York: State University of New York Press. 201–229.

Kernohan, Sally. 2003. 'Penetrating Look at Post-apartheid Attitudes.' *Weekend Post Leisure*. 3 May: 2.

Khumalo, Sibongile. 2005. 'Bleak Start to Year for Township Pupils, Who Face Lack of Stationery, Vandalised Schools.' *Eastern Province Herald*. 19 January: 1.

Kincaid, Jamaica. 1988. *A Small Place*. New York: Farrar, Straus and Giroux.

Kirby, Robert. 2005a. 'Darrel Bristow-Bovey Emeritus.' *Mail & Guardian*. February 4–10: 23.

——. 2005b. 'Cheats, Loots and Thieves.' *Mail & Guardian*. 14–18 February: 28.

Kossick, Shirley. 2003. 'Back on Form.' *Mail & Guardian (Friday)*. 17–24 April: 4.

Krog, Antjie. 2000a. *Down to My Last Skin: Poems*. Johannesburg: Random House.

——. 2000b. *Kleur Kom Nooit Alleen Nie*. Cape Town: Kwela Boeke.

——. 2002 [1998]. *Country of My Skull*. Johannesburg: Random House.

——. 2003. *A Change of Tongue*. Johannesburg: Random House.

——. 2005. *'n Ander Tongval*. Cape Town: Tafelberg.

Lévinas, Emmanuel. 1969. *Totality and Infinity: An Essay on Exteriority*. Pittsburgh: Duquesne University Press.

Lewis, Desiree. 1996. 'The Politics of Feminism in South Africa.' In: Daymond, Margaret (ed.). *South African Feminisms: Writing, Theory and Criticism 1990–1994*. New York and London: Garland. 91–106.

Lockett, Cecily (ed.). 1990. *Breaking the Silence*. Parklands: Ad Donker.

López, Alfred J. (ed.). 2005. *Postcolonial Whiteness: A Critical Reader on Race and Empire*. New York: State University of New York Press.

Lott, Eric. 1999. 'Racial Cross-Dressing and the Construction of American Whiteness.' In: During, Simon (ed.). *The Cultural Studies Reader*. London: Routledge. 241–255.

Mandela, Nelson. 1995. *Long Walk to Freedom*. London: Abacus.

Mann, Susan. 2005. *One Tongue Singing*. London: Vintage.

Martin, Biddy and Chandra Talpade Mohanty. 1997. 'Feminist Politics: What's Home Got to Do with It?' In: Warhol, Robyn & Diane Price Herndl (eds). *Feminisms: An Anthology of Literary Theory and Criticism*. New York: Routledge. 293–310.

Medalie, David (ed.). 1998. *Encounters: An Anthology of South African Short Stories*. Johannesburg: University of Witwatersrand Press.

Melville, Herman. 1986 [1851]. *Moby Dick, or The Whale*. London: Penguin Classics.

Modleski, Tania. 2002 [1982]. 'The Search for Tomorrow in Today's Soap Operas.' In: Hall, Stuart (ed.). *Representation: Cultural Representation and Signifying Practices*. London: Sage. 385.

Mongia, Padmini (ed.). 1996. *Contemporary Postcolonial Theory: A Reader*. London: Arnold.

Moon, Dreama. 1999. 'White Enculturation and Bourgeois Ideology: The Discursive Production of "Good (White) Girls".' In: Nakayama, Thomas & Judith N. Martin (eds). *Whiteness: The Communication of Social Identity*. Thousand Oaks, London and New Delhi: Sage. 178–191.

Morrison, Toni. 1992. *Playing in the Dark: Whiteness and the Literary Imagination*. London: Picador.

———. 1997 [1987]. *Beloved*. London: Vintage.

———. 1999 [1979]. *The Bluest Eye*. London: Vintage.

Mutman, Mahmut. 1992. 'Pictures from Afar: Shooting the Middle East.' In: Mutman, Mahmut & Meyda Yegenoglu (eds). *Orientalism and Cultural Differences*. (Volume Six): Santa Cruz: University of California.

Najmi, Samina & Rajini Srikanth (eds). 2002. *White Women in Racialized Spaces: Imaginative Transformation and Ethical Action in Literature*. Albany: State University of New York.

Nakayama, Thomas K. & Judith N. Martin (eds). 1999. *Whiteness: The Communication of Social Identity*. Thousand Oaks, London and New Delhi: Sage.

Ndlanga, Sabelo & S'Thembiso Msomi. 2005a. 'ANC Praises Afrikaners.' *The Sunday Times*. 22 May. www.sundaytimes.co.za/articles. Accessed 28 May 2005.

———. 2005b. 'White Men Still Rule in Rainbow Nation.' *The Sunday Times*. 22 May. www.sundaytimes.co.za/articles. Accessed 28 May 2005.

Nurse, Justin. 2003. *The Laugh It Off Annual*. Cape Town: Double Storey Books

Peckham, Linda. 1990. 'Ons Stel Nie Belang Nie/We Are Not Interested in Speaking Apartheid.' Ferguson, Russell, Martha Gever, Trinh T. Minh-ha & Cornel West. *Out There: Marginalization and Comtemporary Cultures*. New York: The New Museum of Contemporary Art. 371–389.

Pieterse, N. & B. Parekh. 1995. *The Decolonization of Imagination: Culture, Knowledge and Power*. London: Zed Books.

Pope, Alexander. 1978 [1714]. *The Rape of the Lock: A Heroic-Comical Poem in Five Canto's*. Edited by Geoffrey Tillotson. London: Methuen Educational Limited.

Press, Karen. 1993. 'Interview.' *New Coin*. June: 22–29.

———. 1998. *Echo Location: A Guide to Sea Point for Residents and Visitors*. Durban: Gecko Poetry.

Pretty Woman. 1990. Screenplay by J.F. Lawton, Directed by Garry Marshall.

Rich, Adrienne. 1979. *On Lies, Secrets and Silence: Selected Prose 1966–1978*. New York and London: W.W. Norton and Company.

Richards, Jo-Anne. 2003. *Sad at the Edges*. Cape Town: Stephen Phillips.
Roediger, David. 1991. *The Wages of Whiteness: Race and the Making of the American Working Class*. New York: Verso.
Roof, Judith & Robyn Wiegman (eds). 1995. *Who Can Speak? Authority and Critical Identity*. Urbana and Chicago: University of Illinois Press.
Rosenthal, Jane. 1998. 'The Gifts of Sea Point'. *Mail & Guardian*. 20–26 November: 23.
——. 2004. 'Art and Love'. *Mail & Guardian*. 20–24 February: 5.
Ross, Fiona. 1998. 'From a "Culture of Shame" to a "Circle of Guilt".' *Southern Africa Review of Books*. June. 1–5.
Roy, Arundhati. 2004. *The Ordinary Person's Guide to Empire*. London: Flamingo.
Said, Edward. 1978. *Orientalism*. New York: Pantheon.
——. 1983. *The World, the Text, the Critic*. London: Vintage.
——. 1993. *Culture and Imperialism*. London: Chatto and Windus.
——. 2000. *The Edward Said Reader*. Eds Moustafa Bayoumi & Andrew Rubin. New York: Vintage Books.
Sanders, Mark. 2002. *Complicities: The Intellectual and Apartheid*. Pietermaritzburg: University of Natal Press.
Sandoval, Chéla. 1997. 'Theorizing White Consciousness'. In: Frankenberg, Ruth (ed.). *Displacing Whiteness: Essays in Social and Cultural Criticism*. Durham: Duke University Press. 86–106.
——. 2000. *Methodology of the Oppressed*. Minneapolis: University of Minneapolis Press.
Scales-Trent, Judy. 1999. 'The American Celebration of Whiteness'. In: Cuomo, Chris & Kim Hall (eds). *Whiteness: Feminist Philosophical Reflections*. Lanham: Roman and Littlefield Publishers. 55–56.
Schoonees, P.C. (ed.). 1970 [1947]. *Woordeboek van die Afrikaanse Taal: Eerste Deel A–C*. 3rd ed. Pretoria: Die Staatsdrukke.
Seshadri-Crooks, Kalpana. 2000. *Desiring Whiteness: A Lacanian Analysis of Race*. London and New York: Routledge.
Shaw, George Bernard. 1998 [1913]. *Pygmalion*. London: Viking Penguin.
Shome, Raka. 1999. 'Whiteness and the Politics of Location.' In: Nakayama, Thomas K. & Judith N. Martin (eds). *Whiteness: The Communication of Social Identity*. Thousand Oaks, London and New Delhi: Sage. 108–122.
Sleeter, Christine. 2005. 'Race Traitor'. In: Ingram, David. Toward a Cleaner White(ness): New Racial Identities. *The Philosophical Forum*. 36(3) Fall: 243–277.
Smith, Gail. 2004. 'Getting Beyond the Guilt Trip'. *This Day*. 16 January: 9.
Spillers, Hortense J. 1997. '"All the Things You Could Be by Now, If Sigmund Freud's Wife Was Your Mother": Psychoanalysis and Race'. In: Abel, Elizabeth, Barbara Christian & Helene Moglen (eds). *Female Subjects in Black and White: Race Psychoanalysis and Feminism*. Berkeley: University of California Press. 138–162.

Spivak, Gayatri Chakravorty. 1980. 'Interview.' In: Harasym. S. (ed.). *The Post-Colonial Critic: Interviews, Strategies, Dialogues*. New York and London: Routledge.

———. 1987. *In Other Worlds: Essay in Cultural Politics*. New York: Methuen.

Steyn, Melissa. 1999. 'White Identity in Context: A Personal Narrative.' In: Nakayama, Thomas K. & Judith N. Martin (eds). *Whiteness: The Communication of Social Identity*. Thousand Oaks, London and New Delhi: Sage. 265–276.

———. 2001. *'Whiteness Just Isn't What It Used To Be': White Identity in a Changing South Africa*. Albany: State University of New York Press.

———. 2005. '"White Talk": White South Africans and the Management of Diasporic Whiteness.' In: López, Alfred J. (ed.). *Postcolonial Whiteness: A Critical Reader on Race and Empire*. New York: State University of New York Press.

Storey, John. 1998. 'The "Culture and Civilization" Tradition.' In: *An Introduction to Cultural Theory and Popular Culture*. Athens, Ohio: University of Georgia Press.

Swerdlow, Alan. 2003. 'Interview with Pamela Jooste.' (Transcript of *The Bookshelf*. 1 June). www.safm.co.za/transcripts. Accessed 2 February 2004.

Taylor, Gary. 2005. *Buying Whiteness: Race, Culture and Identity from Columbus to Hip-Hop*. New York: Palgrave MacMillan.

Terry, Peter. 2002. 'Review of *Mental Floss* by Marianne Thamm.' Transcript from SAFM's *The Bookshelf*. www.safm.co.za/transcripts. Accessed 3 April 2005.

Thamm, Marianne. 2002. *Mental Floss: A Collection of 'Unfair Comment' from Fairlady*. Cape Town: Spearhead.

———. 2003. 'Unfair Comment: Let's Hear It for the Wrinklies.' In: *Fairlady*. Cape Town: Media24 Magazine Division. January: 10.

———. 2003. 'Unfair Comment: Welcome to the Matrix.' In: *Fairlady*. Cape Town: Media24 Magazine Division. July: 12.

———. 2003. 'Unfair Comment: Trying for White.' In: *Fairlady*. Cape Town: Media24 Magazine Division. September: 12.

———. 2003. 'Unfair Comment: Barbie's Revenge.' In: *Fairlady*. Cape Town: Media24 Magazine Division. December: 12.

———. 2004. 'Unfair Comment: Fair Play.' In: *Fairlady*. Cape Town: Media24 Magazine Division. February: 12.

———. 2004. 'Unfair Comment: I Do, I Don't.' In: *Fairlady*. Cape Town: Media24 Magazine Division. July: 14.

———. 2004. 'Unfair Comment: The Coalition of the Brainless.' In: *Fairlady*. Cape Town: Media24 Magazine Division. October: 16.

———. 2004. 'Unfair Comment: Collateral Damage.' In: *Fairlady*. Cape Town: Media24 Magazine Division. November: 14.

———. 2005. 'Unfair Comment: Duh, Duh, Duh, Duh.' In: *Fairlady*. Cape Town: Media24 Magazine Division. February: 12.

———. 2005. 'Unfair Comment: Royal Male.' In: *Fairlady*. Cape Town: Media24 Magazine Division. March: 12.

———. 2005. 'Unfair Comment: We've Come a Long Way … Maybe.' In: *Fairlady 1965–2005* (The Anniversary Edition). Cape Town: Media24 Magazine Division. April: 30.

———. 2005. 'Unfair Comment: Just Believe.' In: *Fairlady*. Cape Town: Media24 Magazine Division. May: 12.

———. 2005. 'Unfair Comment: Forked Tongues.' In: *Fairlady*. Cape Town: Media24 Magazine Division. June: 14.

———. 2005. Unofficial Interview with Mary West. Cape Town. July.

———. 2005. 'Unfair Comment: It's All the Same Thing.' In: *Fairlady*. Cape Town: Media24 Magazine Division. July: 14.

———. 2005. 'Unfair Comment: Who Killed Fana Kaba?' In: *Fairlady*. Cape Town: Media24 Magazine Division. November: 18.

Van Niekerk, Anton. 2003. 'Merkwaardige Intellektuele Prestasie.' *Rapport*. 23 November: 24.

Van Niekerk, Marlene. 1996. *Triomf*. Johannesburg: Queillerie Publishers.

———. 2001. 'Klein Vingeroefening rondom die Nosie van Hibriditeit.' In: Van Heerden, Etienne (ed.), *Briewe deur die Lug*. Cape Town: Tafelberg. 147–163.

———. 2004. 'Labour.' In: Chapman, Michael (ed.). *The New Century of South African Short Stories*. Johannesburg: Ad Donker. 301–318.

———. 2005. *Agaat*. Cape Town: Tafelberg.

Van Zyl, Albert. 2005. 'Sidderend Eerlik. *Rapport*'s "Perspektief".' 23 Oktober 2005: 4.

Von Klemperer, Margaret. 2003. 'People We Know.' *The Natal Witness*. 28 April: 7.

Ware, Vron & Les Back. 2002. *Out of Whiteness: Color, Politics and Culture*. Chicago and London: Univeristy of Chicago Press.

Wellman, David. 1977. *Portraits of White Racism*. New York: Cambridge University Press.

———. 1997. 'Minstrel Shows, Affirmative Action Talk, and Angry White Men: Marking Racial Otherness in the 1990s.' In: Frankenberg, Ruth (ed.). *Displacing Whiteness: Essays in Social and Cultural Criticism*. Durham: Duke University Press. 311–331.

Werbner, Pnina & Tariq Modood (eds). 1997. *Debating Cultural Hybridity: Multi-Cultural Identities and the Politics of Racism*. London and New Jersey: Zed Books.

Wicomb, Zoë. 2001. 'Five Afrikaner Texts and the Rehabilitation of Whiteness.' In: Kriger, R. & A. Zegeye (eds). *Culture in the New South Africa: After Apartheid*. (Vol. 2). Cape Town: Kwela Books 159–180

Wiegman, Robyn. 1999. 'Whiteness Studies and the Paradox of Particularity.' *Boundary 2*. Fall: 115–150.

Williams, Raymond. 2001 [1997]. 'Marxism and Literature (Chapter 3: Literature).' In: Leitch, Vincent, B. et al. (eds). *The Norton Anthology of Theory and Criticism*. New York and London: W.W. Norton and Company.

Woolf, Virginia. 1945 [1928]. *A Room of One's Own*. London: Penguin.

———. 1986 [1925]. *Mrs Dalloway*. London: Grafton.

www.babynamesworld.com for the meaning of 'Alida'. Accessed 2 February 2005.

www.inyourpocket.com for information on Vilnius. Accessed 14 August 2004.

www.manataka.org for information on the 'Rainbow Warriors'. Accessed 2 January 2005.

www.pygmalion.org for information on the play and its later film interpretations. Accessed 1 July 2005.

www.scouting.org.za for the English translation of 'Shosholoza'. Accessed 23 March 2005.

www.sing365.com for the lyrics to Nina Simone's 'Pirate Jenny'. Accessed 5 October 2005.

www.wutheringjolie.com for information on actor, Angelina Jolie. Accessed 2 November 2005.

Wylie, Dan. 1998. 'Review of *Echo Location*.' *Mail & Guardian*. 20–26 November: 33.

Young, Robert, J.C. 1995. *Colonial Desire: Hybridity in Theory, Culture and Race*. London: Routledge.

———. 2004 [1990]. *White Mythologies: Writing History and the West*. London and New York: Routledge.

Endnotes

1. Homi K. Bhabha has noted that 'recent writing in cultural criticism has left the prose plainer, less adorned with the props of the argument's staging' (2002: 56). In following Bhabha's lead, I have resisted the temptation to 'scare quote' every reference to race, especially South African delineations of the various racial groupings (black, white, Indian and coloured), which are still in usage despite a growing awareness of the speciousness of such constructions.
2. It is tempting to employ the same parenthesis used in the title of this book, i.e. (post-)apartheid, throughout, to highlight the continuing effect of the racial violence that the regime created, though there are moments when such a strategy is more appropriate than others.
3. The concept is widely used in whiteness studies, but associated most readily with the pioneering work of Ruth Frankenberg (1993), whose contributions are introduced later in this chapter. Other scholars have employed the Lacanian terms 'empty signifier' (i.e. Zoë Wicomb), or 'Master Signifier' (Kalpana Seshadri-Crooks), which are interchangeable with the notion of an 'unmarked marker', also introduced later in this chapter.
4. I have consciously chosen not to capitalise references to the 'west' in order to resist what Emmanuel Lévinas has called the 'ontological imperialism' (1969: 21) of a western will to power.
5. The plural is employed primarily to suggest the multigeneric approach adopted – in other words, the inclusion of texts that would not necessarily be considered as 'literature', or even 'English literature', in conventional usage of such concepts.
6. I acknowledge J.M. Coetzee's seminal contribution to the topic later in this introduction.
7. A concept that gained currency in *l'écriture feminine*, associated with French Feminists, namely Hélène Cixous, Julia Kristeva and Luce Irigaray, to denote the centrality of the phallus and logos in the Lacanian symbolic order.
8. See Sander Gilman's work on the visual markers that equate the highly sexualised western woman and the lascivious black woman, introduced later in this study.
9. In *White Mythologies: Writing History and the West* (1990), a seminal text in whiteness studies, Robert Young plots the history of white western liberal humanism and demonstrates its complicity in colonialism.

10 Jacques Derrida suggests that 'for the notion of translation we would have to substitute the notion of transformation: a regulated transformation of one language by another, of one text by another' (in Krog 2003: 267).

11 The term has been employed increasingly in creative writing programmes to signal the columnist's contribution to journalism, which is arguably less constrained than other types of journalism, in blurring the boundaries between fact and fiction. For example, a recent publication, entitled *Literary Journalism: A Reader* (2001), edited by Jean Chance and William McKeen, consists of a selection of articles from newspapers and magazines and these pieces are hailed as 'some of the finest writing done under the aegis of journalism' (2001: xiii).

12 In *Marxism and Literature*, Williams asks: 'If literature was reading, could a mode written for spoken performance be said to be literature, and if not, where was Shakespeare?' (2001: 1568)

13 '[which] was in effect the final stage in a shift from a para-national scholarly profession, […] to a profession increasingly defined by its class position, from which essentially general criteria, applicable in fields other than literature, were derived. In England, certain specific features of bourgeois development strengthened the shift; the "cultivated amateur" was one of its elements, but "taste" and "sensibility" were essentially unifying concepts, in class terms' (2001: 1568)

14 The collapsing of disciplines, particularly languages and literatures, into unwieldy schools and departments under the auspices of Communication/Cultural and/or Media Studies at many South African universities is at least partially a consequence of Marxist and post-Marxist critiques such as these.

15 Krog's authorial manifesto recorded in *Country of My Skull* is examined in detail in Chapter Three, though it is significant to note here that as a result of her work as a journalist covering the Truth and Reconciliation Commission hearings, the writer's contribution to rethinking the limits of autobiography include her consciously problematising the distinction between the 'personal' and the 'public'.

16 From David Medalie's *Encounters: An Anthology of South African Short Stories* (1998) and Michael Chapman's *The New Century of South African Short Stories* (2004).

17 See Steve Biko's *I Write What I Like* for an explication of Black Consciousness as a response to white racism. This series of polemical essays written in the 1970s urges black South Africans to recognise their own worth, and to understand the ways in which they have been systematically and institutionally disadvantaged. Of note is Biko's charge that '[w]hite liberals must leave blacks to take care of their own business while they concern themselves with the real evil in our society – white racism'. (1987: 23)

18 The term is used here to signal a process of identification, rather than pigmentation, and is qualified as this discussion unfolds.

19 Shome explicitly lists these products and suggests that in addition to the historical and 'physical travel of white imperial bodies colonising "other worlds" […] today's neocolonial travel of white cultural products – media, music, television, products, academic texts, and Anglo fashions – to "other worlds" [has] […] sustained [the] forces of imperialism and global capitalism' (1999: 108).

20 This concept is borrowed from Ruth Frankenberg, whose work is introduced later in this subsection (1993: 290).

21 'Position Two: To acknowledge the fact that you are a victim, but to explain this as an act of Fate, the Will of God, the dictates of Biology (in the case of women, for instance), the necessity decreed by History, or Economics, or the Unconscious, or any other large general powerful idea.'
'Position Three: To acknowledge the fact that you are a victim but to refuse to accept the assumption that the role is inevitable.'

22 A theory elaborated on later in this introduction, and in relation to Marianne Thamm's writing in Chapter Four of this study.

23 Horrell's article, entitled 'A Whiter Shade of Pale: White Femininity as Guilty Masquerade in "New" (White) South African Women's Writing' (2004) offers a complementary reading of writers who do not appear in this study, with the exception of Antjie Krog, whose work she only marginally includes.

24 The proper noun order here denotes the constructedness of femininity, as a role to be learned and performed.

25 An ANC discussion document on 'The National Question' suggests that there is a tendency among 'white Afrikaners [to] have a different emotional, psychological and material relationship to Africa and South Africa compared to other whites'. This is taken as evidence to indicate 'that Afrikaners are embracing the new South Africa and Africanism more readily than English-speaking whites' (Ndlanga & Msomi, 22 May 2005a). This comparison between English and Afrikaans responses to the new political dispensation is in itself a sweeping generalisation but one that offers interesting potential investigations.

26 They note that the universalising aspect of this kind of power 'persists across its particular manifestations, cuts through specificities, and devastates those who fall within its purview. Thus, to say that whiteness is not monolithic and to demonstrate that it is a nuanced construction reflects a disingenuous refusal to acknowledge the destructive effects of white power, which, in its overwhelming effect on the lives of people, carries the weight of the universal. Many contemporary whites steeped in Civil Rights ideologies, disaffiliate from segregationist and white supremacist practices to declare themselves anti-racist.'

27 He argues that '[t]he institutionalisation of "white studies" threatens to inaugurate an invidious intellectual division of labour that designates white scholars to the study of whiteness and people of color to the study of difference. As a result, "white

studies" is relegated to a politically safe form of "race talk," which, rather than pushing the understanding to its limits, erects a racial palisade around the pursuit of wisdom.'

28 This is not to suggest that there are not black enclaves of middle-class respectability emerging in the country, but the emergence of such a phenomenon, in any case, may be related to the transferability of values and norms.

29 David Wellman, in an essay entitled 'Affirmative Action and Angry White Men' suggests that '[u]ntil recently, the categories "white" and "male" were taken for granted. Being white and male was "normal"' and adds that '[t]he taken-for-granted world of white male Americans […] was their *normalcy*, not their whiteness or their gender' (Frankenberg, 1997: 321 my emphasis).

30 Vron Ware has also suggested the ongoing necessity of studying the phenomenon and the complicities it engenders. She points out that 'the study of whiteness offers to all those individuals caught up in racial discourse against their will potentially new opportunities to make sense of their own political location and to recognise a degree of agency in challenging (and therefore changing) the many ways in which the beneficiaries of racial hierarchy are complicit with injustice' (Ware & Back 2002: 31).

31 'White men still rule the rainbow nation' runs the headline of an article in the *Sunday Times* (22 May 2005), on the ANC's discussion document 'The National Question'.

32 Though there are suburban areas in South Africa that are beginning to reflect changes in material circumstances for previously advantaged groups, one need look no further, in many instances, than one's 'own backyard', to witness the persistence of a racially divided economic dispensation. In Port Elizabeth, for example, the sprawling black informal settlement of Walmer Township is adjacent to one of the wealthiest (predominantly white) middle-class suburbs in the city.

33 Though Rich's work is seminal, there are multiple and more recent responses from black feminist scholars, among them bell hooks and Barbara Christian, who have responded to the kind of solipsism that Rich associates with western feminism. In this country the work of Desiree Lewis, and more recently Pumla Gqola (both of whom are cited elsewhere in this study), has significantly added to the debate.

34 Their projects are comparable in the sense that both pursue feminist/lesbian politics to uncover multiple and related oppressions.

35 'In Foucault's scheme', notes Dollimore, 'deviants come to occupy a revealing, dangerous double relationship to power, at once culturally marginal yet discursively central. Even as the sexual deviant is banished to the margins of society, he or she remains integral to it, not in spite of but because of that marginality' (1991: 222).

36 J.M. Coetzee, in an essay from *Stranger Shores,* warns against such celebrations in his reading of the media's representation of the Rugby World Cup in 1995.

'Rainbow-ness', he notes, was in any event borrowed from America, like so much else in South Africa, and was deliberately and certainly too glibly 'set to work to reverse the mindset of a population locked by its former masters into ethnic-political compartments' (2001: 352). Though the phrase has subsequently been discredited, there is evidence that the celebratory gesture it promotes, particularly in advertising practices and pulp fiction, still has currency.

37 I am indebted to Helize van Vuuren for this and other translations from Afrikaans reviews: 'What leaves the reader unsatisfied is the lack of direction in the book. What is it really now – novel, satire, love story with a (unlikely) happy ending? It falls somewhere between all those [genres] and consequently – and it is a great pity – is not a memorable read.'

38 In the *Sunday Times* (6 February 2005), Charlotte Bauer argues that plagiarism is 'a very straightforward kind of theft' and that Pamela Jooste will have to face her own 'failure of imagination'.

39 Kirby's earlier condemnation of Jooste (*Mail & Guardian* 4–10 February 2005) is reinforced in response to academic Michiel Heyns's less damaging reading of the 'grey areas' of plagiarism. Briefly summarised, Heyns (2005: 29) suggests that Kirby overreacted to the incident, which further enrages Kirby in his remark that Heyns's 'sophistry might have gone down well with the less promising among his first-year students' whereas Kirby himself supports Charlotte Bauer's 'refreshingly blunt' consideration of the charge (18 February 2005).

40 Such an observation is unlikely to be received without eliciting a list of famous white South African activists, but it is nonetheless important to weigh up such cataloguing of white contributions in relation to the enormity and anonymity of the figures associated with black contributions.

41 See Eric Lott's reading of the cultural implications of such representations in his polemical essay 'Racial Cross-Dressing and the Construction of American Whiteness', in During, Simon (ed.), 1999, *The Cultural Studies Reader*. London: Routledge.

42 The stereotype in white South African writing of Kaaitjie Kekkelbek – a loud, obnoxious, usually coloured woman, prone to alcohol abuse and signifying the 'Hottentot Venus' – Sarah Baartman.

43 The Jezebel and Mammy figures are interrogated in Toni Morrison's *Beloved*, and in much of the scholarship surrounding the novel.

44 The word is not unconsciously used anomalously: it has been scare quoted to suggest residual associations, in this case the inferiority brought about by Eurocentricity, and in other cases to suggest a tenacious sense of entitlement.

45 Wine Farmers' Association.

46 'Drink Policy': the dispensing of cheap wine to the labourers at night and over weekends to supplement their meagre wages.

47	Underwear.
48	Ditch.
49	Afrikaans 'aunt' – any older woman who is 'oud and getroud' – old and married.
50	The son of a farmer, but more generically, an Afrikaner boy.
51	Translation: '*A Change of Tongue* is too many books brought together in one book.'
52	Translation: 'Krog's book frustrates and confuses one – in the first place because one does not really comprehend why it is a book! However, it remains one of the most remarkable intellectual achievements of our time.'
53	It is important for the purposes of this argument to note that I am tracing residual 'discursive repertoires' that emerge in white women's writing. In the case of Krog, it would be just as interesting and as valid to trace the development of her oppositional stance to patriarchy, to apartheid, and to Afrikanerdom, as it emerges throughout her extensive oeuvre and in her poetry especially.
54	In an interview with journalist Diane de Beer, Krog reiterates her position in relation to the material which she spells out in the Acknowledgments (2003: 369): 'the "I" doesn't always refer to the author; the father and mother quoted in the book are not necessarily her parents and her family not always blood relatives' (De Beer 2003b: 3). Despite this disclaimer, there are obvious parallels between Krog's biographically authentic experiences and the histories she records in the book.
55	The first review appeared in *Rapport*'s 'Perspektief' (23 October 2005), and the book is entitled *'n Ander Tongval* (loosely translated: 'A Different Way of Speaking', flagged as the original version of *A Change of Tongue*).
56	Bhabha argues that the myth of origins and discovery is a 'normalising myth whose organics and revisionary narrative is also the history of that nationalist discipline of Commonwealth history and its equally expansionist epigone, Commonwealth literature (1986: 166).
57	'Yes, I know, it's a story that I constructed from all the other information picked up over the months about other people's reactions and psychologists' advice. I'm not reporting or keeping minutes. I'm telling. If I have to say every time that so-and-so said this, and then at another time so-and-so said that, it gets boring. I cut and paste the upper layer, in order to get to the second layer told, which is actually the story I want to tell. I change some people's names when I think they might be annoyed or might not understand the distortions.' 'But then you're not busy with the truth!' 'I am busy with the truth…*my* truth! Of course, it's quilted together from hundreds of stories that we've experienced or heard in the past two years. Seen from my perspective, shaped by my state of mind at the time and now also by the audience I'm telling the story to. In every story there is hearsay, there is a grouping together of things that didn't necessarily happen together, there are assumptions, there are exaggerations to bring home the enormity of situations, there is downplaying to

confirm innocence. And all of this together makes up the whole country's truth. So also the lies. And stories that date from earlier times.'
'And the affair that you describe in here. Is that also true?'
'No, but I had to bring a relationship into the story so that I could verbalise certain personal reactions to the hearings. I had to create a new character who could not only bring in new information but also express the psychological underpinning of the Commission. Surely I can't describe how I eavesdropped and spied on others? What gives a story its real character is the need to entertain – to make the listener hang on your lips.' (2002: 170–171)

58 'We think back through our mothers if we are women. It is useless to go to the great men writers for help, however much one may go to them for pleasure.' (1945: 76)

59 The epigraph of the book records Chomsky's transformational rule which is reiterated on page 205. 'Transformational Grammar has stipulated two levels of syntactic structure: deep structure (an abstract underlying structure that incorporates all syntactic information required for the interpretation of a given sentence) and surface structure (a structure that incorporates all the syntactic features of a sentence required to convert the sentence into a spoken or written version). Transformation links deep structure with surface structure.' (2003: epigraph)

60 The term Dreama Moon coins in 'White Enculturation and Bourgeois Ideology' (1999: 188).

61 See Rey Chow's 'Where Have All the Natives Gone?' in *Contemporary Postcolonial Theory: A Reader* (1996), edited by Padmini Mongia for an elaboration of this debate.

62 The book that Krog translated into Afrikaans, a process no less difficult to negotiate than either of the journeys evoked in the walking metaphors above.

63 Summarised in the Krog text as the third consequence of racism, i.e. what happens when the native is required to be 'agreeable' – the black person who having made it in a white world now feels that he/she has been co-opted into docility and acquiescence (2003: 151).

64 Both Afrikaans expressions indicate being 'fucked up'.

65 'It is frightening to see how people here cling to an Afrikaner identity that has long ceased to exist in South Africa. I told Katrien, you know, those of us who have remained behind, we adapt, we die, we sacrifice, give away, compromise, we fight a bit too much here on the off side, a bit too little there on the on side, but hell, we know how to change from mean-whiskered bully to arse-kissing poodle, from God Almighty to Father Christmas. Whatever is required at the moment. Our children go to mixed schools, read from books about Bongi and Thandi, we click our clumsy tongues around Ngconde and Nongqawuse and Xolile, and we know how to make ourselves scarce.

I said to her, the danger is that one day you suddenly realise you've kept faith with an imaginary country, a country constructed purely from your longings and your memories. Has the South Africa of which you speak not disappeared already? You long for and want to go back to a place that doesn't exist anymore, and that makes you a bit like a refugee who cannot go home again.
But Katrien said she preferred the refugee kind to the Afrikaners who tried to assimilate. They have an obsession with bad news from South Africa, they keep the negative stories alive like babies in incubators, to justify their leaving and their staying away.' (2003: 71–72)

66 'oh shame!' – a complete translation of the poem is included in the Addendum.
67 'male vanity that always has the last word on the prerequisites of belonging to them'.
68 'in a language stripped of the grammar of humanity and regret'.
69 'the new barcounter of identities'.
70 We have already encountered, in Dot Serfontein's history, the Boer described by the English as 'orang-utans' (2003: 150). The cumulative effect of these images is a sense that Krog is situating Afrikanerdom as alterity, and reinforcing the psychological double bind in which the Afrikaner is simultaneously victim and perpetrator.
71 'Complexion' is a word with an interesting etymology. In most usages cited in the *New Shorter Oxford English Dictionary* it includes an overt sense of physicality, including tone, texture, 'nature' and the four bodily humours: heat, cold, moisture and dryness.
72 This is not to suggest that a similar indifference is not also evident amongst black South African youth, only that those responses are not under scrutiny in this study.
73 The parts italicised are from *Country of My Skull*.
74 'After Land Invasions in Zimbabwe' – the entire poem and an English translation is included in the Addendum.
75 Robert Young offers a convincing contextualisation in *White Mythologies* of the ways in which humanism has always been paradoxically anti-humanist, and plots humanism's involvement in the history of colonialism (2004: 158–165).
76 Translation from the *Woordeboek van die Afrikaanse Taal: Eerste Deel A–C*: 1. A white man on a farm who does not really earn a fixed salary but enjoys certain advantages such as a free house and grazing, etc., in exchange for certain services. 2. Somebody settled in a country as a stranger or living with someone as a subordinate.
77 'one belongs to she who daily and wordlessly/weaves new wool into the carpet'. The entire poem and a translation of it is included in the Addendum.
78 The title might be translated as 'horror' and describes defecating in a shower.
79 These emerge particularly in the italicised lyrical descriptions that serve as

partition breaks between each of the six sections of the book: *rain, giraffe, moon, willow, river, child, wing* (2003: Contents Page).

80   These are regretfully omitted from this project, though they would be elucidating reflections of sexual awakening that an exclusively feminist reading of the novel could find charged with relevance, and they provide another research opportunity on completion of this project.

81   'turdwhite and pissblack'. A translation of the poem is included in the Addendum.

82   These unofficial introductory comments are provided only as contextualising asides and are not meant to suggest any qualitative or quantitative certainty.

83   It received the Sappi Pica Award for best women's general interest magazine in 2003 and 2004, and the Admag Award for best women's magazine in 2003.

84   A word Marianne Thamm has employed to describe her role in the magazine (Unofficial interview: July 2005).

85   See Thamm's feature article entitled 'The Political As Personal' in which she provides an historical overview of the contributions each of *Fairlady*'s editors has offered in challenging South African politics, albeit 'between pages of powder and perfume, between advertisements that reflected the racist and sexist society that South Africa was [and still is]' (April 2005: 82–89).

86   Interesting work, beginning with Robyn Lakoff's in the seventies, has been done on the implications of the designation 'lady' in relation to a set of value-laden behavioural prescriptions regulating normative western womanhood. These linguistic insights may be found in the recent study called *Gender and Language* by Penelope Eckert and Sally McConnell-Ginet (2003). Likewise, see Christopher Kelen's polemical essay on the implications of the designation 'fair' in the Australian national anthem, 'Advance Australia Fair', which he reads as 'Keep Australia White' (2005: 216).

87   Facts gleaned from www.pygmalion.ws

88   Quoted in John Storey's analysis of the politics involved in definitions of 'Culture' from his essay called 'The "Culture and Civilisation" Tradition' (1998: 23).

89   The year 2005 saw two celebratory issues of the magazine, the Anniversary Edition and *The Fairlady Collection* (a book), both of which have endeavoured to prove that *Fairlady* has always been a monthly with a social conscience, and both of which have involved Marianne Thamm's editorial experience. Neither, however, detracts from the general thrust of the magazine, which is still predominantly about how to be(come) a 'fair lady'.

90   Borne out by the response in the only review the book received, from Peter Terry on SAFM's *The Bookshelf*: 'You won't always agree with her. There are times when she'll probably even get you tweezer-lipped. Indeed a few of her opinions and attitudes stick in my throat. But, boy, she is one stimulating lady!' (10 November 2002).

91   The interview was not transcribed, but will be mentioned in this study, with Thamm's consent.
92   Marianne Thamm was voted Journalist *and* Columnist of the Year at the Media24 Excellence Awards Ceremony in 2005 (Ed's Notes, *Fairlady*, August 2005: 10).
93   A contested terrain which John Storey defines as 'mass produced commercial culture', homogenised and 'Americanised' (1998: 8–12), but characterised as a 'site of struggle between the forces of "resistance" of subordinate groups in society, and the forces of "incorporation" of dominant groups in society' (1998: 13–14).
94   Kerkorrel was an alternative Afrikaans rock singer whose homosexuality was only publicly acknowledged after the singer had committed suicide.
95   See 'Let's Hear It for the Wrinklies' (January 2003: 10) for an additional example of such strategies. Amongst others, she invokes David Cassidy as an example of a pop star she found attractive in her youth: 'The other star who got me hot was David Cassidy [...] but for many years I was under the impression he was a girl. It was a difficult adolescence, you see.'
96   The piece is rendered even more dangerous given that Thamm had already been berated by a reader for bashing marriage in an earlier column, 'Untying the Knot' (2002: 53). The reader says: 'By giving space to Marianne Thamm's Unfair Comment, you are lending credence to her jaundiced views on life and helping to erode the little bit of hope we have left. The Woman I Want to Be went in love to my daughter's wedding, the Woman I Am went in celebration to my son's wedding [...] I dare not buy your next issue, perhaps Marianne is planning to tell my grandchildren that there's no Father Christmas, and what's left after that, the Easter Bunny?' (2002: 55).
97   From the poem by Lord Alfred Douglas addressed to Oscar Wilde, written in 1894 and published originally in *The Chameleon*.
98   Thamm mentioned this in the interview (July 2005).
99   The lyrics and translation of 'Shosholoza' may be found at www.scouting.org.za/songs/
100 Ample research has been done on the role of the mass media as an institutional apparatus that promotes western normativity. See, for example, John Downing and Charles Husband in *Representing 'Race': Racisms, Ethnicities and Media* in which they plot 'the perpetuation of racist structures' and 'racist rhetoric' (2005: 82) across mainstream multimedia practices.
101 Thamm deliberately plays on the sensitivities around labelling global co-ordinates in 'Welcome to the Matrix' (July 2003: 12) by referring to a man 'sitting in the cosy living room of his developed world home [...] witness[ing] footage of some fresh, unfolding horror in the developing world'.
102 Jolie's mother is purported to be an indigenous American (www.wutheringjolie.com).
103 Though the magazine prides itself on having refused to advertise dieting products

(and has lost huge sums of money as a result), it still obsessively features 'How To' articles on maintaining an acceptable physical shape, and the fashion pages still feature anorexically thin models.

104 'There is an aspect of South African journalism that is beginning to disturb me [...] Marianne is one of many who regularly insult George W. Bush [...] If I were American, particularly a Christian Republican, I doubt my views would be "enlightened" by some journalists using [derogatory] terms to describe me.'
'I think Marianne should show some consideration for the beliefs and faith of others [...] Just because people choose to be Christians does not make them like Bush.' ('What's On Your Mind?' July 2005: 12)

105 An allusion to Albie Sachs's call to acknowledge the extent of white privilege, in suggesting that if white South Africans 'cannot see what apartheid did to [their] fellow South Africans, [they] must be dead or living in Canada' (2002: 18).

106 Morrison's afterword reinforces the necessity of columns such as this that target capitalist consumerism as mass-producing notions of beauty (and ugliness), when she says that her project was to 'hit the raw nerve of racial self-contempt, expose it, then soothe it not with narcotics but with language that replicated the agency I discovered in my first experience of beauty' (1999: 168).

107 She mentions in particular the launch of the MissDela doll range, the founder of which is Judith Oosthuizen.

108 Though I have suggested that Thamm only cryptically hints at her sexual orientation so as not to offend the sensibilities of the *Fairlady* readership, the most conservative moral hound-dogs would have sniffed this out.

109 These are discussed in more detail in the concluding section of this chapter.

110 That the practice of selection and omission has been employed is duly noted. However, these snippets are unadorned, uncontextualised and rendered as authentically as is possible.

111 I have read many of the poems that deploy the first-person pronoun as representing, however imperfectly, the subjectivity of Karen Press, a white middle class woman who occupies a flat in Sea Point, writes poetry and designs textbooks for children. Though this reading cannot be proved with any empirical certainty, it is at least probable, especially in relation to the first- or third-person poems surrounding them, in which the speakers or those described are clearly imagined or represented personas, as is the case in the poems featuring Alida (1998: 72) or Sergeant Oliphant (76), for example.

112 Translated: '*Your mother's cunt! .../You piss cunt! piss/cunt! You – you – /I'll fucking screw you!/You fucker! Yes, you! You!/Don't walk away!/You fucker!*'

113 Loosely translated from IsiXhosa: *S/he said that the child can stay during school time, but should not be allowed to bathe.* I am indebted to colleagues, Ron Endley and Simphiwe Sesanti for these and other translations.

114 I am indebted to Beth Jeffrey for this image (of the white writer gazing down on South African realities from the elevated safety of the apartment balcony), an image that she has examined in relation to white South African poets in an unpublished conference paper. Though there are many white poets who arguably do not fall easily into this category (for example, those who have been imprisoned, and those who have chosen exile), it may be regarded as a recognisably common positionality of the white South African writer.

115 Translated: 'liberal' and 'conservative', respectively.

116 A website called 'In Your Pocket: Essential City Guides' records the following information about Vilnius, capital of Lithuania: 'It may not be the centre of the universe, or the centre of culture, but you might be surprised to learn that Lithuania is in fact the smack dab centre of Europe [...] In 1989 [...] the French Geographical Society placed the exact centre of Europe (after a re-estimation) at 54 54' N latitude, 25 19' E longitude', just outside Vilnius (www.inyourpocket.com 'The Monkey in the Middle').

117 Perth is a favourite destination for white South Africans who cannot adjust to the new dispensation, an occurrence so routine that it has already become proverbialised in the phrase 'packing for Perth'.

118 It records what may be a historically verifiable incident in which human remains are found buried in an abode, and Press is clearly also playing on the idiom of 'finding skeletons in the closet': '"What's worse than finding a body in your cupboard?"/ – "Finding a half a body"'. Schoolboys swap skeleton stories' (1998: 36).

119 www.babynamesworld.com is one of the websites consulted.

120 An unofficial source has translated 'naches' as joy or pleasure, and 'schoch' as derogatory for black man in Jewish colloquial speech. Sea Point has always attracted a large Jewish community.

121 The companion poems 'Exotic Entertainment 1' and 'Exotic Entertainment 2' (1998: 46–47) both mimic the discourse of advertising erotica to be found in the Smalls of newspapers, and echo Press's baseline strategy.

122 'Madam' is the title afforded to the white woman in charge of domestic labour.

123 Elaborated on in Dominic Head's study of the modernist short story as the 'psychological story [... in the] Chekhovian tradition' (1992: 16).

124 Simon Dentith defines 'mock heroism' as a form of parody that relies on 'the incongruity between manner and matter' in order to 'negotiate a cultural situation in which inherited prestigious forms continue to carry authority but can no longer convincingly be deployed unironically in the contemporary moment' (2000: 192).

125 Or, if he is seen at all, it is only as an 'object, in the midst of other objects. Sealed into that crushing objecthood' (1967a: 109).

126 In her examination of Hollywood's Vietnam stories as *American* stories: 'Indochina

provided the lush, tropical backdrop against which the United States played out its fantasies … The Vietnamese, the Cambodians, and Laotians were only script props. Nameless, faceless, slit-eyed humanoids. They were just the people who died. Gooks' (2004: 63).

127 Invoking James Joyce's notion of the literary epiphany, Dominic Head examines the effects of the 'equivocal epiphany' in relation specifically to Katherine Mansfield's 'Bliss' where Bertha's 'epiphany' is read as 'semi-revelation [which is] greatly compromised by the personal confusion and alienation simultaneously uncovered' (1992: 29).

128 See, for example, the fiction of Margaret Atwood and Angela Carter, and the poetry of Anne Sexton. There are many scholarly responses to these artistic interventions and much of the summarised overview of the fairy-tale above is indebted to a collective engagement with the genre and the critical work it generates.

129 The title of the anthology might be translated as 'Airmail'.

130 'Small finger exercise on the notion of hybridity'.

131 See the *Laugh It Off Annual* (2003), edited by Justin Nurse.

132 'The black threat'.

133 The Rainbow Warriors emerge in indigenous American folklore and are depicted as children who learn to love the world anew, and all its beings, after it has been all but destroyed by the white man. Many versions of the story exist and may be gleaned from the Manataka Indian Council website: www.manataka.org

134 An extract from the lyrics of 'Pirate Jenny' (Brecht/Weill), as sung by Nina Simone:
'You people can watch while I'm scrubbing these floors
And I'm scrubbin' the floors while you're gawking
Maybe once ya tip me and it makes ya feel swell…
But you'll never guess to who you're talkin'.
No. you couldn't ever guess to who you're talkin'.
Then one night there's a scream in the night
And you'll wonder who could that have been
And you see me kinda grinnin' while I'm scrubbin'
And you say, what's she got to grin?
I'll tell you.
There's a ship
The black freighter
With a skull on it's masthead
Will be coming in' (Lyrics accessed from www.sing365.com).

135 A popular urban myth circulating currently is that when (white) suburban homes are burgled, the robbers inject some kind of sleeping spray into the keyhole to ensure that the occupants of the house remain in a deep sleep for the duration of the burglary.

136 Hephaistos is a Vulcan, a 'blacksmith' by trade, ironically, and in this context, a prerequisite of his trade is cheap black labour.
137 Van Niekerk is vigilant in her uncovering of idioms, and even if they are not articulated in the story they are nonetheless implied.
138 The expression, translated into English, loses much of its authenticity, and less directly translated might be something like 'kind of' or 'sort of'.
139 Van Niekerk is foregrounding the stereotype of a black South African fear of snakes and simultaneously using it to protect her property.
140 See the incident in *Triomf*, in which the lesbians across the road from the Benades 'eat forbidden fruit'!
141 Reminiscent of Frieda Kahlo's self-portraits with a monkey on her shoulder and defiantly celebrating Woman's association with Nature as opposed to Culture in the binaries governing gender.
142 'What we are calling a hybrid construction in an utterance that belongs, by its grammatical and compositional markers, to a single speaker, but that actually contains mixed within it two utterances, two speech manners, two styles, two languages, two semantic and axiological belief systems ... In such discourse there are two voices, two meanings and two expressions. And all the while these two voices are dialogically inter-related. They – as it were – know about each other (just as two exchanges in a dialogue know of each other and are structured in this mutual knowledge of each other). Double-voiced discourse(s) (are) always internally dialogised. A potential dialogue is embedded in them, one as yet unfolded.' (Bakhtin 2001: 147)

Index

Entries in italics are either non-English words, or publications, films or other titles.

100% Silk 145–146, 155
19th Century Gratitude 137, 139
2002 SA Conference of Racism 88
A Change of Tongue 7, 25, 89, 91, 94, 96, 99 117, 187, 189, 190, 191, 194
A Hard Drive 75–76, 87
A Journey 97
A Most Desirable Location 131, 150
A Room of One's Own 13
AA 118
abuse 145
academic knowledge, imperialistic nature of 12
accountability 88
Achilles and Paris 141
adultery 58, 59, 60, 68
Africa
 identification with 90
 pre-colonial 119
 western attitudes towards 116
African Americans 120
representation of by white writers 15
African Facts 148
African, definitions of 95
African, resignification of 96
Afrika man 95
Afrikaan vs Afrikaner 95
Afrikaans 57
 and English, divide between 173
 fiction 173
Afrikaner-bashing 56
Afrikaner Weerstandbeweging 88
Afrikanerdom
 parochialism of 191
 re-narrativisation of 182
Afrikaners 102

history of 101
 settlerhood of 102
 vs Africans 95
 persecution of by English 75
 stereotypes of 56, 57
Afros 112
After Land Invasions in Zimbabwe 197–198
Agaat 188
agentless passivity 17
ai tog 94, 98, 198
alcohol 185
Alida 143, 145–146, 155
Alida at Home 145, 156
alienation 25, 97
Althusser, Louis 17
Alzheimer's 45, 46
Amandla! A Revolution in Four-Part Harmony 111
ambivalence 65, 193
 of contemporary SA women's writing 192
American Celebration of Whiteness, The 116
anal retention 97
ANC Youth League 124, 125, 165
Anderson, Benedict 15
anorexia 119
anti-apartheid activists 45
antiretrovirals 128, 129
apartheid 24, 87, 170
 beneficiaries of 23
apartheid-era South Africa 187
apartment blocks 149
appropriation and closure of land 132
Armstrong, Nancy 29, 64,120, 159, 179
Arnold, Mathew 107
Asmal, Kader 118
assimilation 80
 and integration 22
At the End of the Story 133, 156, 157

Atwood, Margaret 1, 12–13, 15, 65, 172
autobiographical catharsis 25
autobiographical nature of all writing 67
autobiographical novels 9
autobiographies 66
Awerbuck, Diane 9, 38
Babb, Valerie 14, 18, 19, 57, 133, 195
Back, Les 21
bagels 133
Bakhtin, Michail 109, 187
Bakhtin's carnival 109–110, 129
ballet 140–141
Barbie ideal 115
Barbie's Revenge 124
Barnett, Adrian 34
Barthes, Roland 22, 150
bathers 148
Bauer, Charlotte 41
Bauer, Dale 109, 129
Bauer, Katy 38
beach walks 139, 148
Beauty and the Beast 183
Beckham, David 113
Behr, Mike 105
Bell, Vikki 17, 29, 30, 127, 178
belonging 13, 26, 93, 101, 131
 in white suburbia 140
 yearning for 98
Beloved 93, 171
benevolent liberalism vs conservative culpability 173
Berman, Kelly 130, 157
Beyond Borders 116–117
Bhabha, Homi K 19, 20, 21, 22, 36, 67, 74, 95, 125, 132, 173, 184, 185
big-phallus status 129
Biko, Steve 11
binaries, tyranny of 37
binarism 76
birds 142

black characters, one-dimensionality of 49
Black Consciousness 11, 114
black defensiveness 127
black female characters 43
black labour, rules pertaining to 50
black labour, white guilt 174
black life of risk 93
black power 11
black pride 114
black resentment, as a response to white entitlement 93
Black Skin, White Masks 21
black solidarity 127
  as a response to white entitlement 93
black South Africans 63, 64
black women
  different roles of 48
  white women's responses to 43
Black, Les 14
blacks
  good and bad 85
  persecution of by other blacks 75
Blixen, Karen 179
Bloch, Graeme 65
Blood and Belonging – Croatia & Serbia 196, 197
blue overalls 144
bodily discipline 120
body language 99, 102
Boehmer, Elleke 135
Boer War 75–76
boere 56
Boers 76
Bonnet, Alistair 18, 85
Booth, Michelle 9
Bottom Billing 118
bourgeois decorum 31, 64
  tyranny of 17
boys, behaviour of 141
breast cancer 42, 46
Bremner, Lindsay 41
Briewe deur die Lug 172
Brink, André 53, 58
Brown, Wendy 29
Bublé, Michael 111
Burden of Whiteness 9
burka 120, 121
Bush, George W 37, 120
Butler, Judith 17, 32, 113, 114
Caledon 184
Calvinists 55
Camera Lucida 22
Campbell, Naomi 124
campus security 165

canteens 151
Cape coloured-ese 138
Cape Times 40
capitalism 174
capitalist global world economy 192
car alarms 165
carbon-based beings 136
caricatures 62, 64
Carreira, Vanessa 125–126
cars 178
Cartesian subjectivity 4
castle 77, 195
cattle 147
Caucasian hegemony 1
celebrity visits 148
chameleons 186
chaos 77
Chapman, Michael 160, 161, 173, 187, 190
characters, unpopular 59
chauvinism 115
cheap black labour 194
  reliance on 182, 188
children 72
  stories for 168
Chomsky, Noam 37, 72
Chow, Rey 74
Christian National Education 118–119
chronology 154
Cilliers, Cecile 39–40
Cixous, Hélène 186
class 153
  and race 29–32
  centrality of in racial dynamics 90
class dynamics of power relations 56
classic realism 46
clichéd characters 61
clichés 42, 44, 56, 185
Coalition of the Brainless, The 116
Coetzee, JM 13, 24, 103, 107, 108, 109, 126, 129, 133, 183, 187
Coke ad 155
Collateral Damage 119
collective consciousness of white South Africans 119
collective racial heritage 177
collective unconscious, white 122
colonial cringe 60
Colonial Desire: Hybridity in Theory, Culture and Race 20
colonial oppression 128
colonialism 132

colonising history 95
colour, in Thamm's work 114
coloured despair 139
coloured gardener 176
coloured labour, employers of 177
coloured maids 150
coloured men, stereotype of 54, 55, 56
coloured women 139
commerce, etymology of 153
competitive individualism 114
complexion as dominant signifier 85
complicity 12, 195
  and culpability 191
  in maintaining white normativity 192
compulsory procreation 169
Comrades 160, 161, 165–168, 172
confessional reconciliatory post-apartheid fiction 25, 64
Conrad, Joseph 98
conservative culpability vs benevolent liberalism 173
conspicuous consumption 169
conspiratorial wink/gesture 180, 181
consumerism 26, 127
consumerist branding, subversion of 180–181
CONTACT ZONE 146
continuum of awareness of whiteness 189, 192
convergence 133
Conversations with Women 193
cosmetic surgery 121
Country of My Skull 5, 7, 66, 67, 68, 88, 89, 92, 99, 173
  lack of narrative closure in 99
court jesters 109, 110, 193
  compromised position of 122
  the role of 107–110
cricket 167
crime 88, 151, 178
Crocker, Jennifer 39
Cronin, Jeremy 157, 193
cuisine 152
cultural chauvinism 27
cultural imperialism 115
cultural studies vs literary studies 6
culture, location of 132
Darwin, Charles 146
Davy, K 31, 32
De Beauvoir, Simone 30
De Beer, Diane 39
De Vries, Fred 8, 9, 38, 58, 61

Dead or Living in Canada 122
deep century 156, 157
deep structure 72
defecation 96
Delphi, oracle of 132
Democratic Alliance 115
depraved luxury 166, 167
Derrida, Jacques 20, 131
Derry, Debbie 39
detour, a bloody long 143
detox 153
Dhairyam, Sagri 32
die swart gevaar 174
dieting 153
Dimitriu, Ileana 161
Dingaan and Pretorius 141
Discipline and Punish 29
disempowerment 128
Disgrace 24, 183, 187
Disgrace-lite 52
Disloyal to Civilisation: Feminism, Racism and Gynophobia 30–31
displacement 45, 46, 94
  vs alienation 179
Displacing Whiteness: Essays in Social and Cultural Criticism 16–17
dissent from within ranks of whiteness 109
District Six 174
divorce 113–114
Doane, Mary Ann 33
dog attack 78
dog pound 183
Doggies' Loo 147
dogs 167
  defecation habits of 148
  walking of 138
Dollimore, Jonathan 32, 33, 114, 129
dolls 123
domestic cleaners, teams of 176, 179, 184
domestic disputes 139
domestic violence 55
dopstelsel 55
double bind 77, 109
Down to My Last Skin 72, 82, 96
drag 113
dragon's teeth 171
dreadlocks 112
dream homes 151
Dreams Do Come True 151
Driver, Dorothy 36
drolwit en pissswart 98
drowning 136, 137
drunken coloured men 54, 55, 56, 64

Du Bois, WEB 1
dualism 68
Duchamp, Marcel 134
Duh, Duh, Duh, Duh 111
dump 183
duplicity 110, 121, 193
Dyer, Richard 22, 23, 158
Dylan, Bob 111
East Africa 117
Eastern Cape 99
Eastern Cape Herald 2
Echo Location 7, 8–9, 190, 193
  baseline text of 152–155
Eckstein, Barbara 162
Eeny Meeny Miny Mo 179
Elam, Diane 23
elderly women 164
  empty lives of 172
  journeys of 163
  elections in Africa 117
Eliot, TS 132
Ellison, Ralph 31
Eminem 111
emptiness 158
Encounters: An Anthology of South African Short Stories 160
Enemies 160, 161, 162–164, 172
English book as signifier 67
English country gardens 179
Englishness 27
entitlement 179, 188
  a sense of 4, 26
  and ingratitude 137
equality 95, 96
Erasmus, Desiderius 109, 193
eucalyptus trees 92, 95
eunuchs 108
euphemistic whitespeak 17, 174
Eurocentrism 54, 124, 179
European civility 57
European descent 114
European displacement 78
European liberal largesse vs settler conservatism 54
European Marxism 20
European settlers 11
European white masculinity 59
European, traditional food 153
euthanasia 46
excrement 96, 199
fact and fiction, relationship between 67
Fair Play 123
Fairbairn, Tessa 39
Fairest Cape, The 133
Fairlady 6, 7, 103, 104, 120, 126, 129, 193
  anniversary edition of 106

male readership of 105
taglines of 105–106
target market of 104–105
fairy-tales 190
  format of 169
  subversion of 168, 169, 170
  revisions of 171
Fanon, Frantz 21, 74, 76, 90, 166
Farred, Grant 25–26, 162
fast-food multinationals 153
fear 136, 137, 188
  of dark villains 170
female physicality 60–61
femininity
  specularity of 121
  unreachable ideals of 106
feminism 106
Feminist Imagination 29
feminist lesbians 110
Feminist Politics: What's Home Got to Do With It! 158
feminist recovery 101
feminist theory 32
fiction 159
fictional nature of all writing 67
firearms 178
first-person narration, in *Labour* 175
First Thirty-Seven Years, The 139
food 152
  western obsession with 154
fool's staff 121
foreign white people 61
forgiveness 24
  asking for by whites 89
Forked Tongue 119
forked tongue 175, 178, 185–186, 195
Foucault, Michel 29, 32, 33, 36, 108, 149, 177
found poems 134, 139, 144, 146, 193, 194
Fountain 134
four basic victims position/grid 13–14, 65, 172
Frankenberg, Ruth 14, 16, 17, 36, 39, 56, 174
freak displacement 94
freedom struggle 87
Fresnaye 148
Freud, Sigmund 33
Friedman, Susan Stanford 131
frontier, the 13
fruit 167
funeral of Krog's father 101
Gallagher, Charles 18
Gambler's Anonymous 118
garden in Africa 178–179
Garden of Eden 186

gardening services 182–183
gay marriage, a joke about 113
gender 17, 153
  and race 105
  performativity of 32–33
  norms 58
  politics 169
gender dynamics of power relations 56
Gender in Bakhtin's Carnival 109
gendered oppression, non-victims of 66
genes using ships 143
Gerald and the rat 141–142
Ghangha 88, 90, 91, 99
Gill, AA 118
Gilman, Sander 31, 51, 135
Glimpses of Women in Overalls 144
global media industry 111
goblin boots 110
Golding, Pam 118
good black people 50
good white people 61
Gordimer, Nadine 5–6, 8, 9, 40, 93, 126, 160, 172, 187, 189, 190, 194
Grand old Duke of York 119
granite 146
Green Tin 133
Grobin, Josh 111
guide books 135, 152, 193
guilt 43
  the white man's burden 24–25
  the white women's burden 26, 65
guilt-ridden white women 38
gynophobia 31
hair, talking about 112
half-and-half 184, 185
Hall, Stuart 6
Hamilton-Paterson, James 136
hand, Krog's, paralysed by a stroke 86
handbags, locking away of 177
hang-gliding 154–155
happily-ever-after 168
Harding, Sandra 83, 84
Head, Dominic 161
headscarf 120
Health Minister 127, 128, 129
Heart of Darkness 98
Hephaistos 184
Her Watery Legs Led Him Deeper 145, 146
heterosexual romance, the violent underpinnings of 53
heterosexual status quo 109

heterosexuality 169
  hegemonic 113
Heyns, Michiel 172
high literature 7
hijab 120
Hill, Mike 22
Hillebrand, Candice 115
Hirson, Dennis 72
History of Sexuality 32
history, inheritance of 16
HIV/Aids 100, 127, 128, 129
  an African solution for 129
Hollands, Barbara 39
Hollywood 116
homeless people 151–152
homophobia 122
homosexuality 32, 33, 113, 151
honey 92
hooks, bell 31, 64
Horrell, Georgina 17
hospital 99
housemaids 138, 170
human tragedy, personalising of 69
hunger 166, 167, 185
I Do, I Don't 112, 114
ice creams 139
identities 138
  signification in shaping of 48
identity crisis of white South Africans 191
idioms 177, 184
Ignatieff, Michael 196, 197
Ignatiev, Noel 21
Ignorance was Bliss 118
Iliad, the 141, 142
In Those Days 139, 142, 150
incest 62
inequalities, structures that perpetuate 181
ingratitude and entitlement 137
innocence 63
  of whites in respect of apartheid 87
Insig 65
insularity 58
interracial politics 56
irony 58
island, the 13
It Never Stops 144
It's all the Same Thing 119, 120
Ivory Coast 117
Jacobson, Celean 41
Jolie, Angelina 116–117
Jooste, Pamela 6, 32, 36, 38, 59, 63, 64, 190, 191
July's People 161
Just Believe 126
kangaroo 92

Kerkorrel, Johannes 111
Kernohan, Sally 39, 40, 52
Kincaid, Jamaica 135
Kirby, Robert 6, 38, 41
Klein Vingeroefeninge Rondom die Nosie van Hibriditeit 173
Kleur Kom Nooit Alleen Nie 80, 89, 94, 96
Klip in die Bos 146
Kossic, Shirley 39
Kota, Namfanelo 124
Krog family farm 91
Krog, Antjie 5, 7, 25, 32, 40, 109, 117, 126, 131, 160, 173, 187, 189, 190, 191, 192, 194, 195
  funeral of father of 101
  scatological preoccupation of 192
Kroonstad 70, 72–75, 83, 91, 96, 100, 101
  mayor of 82
Labour 19, 172–187, 188, 194, 195
labour 174, also see cheap black labour
land
  as property 132
  redistribution 85
landownership 177, 198
language 67
  power of 102
  vigilance in the use of 116, 124
leftist liberal activists 165
leisured classes, sense of entitlement of 147
Leon, Tony 115
lesbians 19, 108, 186
Lévinas, Emmanuel 20, 54
Lewis, Desiree 47
Lewis, Patricia 115
liberal humanism 4, 17
lies, making them visible 182
lift to town 165
Light My Fire 112
literary journalism 6
literary studies vs cultural studies 6
literature 7
  accessibility of 190
  classification of 68
  nature of 6
live-in maids 144
Llandudno 155
locations 132
loneliness 136
Loneliness of Noam Chomsky, The 37
Long Walk to Freedom 69, 76, 94

translation of into Afrikaans 95, 98
Lopez, Alfred J 1, 14, 35
Lott, Eric 15, 150
love that dares not speak its name, the 113
Lacan's symbolic order 34
Lumley, Joanna 112
lunch, inviting comrades home for 167
Madam and Eve politics 176
Madamhood 13, 164, 178, 172, 173, 185, 194
Madams 160, 176
Madibaland 116
magazines 7
maids and caretakers 143, 144
Mail & Guardian 6, 9, 10, 38, 40
Malay chauffeur 162
Mamukwa 88
man in white coat, photograph of 148
Mandela, Nelson 45, 69, 76, 84, 94, 95, 98, 152
  address of to UN 81
manic-depressive character of SA 9
Mann, Susan 6, 18, 32, 38, 52, 63, 190, 191
manservant 162
Mansfield, Katherine 168
marriage 68
  vs the wedding 112
Martin, Biddy 158
Masai 117
mass conformity 119
master signifier 28, 33, 34, 39
master/servant dialectic 176
materialism, violence on which it is premised 170
Mayekiso, Professor 81
Mbeki, Thabo 26, 89, 127
McMusic 111
Medalie, David 160, 161, 187
Medusa 186
Melua, Katie 111
Melville, Herman 34, 35
Mental Floss 6, 104
metamorphosis 70, 72
methodology of the oppressed 27, 28
middle-class frame of reference 63
middle-class realities 188
middle-class respectability 22
middle-class white suburbia 139
mimes, power of 184
mimicry 184, 185
miscegenation 62
miscreants 147
Miss South Africa 124, 125
mixed schools 79
mixed-race relationships 62
Moby Dick 34
Modleski, Tania 46
Mohanty, Chandra 158
Mol, Michael 113
monk's cowl 121
Moon, Dreama 17, 26, 122, 174, 177
moralising monk 124
morality 128
Morrison, Jim 112
Morrison, Toni 14, 15, 19, 93, 118, 123, 171
Mother Africa figure 51
mothers and daughters 70
Mqhayi, SEK 81
Mrs Dalloway 42
Mugabe, Robert 85
multiculturalism 192
multi-lingualism 80
music in SA travel ad 117
Muslim culture 121
Mutman, Mahmut 120–121
My Fair Lady 107
My Son's Story 93
myopia of US and UK 117, 118
myopic white sensibilities 125
mythic misperception 31
Ná Grond-Invasions in Zimbabwe 89, 196–197
Najmi, Samina 21
name changes
  of black people 49
  of SA towns 50
Namibia 117
Namibian border war 79
naming, power of 145
nature vs nurture 113
Ndebele, Njabulo 84, 85
neighbourhood watches 159
New Abuse for Drain Covers 151
New Century of South African Short Stories, The 160, 173
New Gay Club for Sea Point 151
New Seekers in Cape Town 147
New York Times 21
New Yorker, the 113
newspapers 7
normalcy 9
normativity 19, 23
  vs multiculturalism 104
norms, racial and gender 169
Northwest Breeze 176, 179
nuclear family 162, 171, 195
  bourgeois 169
  politics of 140
objectification of women 4
old men playing cards 142–143
Oliver, Jamie 113
Once Upon A Time 160, 161, 162
One Tongue Singing 6, 38, 39, 52, 63, 191, 194
ontological imperialism 20, 54
oral transmission of fairy-tales 171
Orientalism 12
Other, the dehumanising image of 166
Oupa Boela 157
Out of Africa 179
Out of Whiteness: Color, Politics and Cutlure 14
overalls 144
overheard conversations 134, 148
ox, slaughtering of 81
panopticism 29
paradise lost 186
Paris and Achilles 141
past, divisions of 156
patriarchal oppression 164
patriarchy 4
Peckham, Linda 24
Peet and Rina 77–80
People Like Ourselves 6, 38, 39, 41, 51–52, 63, 191, 194
perception as a convention 76
personal is political 67, 68, 157
petit bourgeois vulgarity 163
phallocentricity 4
phallus 193
  as transcendental signifier 108, 110
  little vs big 108, 129
pigeons 144
pink hat, 85–86
Pirate Jenny 180, 181
Pityana, Barney 123
plagiarism 39, 40 41, 51, 191
Playing in the Dark: Whiteness and the Literary Imagination 14, 15, 118
poetry 7–8, 9, 25
  repackaging of 131
polarised discourses 134
political correctness 116, 124
Politics of Feminism in South Africa, The 47
politics of privilege 10, 11
Pop Idols 112
Pope, Alexander 162
popular culture 110
popular fiction 9
poquismo 19
possessions, acquisition of vs humanity 114

230 ■ White Women Writing White

post-apartheid generation 191
post-apartheid power relations 83
post-apartheid South Africa 131, 173
post-apartheid weepies 6, 9, 38, 64
Postcolonial Whiteness 14, 35
post-Enlightenment man 20
post-liberation black bourgeois 90
poverty 153
power relations in post-apartheid South Africa 131
Praise of Folly 103, 108
precedents, setting of 176
prejudices 164
Press, Karen 7, 8–9, 25, 40, 189, 190, 193, 194
Pretorius and Dingaan 141
Pretty Woman 107
previously disadvantaged individuals, interviews with 82
prince, in *Sleeping Beauty* 171
private vs public 68
privilege 5
property 25, 132, 175
property developers 141
prostitutes 145
Provence 179
pseudo-marketing 153
psychoanalysis 33
psychological double bind 77, 109
psychological emigration 10
psychological regression vs social transformation 98
publishing industry 190
pulp fiction 46, 51, 64
Purple 134, 137–138
Pygmalion 107
queer theory 32
queer transgressive aesthetic 32, 33
queer whiteness vs raced queerness 32
race 128, 153
 continuity of positions on 16
 preoccupation with 4
 Thamm's focus on 104
 vs class 89
race/class divide in SA 181
race dynamics of power relations 56
racial hierarchies 5, 19
racial markers, visual 1–2
racial prejudice, non-perpetrators of 66

racial shaming 62
Racing the Lesbian, Dodging White Critics 32
racism 16, 31, 74, 83, 122
 psychological consequences of 76
 unconscious 17
 vs sexism 193
racist rhetoric 74
rainbow nation 3, 34, 52, 84, 180, 187
rainbow warriors 180, 181
rape and murder 53, 54
 suspects of 55
rats, 141–142
ravenous materialism 114
real estate, prime 151
recipes 137
reconciliation 11
Reconciliation 143, 144
Reconstruction and Development Programme 151, 152
Recorded History 147
Recreation 146
Rehearsal 140
religion and tradition 121
reproduction of labour 174
Rich, Adrienne 30, 31, 32, 43, 64
Richards, Jo-Anne 9, 38
richman poorman beggarman thief 178, 179, 184
Roediger, David 14
Roodt, Dan 126
Rosenthal, Jane 53, 60, 61, 154
Ross, Fiona 69
Rotten Fish 145, 146
Roy, Arundhati 37, 166
Royal Male 124
ruffled collars 110
ruin 77
Rules Binding on all Owners and Residents 134, 149, 150
Rwanda 75–76
SABC3 112
Sachs, Albie 125
safe sex 128
Said, Edward 12, 19, 36, 65
salad 176, 178, 181
Sandoval, Chela 27, 28
sangomas 59
Sarie 70
satire 43
savagery 61
Scales-Trent, Judy 116
scatological nature of Krog's work 96–100
scatomancy 96
Schenk, Celeste 131

Schiavo, Terry 119, 120
schizophrenia 45
Schonstein, Patricia 38
school desks 85
school sport 73
school, enquiring about 167
schools, racial differences in 2–3
Sea Captain 139, 142–143
Sea Point 130–158
 as a colonial country club 147
Seaworthy 156–157
selective memory 76
Serfontein, Dot 70, 76
serpent symbolism 186
servants' quarters 139
Seshadri-Crooks, Kalpana 33, 34, 35, 64
settler/native encounters 146
settler-descendants 193
settlers 133
 literary preoccupation of 15
 vs tourists 131
Seven Tenths: The Sea and Its Thresholds 136
seven-day eating plan 152–153
sewerage disposal 100
sexism 122
sexual abuse 55
sexual deviance, rational theory of 113
sexual orientation 110
sexually rapacious Man of Color 176
sexually vulnerable White Woman 176
shacks, chicest 118
Shaik, Shabir 127
shared equality 96
Shaw, George Bernard 107
sheep 92
Sheridan 83, 84
Shome, Raka 12
short stories 9, 160
Shosholoza 115
signifying practices, alternative 131
Signs Taken for Wonders 67
silk 145
Sindane, Happy 1, 3, 114, 115, 125
Single White Female 8
Singular White Females 8, 9, 38, 58
skin colour vs ideological identification
slate 146
slaves 147
Sleeping Beauty 169, 171
Sleeter, Christine 114

Small Finger Exercises on the Notion of Hybridity 172–187, 195
Smith, Gail 10
Smith, Will 113
snakes 180, 181, 182, 185, 186, 195
Snow White 169
snow-covered peaks 185
soap opera 51
social contract 178
Social Construction of Whiteness, The 14, 16
social order, expense of maintaining 171
soldiers, divine protection for 166
soles 71–72
solipsism 31
Sophiatown 174
Spillers, Hortense 33
Spivak, Gayatri 19, 130, 131, 136, 181
squalor 97
Srikanth, Rajini 21
stability 140
Stellenbosch 174, 179, 182
stereotypes 48, 63, 165
  black 47
  gender and racial 122
  perpetuated in women's magazines 111–112
  white 43
Stewart, Rod 111
Steyn, Melissa 25, 26, 87, 173, 180
strangulation 180
Style magazine 61–62
suburban myths 172
suburbia 8, 139, 159, 168, 174, 194
Sunday Times 40
Sunday Times Lifestyle 41
survival 13
survival strategies, subordination of 33
Swahili 82
Swerdlow, Alan 52
Sybil 132
symbolic motifs 13
Talbot, Margaret 21
Taliban Feminist Mommy 119
Taylor, Gary 38
telegrams 163
Thamm, Marianne 6, 7, 18, 32, 33, 105, 109, 110, 131, 189, 192, 193, 194, 195
  oppositional stance of 106
The More Things Change 111

The Rape of the Lock 162
The RDP Comes to Sea Point 144, 151
Them 183
Theme Park City 41
They 177
third-person narration, in *Labour* 175
This Day 8, 10, 38
thorny briars 170, 171, 195
Tikaram, Tanita 117
Timbuktu 82, 97
time, linear 154
To Be or Not To Be – PC 116, 124
Toilet Poem 96
Tokoloshe 169
Top Billing 118
tourist brochures 135, 152, 193
tourists 131
  envy of 135
Tramps In and About the Peninsula 136
Transcaucasia 1
transformation
  vs masking 79
  white SA response to 7
transgressive aesthetic 32, 33, 193, 195
Transkei 99, 100
transparency of the sole 72
travelogues 135, 193
Triomf 5, 177, 188
Truth 146
truth
  and fiction, blurring of boundaries between 69
  one universal vs multiple conflicting 68
Truth and Reconciliation Commission 2, 66, 86, 87, 92, 99, 193
Trying for White 114
Tshabalala-Msimang, Manto 127, 128, 129
Tsotsi 169
tunnel vision 31
turtle doves 92
Tutu, Desmond 84, 180
Twinkle Twinkle Little Star 154, 155
Twist in my Sobriety 117
tyranny of the transparent 177
ubuntu 88
Umkhonto weSizwe 166
unbelonging 172
uncertainty 65
Unfair Comment 6, 103, 105, 121
unhomeliness 26, 140, 162, 168, 188

universality principle, Gordimer's use of 169, 170
upside-down world 184
Us/Them dialectic 79
vagrancy 151
Van der Merwe joke 169
Van der Watt, Liese 10
Van Heerden, Etienne 172
Van Niekerk, Anton 65, 66
Van Niekerk, Marlene 5, 6, 8, 9, 19, 25, 30, 33, 36, 160, 172–187, 188, 189, 190, 194, 195
veil 120–121
Verskrikking 96, 98
victim as perpetrator 76, 79
View 142, 156, 194
Vilnius 143
violence 26
  and alcohol abuse 55
Virginia Slims 105
Volksblad 39–40
Von Klemperer, Margaret 39, 52
voyages of personal discovery 66, 192
vulnerability 98
Wages of Whiteness 14
Waiting for the Barbarians 13
walls and barbed wire 172
Ware, Vron 14, 21
washing, displaying of 150
Waste Land, The 132
wedding ritual, response of heterosexual women to 113
Wedding Show, The 112
Welcome to the Matrix 118
Wellman, David 83
western femininity vs progressive social and political engagement in *Fairlady* 104
western feminism, three waves of 28
western mass consumerism 127
western normality vs eastern otherness 120
wheelchair, girl in 140–141
Wherever Land Begins 136, 137
white academia 165
white Africans 24, 191
white alienation 42
white anxiety 9, 165
white behaviour, communal 114–115
white culture, non-existence of 115
white displacement 9, 26, 102, 191, 195
  and white normativity 131

white English-speaking South Africans 58
white experience, shared, assumption of 180
white feminists 23
white guilt 82, 165, 167
white hegemony vs black corruption 83
white identity
  historical development of 18
  paradoxes upon which it is built 115
  re- and de-constructing of 70–71
white labour 183
white masculine mythologies of conquest 141
white middle-class insularity, defensiveness of 115
white money 127
White Mythologies: Writing History and the West 19
white normativity 3–4, 5
  vs black deviance 64
  vs transformation and reconciliation 189
white pride 114
white privilege 101, 128, 167
  juxtaposed with coloured despair 139
white racism 11
white right 127
white skin 97, 198
white solidarity, premised on a sense of displacement 191
white solipsism 31, 64
white South African men 59, 80
white South African middle-class women 172
white South African womanhood 164
White Stuff, The 20, 173
white subjectivity 9
white suburbia 159
  dis-ease of 168
  gentility of 174
  privilege of 194
white supremacy 11
White Talk 25
white trash 183
white western hegemony 23, 192
white western heterosexual status quo 191
white western womanhood 27–28
White Woman 175

White Woman, White Man, Man of Color, Woman of Color 174–175
white women's writing, ambivalence in 122
White Writing 133
whiteness
  ambivalence and normativity of 107
  and middle-class womanhood 106
  as a complex dynamic of identification 16
  as a cultural force 12
  as emptiness 22
  as a global affiliation 110
  as a lived experience 189
  as a mindset 91
  as a post-colonial concern 10, 19–24
  as a signifier 189
  as an aspiration 11
  as master signifier 28, 33–35, 39
  as normative 191
  black responses to 81–82
  crisis of 173
  defensiveness of 11
  defining of by exclusion 133
  European vs South African 191
  exposing of 23
  hierarchy of 18
  historical privilege of 5
  in contemporary SA 11
  monolithic vs shades of 66, 102
  nature of performance of 17
  no longer to be cherished 158
  paradox of 19, 35
  photographic interrogation of 9–10
  post-colonial study of 23
  preferred form of 57
  redefining of 94–96
  shades of 75–88
  universal power of 21, 22
  universal sanctity of 83, 84, 87
  writers' negotiation of 192
Whiteness Just Isn't What It Used To Be 26
whiteness studies 3, 5, 10, 12, 189, 195
  in SA 10, 21–27
  in USA 10, 14–19
  point of 23
  vs race studies 19, 21

Whiteness: The Communication of Social Identity 25
Whiteness Visible 14, 18
whites
  alien position occupied by in post-colonial SA 24
  as the Other 90
  good and bad 85
  exodus of post-1994 25
whitespeak 27, 79, 177
Who Killed Fana Khaba? 126, 128, 129
Wicomb, Zoë 1, 2, 24, 35, 133, 158, 173, 182
widows and wives 172
Wilde, Oscar 33
Williams, Raymond 6
window-dressing 83
Winfrey, Oprah 117
winter 181
Wise Fool 7, 108, 109, 124
Woman Alone 175, 186
woman in bikini, photograph of 148
Woman With Another Woman 186
Woman Without Man 186
women
  alienation of in western society 13
  Muslim 121
  objectification of 4
women's magazines 9, 104
Woolf, Virginia 12–13, 15, 42, 70, 168
workers in back of truck 183
working class black men 49
  and women 64
worlding 135, 137
wounded attachment 29
wreaths 137
wrestlers 183–184
writing by white SA women 3
Wylie, Dan 157
xenophobia 149
You've Come a Long Way ... Maybe 105
Young, Robert 19, 20, 90, 132, 153, 185, 195
Young, Will 112
Zimbabwe 127
Zimbabwe land invasions 196, 197, 198
Zulu customs 124
Zwelithini, King Goodwill 124